The
ORVIS®
Ultimate Book of
FLY FISHING

These books can be purchased at any Orvis® store or through The Lyons Press at www.LyonsPress.com.

The Orvis® Pocket Guide to Dry-Fly Fishing
    By Tom Rosenbauer

The Orvis® Pocket Guide to Fly Fishing for Bass
    By William G. Tapply

The Orvis® Pocket Guide to Fly Fishing for Bonefish and Permit
    By Jack Samson

The Orvis® Pocket Guide to Fly Fishing for Steelhead
    By John Shewey

The Orvis® Pocket Guide to Fly Fishing for Stillwater Trout
    By Jim Lepage

The Orvis® Pocket Guide to Fly Fishing for Striped Bass and Bluefish
    By Lou Tabory

The Orvis® Pocket Guide to Great Lakes Salmon and Steelhead
    By Matthew Supinski

The Orvis® Pocket Guide to Nymphing Techniques
    By Tom Rosenbauer

The Orvis® Streamside Guide to Approach and Presentation
    By Tom Rosenbauer

The Orvis® Streamside Guide to Fly Casting
    By Tom Deck

The Orvis® Streamside Guide to Leaders, Knots, and Tippets
    By Tom Rosenbauer

The Orvis® Streamside Guide to Trout Foods and Their Imitations
    By Tom Rosenbauer

The
ORVIS®
Ultimate Book of
FLY FISHING
Secrets from the Orvis Experts

Tom Deck
Jim Lepage
Tom Rosenbauer
Jack Samson
John Shewey
Matthew Supinski
Lou Tabory
William G. Tapply

ILLUSTRATIONS BY
Dann Jacobus
Jeff Kennedy
Rod Walinchus

The Lyons Press
Guilford, Connecticut
An imprint of The Globe Pequot Press

Originally published by The Lyons Press as
The Orvis Pocket Guide to Dry-Fly Fishing
The Orvis Pocket Guide to Fly Fishing for Bass
The Orvis Pocket Guide to Fly Fishing for Bonefish and Permit
The Orvis Pocket Guide to Fly Fishing for Steelhead
The Orvis Pocket Guide to Fly Fishing for Stillwater Trout
The Orvis Pocket Guide to Fly Fishing for Striped Bass and Bluefish
The Orvis Pocket Guide to Great Lakes Salmon and Steelhead
The Orvis Pocket Guide to Nymphing Techniques
The Orvis Streamside Guide to Approach and Presentation
The Orvis Streamside Guide to Fly Casting
The Orvis Streamside Guide to Leaders, Knots, and Tippets
The Orvis Streamside Guide to Trout Foods and Their Imitations

Chapters 1–7
Illustrations by Rod Walinchus. Photographs by Tom Rosenbauer.

Chapters 8–11
Illustrations by Rod Walinchus. Photographs by Tom Rosenbauer.

Chapters 12–15
Illustrations by Rod Walinchus. Photographs by Tom Rosenbauer, Ted Fauceglia,
Carl Richards, and Ross Purnell.

Chapters 16–17
Illustrations by Rod Walinchus. Photographs by Tom Rosenbauer.

Chapters 18–19
Illustrations by Rod Walinchus. Photographs by Tom Rosenbauer and Henry Ambrose.

Chapter 20
Illustrations by Rod Walinchus

Chapter 21
Photographs on page 142 by The Orvis Company. All other Photographs by Jim LePage.

Chapter 22
Illustrations by Jeff Kennedy. Photographs by Matthew and Laurie Supinski.

Chapter 23
Illustrations by Rod Walinchus.

Chapters 24-26
Photographs by Will Ryan and Vicki Stiefel.

Chapters 27–28
Illustrations by Rod Walinchus. Photographs by Tom Rosenbauer.

Chapters 29–32
Photograph on page 213 by Carl Richards. Photograph on page 221 by Cam Sigler.

Chapters 33–34
Illustrations by Rod Walinchus.

Printed in China.

ISBN 1-59228-584-8

10 9 8 7 6 5 4 3 2 1

Production by Print Matters, Inc.
Design by Compset, Inc.

Library of Congress Cataloging-in-Publication Data is available on file.

CONTENTS

INTRODUCTION

The moniker "Ultimate Fly Fishing Guide" is a little inflated but if you want to get published these days, it's wise to let publishers have their way. But to be fair, this book is as good as it gets for learning tricks from some of the best teachers around. When Nick Lyons and I first kicked around the idea of an Orvis series of field guides, we decided we wanted only the best contributors and experts. And by the best we didn't mean the biggest names. We went after those fly fishers who were the best teachers, the best communicators. I'm proud of the contributors we convinced—and sometimes cajoled —to write books for the series.

I'm pleased to be part of that group. I'm here not because I'm such a great fly fisher or great writer. I'm here, and I chose the other contributors, because as a group we've never lost sight of what it's like to be a novice standing in the middle of a river or ocean far from home with very little idea about what to do with that long skinny pole in our hands. All of us have days, after thirty or forty years of fly fishing, when we feel like we don't have a clue how to catch a fish, as if we've started all over. No one in this book has anything to prove or any hidden agenda, beyond the satisfaction of helping other people solve problems on a trout stream, steelhead river, or saltwater flat.

The authors in this book are people who took up fly fishing long before it was fashionable, in fact when fly fishing was considered a silly and inefficient affectation better reserved for old guys who wore tweeds, smoked a pipe, and appeared on the June photo in gas station calendars. We are all lifers, people who would rather fish than eat.

Matt Supinski is on rivers over three hundred days a year, guiding, fishing, or taking photos. Jack Samson has been fly fishing for eighty-two years; he's fished with Bing Crosby, Joan and Lee Wulff, Ed Zern, and Gene Hill, from Scotland to Australia to Japan. Bill Tapply grew up fishing bass from a rowboat on the Charles River with his father, H.G. Tapply, better known as the author of "Tap's Tips," one of the most popular columns in *Field & Stream* magazine for decades. Tom Deck, as the director of the Orvis Fly Fishing Schools, has taught many thousands of people to cast a fly.

John Shewey has written fourteen books and contributed hundreds of articles to the outdoor press but he's best known for his pursuit of summer steelhead with his elegant fly patterns. Lou Tabory, one of the true modern pioneers of saltwater fly fishing in the Northeast, was catching fish on the Atlantic coast when most of the people who watched him had never even seen a fly rod. And my fishing buddy, Jim Lepage, is relentless, relentless in his pursuit of anything with fins and relentless in his generosity when sharing secrets with other anglers.

This volume is a collection of the best parts of *The Orvis Streamside Guides.* You can use it to learn the basics of fly fishing, or how to identify the broad group of aquatic insects, or

how to learn the few knots you need for trout fishing. You can enjoy its photographs of the more exotic fish or locations, leave the book on the shelf for six months, then pick it up in the middle of winter to dream about catching a steelhead or bonefish, or refresh your memory on how to tie a nail knot. Down the road you might have use for other chapters. Maybe your college roommate invites you on a Bahamas bonefish trip. Perhaps your daughter moves to Cleveland and you discover there are steelhead rivers within the city limits of that city, and you can slip away to fish on family visits. I'm hoping you'll find reasons to pick up this book many times over the years, and pick up fresh nuggets every time you do.

Because I'm the editor of this series and writing this introduction, I get to stand on my soap box and proselytize about two subjects no one will buy a book about. But both subjects are important parts of any fly-fisher's education. The first one is waterside etiquette.

You may notice me on a trout stream if you get too close. I'm the short, unimposing guy who might turn to you and ask "Am I crowdin' ya?" if you step into a pool too close to me. Despite the fact that I'm not very big, seldom lose my cool, and haven't thrown a punch in anger since high school, I have a big problem with other fly fishers who show boorish behavior. Spin fishermen take a few casts and move on quickly, bait fishers usually sit in one place and seldom fish the same water I do, but a fly fisher who moves in on me and casts over the same fish is a "very stinky fellow," as a Japanese friend of mine often says. There is just no excuse for crowding another fly fisher. Despite the whininess of people who say today's trout streams are getting too crowded, there is always someplace else to go where you won't be disturbing someone else.

Don't think this stuff is restricted to novices who don't know any better. This spring I was fishing the Farmington River in Connecticut, a heavily fished river just outside of Hartford. It was a cold, rainy weekday and perhaps the river was less crowded than usual. My friend Andy Haberman and I had a stretch of several pools to ourselves with no one else in sight.

Andy took the upstream pool and I took the one below. After a few minutes, I looked up to see another angler standing about forty feet from Andy, casting into virtually the same spot. There was no one else in the one hundred-yard pool and plenty of good water for miles upstream and down.

I decided to be my usual obnoxious self in this kind of situation. Andy is a big, young, very fit man and I figured he could take care of himself if things got hot. Besides, the guy horning in on him was short and squat and over retirement age. He probably fished the same spot every day and, by golly, he wasn't going to let someone else bother his fish. I walked up the bank and yelled to Andy, "Must be a popular spot you picked." No response from the old guy. I could see he was a decent caster and wore an old weathered vest, so he obviously knew better. "Do people always fish so close together here?" I asked. Andy, embarrassed by me, muttered "Not usually." "What a weird place," I said. The old boor suddenly exploded. "There's plenty of room here!"

Andy left the pool, I apologized to him, and we left to find more pleasant conditions. That guy never left his spot and never stopped casting.

What bothers me most about anglers who get too close to me is not that I'm anti-social. Or that they might catch "my" fish. Fish, stream trout in particular, are spooky animals and I spend half my time on rivers trying to get close enough to feeding fish with letting them know I'm there. When someone else walks into a pool, it ruins all my efforts and spoils it for both of us. The same goes for people who walk along a bank you are fishing, peering into the water, helpfully telling you where the fish are (as they dart for cover).

Another equally obnoxious habit comes from guides who aren't respectful of other boats or of wading anglers. Guides are supposed to be our heroes, to set the example for us civilians. If a guide in a drift boat tells you to cast close to another boat, or in a pool that wading anglers are in, tell him you'd rather not. You're paying the bill (and the tip!). The better guides will warn you, "Pull in your line, we've got some wading fishermen up ahead" and will then ask the fishermen in the pool which way they'd like him to go around. Thankfully, guides who let their anglers fish in front of other people are not abundant but common enough to give some outfitters a bad name.

If you see someone in the middle of a big pool and every other pool is occupied, ask him if he's planning on moving upstream or downstream. Then go to the head or the tail and leave him plenty of room. If you see someone sitting on the bank looking into a pool, give her the same respect you would if she were out in the middle. She is probably resting a fish or waiting for a hatch. She got there first and deserves your courtesy.

So be generous with your time on the water. Be respectful of someone who arrived before you. If there is an empty pool nearby, go there. Fish some pocket water or riffles instead of a pool. Do some walking and explore new water.

My second and last piece of unsolicited advice is on the protection of our resources. One of my opinions might surprise you: Catch-and-release fishing is totally unimportant to the future of our fishing resource. Statements like "I don't kill any trout so my children and grandchildren can enjoy fishing" are misguided and may even be damaging to the future of fly fishing. No-Kill fishing is merely a temporary stockpiling of adult fish in a population so they can be caught more than once, thus giving more people an opportunity to stalk and catch them. It is nearly impossible to over-fish a population with rod and reel to the point of extinction. Even if a stream or lake

with natural reproduction is over-fished to the point of making it unattractive to anglers, there will always be some fish left to spawn—those that live in deep water, or under nasty logjams, or the ones that only feed at night. Leave them alone for a few years and a healthy population will return—if the habitat is healthy.

And that is the point: Habitat and water quality are the only factors needed for a healthy sportfish population. Problems occur when misguided anglers put their energy into promoting or defending catch-and-release fishing with no time or money left over to defend what's critical. Few people these days have enough time to fight on multiple fronts so we choose our battles according to how much they mean to us. I've seen too many trout streams where fly fishers come to blows with bait fishers over regulations, while cattle overgraze the banks or tributaries get channelized or parking lots with inadequate storm drainage get built close to riparian zones. If these groups work together on protecting and improving the habitat there will be enough fish for everyone and gear restrictions won't be necessary!

If my sermon upset you, I apologize. Fly fishing is just a game but it's a game that arouses passions at all levels. I promise you that the rest of this book will be just plain fun and I hope you learn much that makes your time on the water the best it can be.

—Tom Rosenbauer

PART I

GENERAL

CHAPTER ONE

DEFINING THE CASTING ARC

— TOM DECK —

The casting arc is the distance the rod travels throughout the casting stroke. If you can control the distance and shape of this arc, your overall fly casting will be greatly improved.

One of the most frequently used descriptions of the fly-casting arc is the old **clock method,** immortalized in books and even in movies. If twelve o'clock is vertical (straight up), then according to the clock method, the rod should travel from ten o'clock out in front to two o'clock behind. This description, though accurate, is somewhat incomplete for fly-casting instruction.

First of all, the size of the arc is dictated by the amount of line that you are casting. The shorter the line you are casting, the less distance the rod tip travels. Conversely, the longer the cast, the farther the tip must travel through the casting arc. The casting arc is ever-changing: As fishing conditions change so does the path of the rod.

Let's start with shorter casts, which require less rod movement because shorter lengths of line require less energy to drive them through the air. When you are casting shorter distances, the rod will not bend or flex greatly— in fact, just the *tip* of the rod will flex. New fly casters often want to wave their hand back and forth excessively, which will move the rod tip too far back and too far forward. The key is that rod movement should be minimized when casting shorter distances. Less is, in fact, more.

To cast longer distances, your casting arc must progressively increase in size. If you want to cast more line, you must put more energy into the rod, and that comes from bending or flexing the rod. The more distance you want to cover, the more the rod must flex during the casting stroke, which means you must increase the size of the casting arc. For medium-distance casts of thirty to forty feet, in other words, the size of the arc will increase and the rod tip will travel further, through a longer casting stroke. The rod flex will also extend down into the middle section of the rod. More flex will translate into greater line speed and distance.

For your longest casts, the arc must open up even more and the flex must extend all the way down into the butt section of the fly rod. The butt section is the stiffest part of the rod and it will hold the most energy. If you want to lay out a nice long line, you need to harness that energy.

Another point to be aware of is that the arc in fly casting can tilt slightly forward or backward. Tilting the arc backwards may be used to help shoot more line on the front cast when the wind is at your back, for example. You can also adjust the angle of the casting arc forward by lowering the front cast (bringing the rod tip closer to the water) and stopping the rod vertically, at about twelve o'clock on the backcast. This will effectively propel the line up and back rather than behind you, which can be helpful for elevating line up over trees or shrubs that would otherwise be in the path of

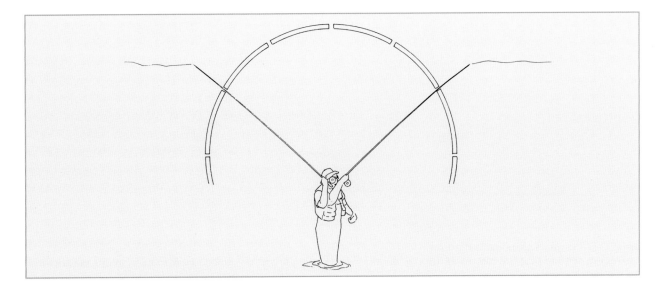

Don't learn fly casting solely by the points on a clock
The "clock method" is rigid and somewhat incomplete for fly-casting instruction. The casting arc is not set in stone from ten o'clock to two o'clock. The size of the arc changes according to the length of line you are casting.

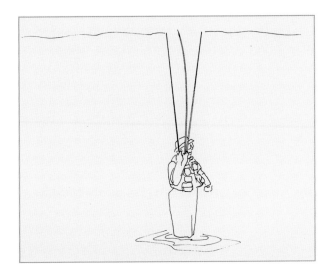

Short Cast / Smaller Casting Arc
Casting a shorter length of line requires less energy from the rod. There is often enough flex in just the tip of the rod to lay out a shorter cast.

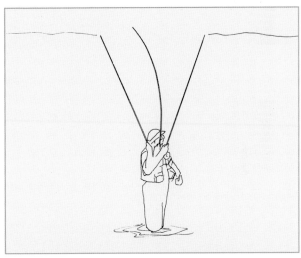

Medium Distance Cast / Medium Casting Arc
As the range of your casting increases, so does the casting arc; the flex extends down to the middle of the rod.

a conventional backcast stroke. Shortening the backcast and lowering the front cast can also help when you are casting into a head wind. It will decrease the amount of hang time the line has over the water at the completion of the forward cast, which in turn will prevent the wind from blowing your presentation off its mark.

Adjust the angle and size of your casting arc for the amount of line you are handling. It will make your casting stroke smoother and more consistent.

Long Cast / Larger Expanded Casting Arc
Long casts require that the rod travel through an expanded casting arc, which will allow it to bend all the way down to the butt section.

The casting arc may have to tilt backwards in order to shoot more line on the forward stroke. This is not advised for beginners trying to learn the basics.

The casting arc may be tilted forward in order to propel the backcast higher and the forward cast lower. This can be very effective when casting directly into the wind.

CHAPTER TWO

CASTING LOOPS

— TOM DECK —

he size of the casting arc is critical, but the path the rod tip travels through the casting stroke is just as important, if not *more* important. Your casting arc may be the proper size, but if the track or path of your casting stroke is incorrect, the line will not straighten out completely. It is important to note that the rod tip dictates where the line will go. If the rod tip travels in a straight line throughout the casting stroke, you will have a perfect straight-line cast. The path the rod tip travels also determines the size of the casting loop. What does a correct casting loop look like? If fly line had stripes on it, then good fly-casting loops would look like candy canes. As a rule, the smaller or narrower the loop at the end of the candy cane, the better. Narrow loops tend to fly or cut through the air better than larger, more open loops.

First let me describe what *not* to do because if you can avoid the negative you can then focus on what the correct rod path should be. At the Orvis Fly-Fishing School I have had the benefit of critiquing hundreds of fly casters on video. Most of the problems beginning fly rodders exhibit stem from the trouble they have controlling the path of the rod.

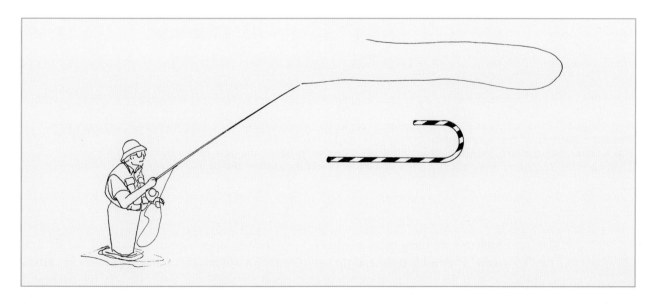

A nice cast with a classic candy cane-shaped loop. A correct fly-casting loop will have a candy-cane shape to it as it unfurls.

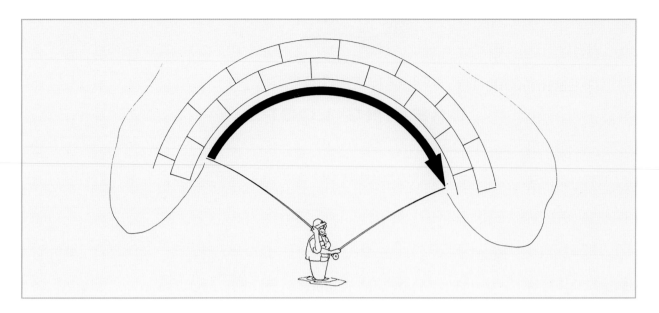

Do not IGLOO CAST.
Avoid painting the ceiling of an igloo with the rod tip. This will lead to excessively open loops, which will cause the fly cast to falter.

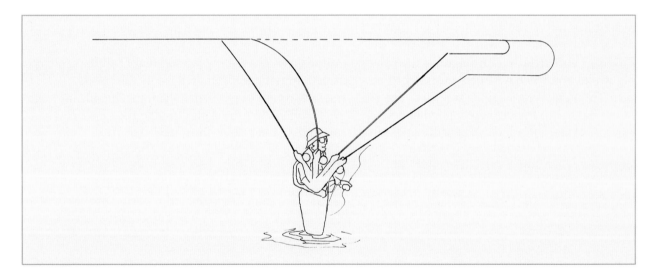

Note the path of the rod tip as it travels through a correct fly-casting stroke. The path is straighter and more direct. This is the opposite of the "igloo cast."
1. A narrow casting loop is formed by stopping the rod tip cleanly below the path of the fly line.
2. An open loop is caused by stopping the rod tip farther below the path of the fly line.

The one problem I see most often is what I call the "igloo cast." Pretend that the rod tip has a paintbrush on it. If the paintbrush moves in a semicircular path overhead, as if you were painting the ceiling of an igloo, you will have extremely open casting loops and the fly line can not unfurl completely. Most new fly casters tend to drop the backcast too far back and drive their front cast too far forward. Some beginning fly casters may have a proper back-

A nice cast with a classic candy cane-shaped loop.

cast position but they paint the ceiling of an igloo on the forward stroke. An interesting fact to note is that one can have the correct-size casting arc, but if the tip of the rod moves in this "igloo-cast" fashion, the fly cast will still falter. Avoid painting the ceiling of an igloo at all costs.

The size of your fly-casting loops is determined by the way you stop the rod. There is very little follow-through in fly casting, especially when dealing with a shorter length of fly line. You must smoothly bring the rod to an abrupt stop at the finish of each casting stroke. This is difficult for most people to do. In sports that have an arcing swing, such as golf or tennis, follow-through helps. In fly casting, too much follow-through causes loops to open up. Once the rod tip passes over the rod grip, the casting loop has been formed. The rod tip

must tilt and drop a little below the flight path of the fly line. If it does not, the line will run into itself. Open loops are caused by excessively pulling or pointing the rod tip downward and failing to stop the rod decisively at the end of the cast. Remember, if you "igloo cast" just a little at either end of the casting arc, your loops will be too large and too open.

By drawing the rod tip in a straighter, more direct path, and driving it to a complete stop, your loops will become narrower. Stop the rod tip quickly after it has traveled over the casting hand and you will have nice, tight casting loops that will cut through the air and travel more efficiently.

Whether you are casting twenty feet of line with a narrow casting arc or laying out fifty feet with an expanded arc, the rod tip must stop cleanly just below the path of the fly line.

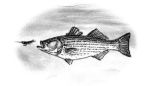

CHAPTER THREE

THE PICK UP-AND-LAY DOWN CAST

— TOM DECK —

The pick up-and-lay down cast has three primary parts: The pickup, the backcast, and the front cast. This is the first and most important cast in the Orvis Progressive Casting Method. Mastering this stroke will allow a caster to progress rapidly, while building upon solid fundamentals. If you are a beginner, practicing this cast will help you develop your casting stroke. This cast, however, is not only for beginners: It's perfect for correcting bad habits because it can reprogram your muscle memory in a better way. If you are an accomplished caster, this cast may help you develop a feel and timing for a new rod.

The goal of the pick up-and-lay down cast is to have the line straighten out entirely above the surface of the water, then touch down quietly. The pick up-and-lay down drill is actually made up of two casts: First is the backcast, which will project the line up and back; then a front cast, which will lay the line out over the water. Both the front and backcasts are equally important and must work together for your cast to succeed. The backcast is critical because the way you project the line behind you in turn dictates how well the front cast will lay out in front of you.

GETTING STARTED

You cannot start casting with just a few feet of fly line beyond the rod tip, as the leader won't have enough weight to put a bend in a rod. For that matter, don't even practice casting without a leader. The line will not behave as it should without an air-resistant leader on the end to slow it down. You don't need to practice with a fly, though—just a piece of yarn or no fly at all will do fine. Plus, it's much safer.

Do whatever you can to get fifteen to twenty feet of line outside of the rod tip. Thrash the rod around and strip line off the reel. Peek ahead in this book and see how to do a roll cast to get the line out. Or just lay the rod on the ground and manually pull the line out. When you become more proficient, you'll be able to make brisk little false casts while pulling line off the reel but right now any method that works is just fine.

I have often noticed that beginners either start with too much line or too little. As a general rule, start with two rod-lengths of line. The average trout rod is eight and one-half feet long. Two rod-lengths will give you almost twenty feet of line, which is perfect to begin with. Don't start with less than fifteen feet of line because things just can't get rolling without some line heavy enough to bend the rod tip. Also, don't start with more line than you can handle smoothly—this will most likely lead to some bad habits. Besides, most fish on the river are caught within thirty feet or less.

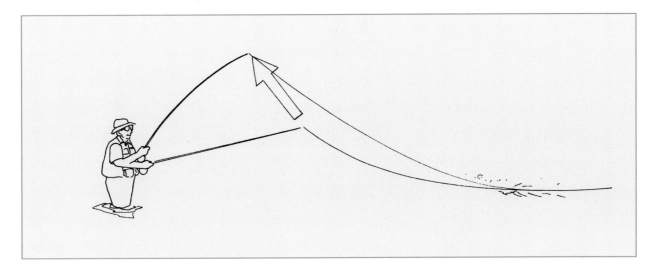

The Pickup
Don't rip the line off of the water! Slide it off gracefully.

THE PICKUP

Get your grip and stance settled and comfortable. Lock the line against the cork grip with the index (trigger) finger of your casting hand. Start with the rod tip very low so that it is almost in the water. Raise the rod slowly so that the line begins to slide on the water. Accelerate smoothly but aggressively through the pickup. Don't rip the line off the water. Slide it off gracefully.

Pickup Tips

The pickup is executed primarily with the forearm. Start with the thumb on top of the grip and have the rod angled so the tip is very close to the water. Cock your wrist forward so that the thumb points down the rod shaft and the butt of the rod is parallel with your forearm. Raise the rod by lifting exclusively with your forearm so that the line begins to slide on the water. Your casting hand should rise up to neck and shoulder level as you lift the rod with your forearm.

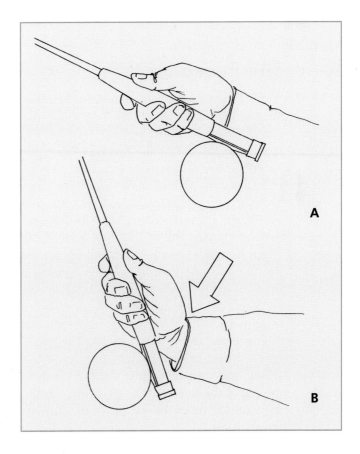

A: Correct Pickup. Lift the rod with the forearm during the pickup.
B: Incorrect Pickup. Do not break the wrist during the pickup.

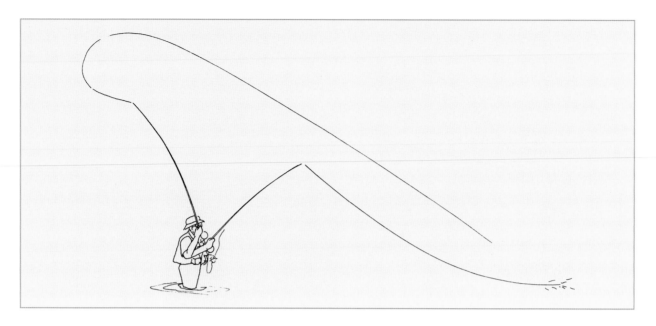

The Backcast
As the rod approaches the vertical position, accelerate to a crisp stop. Note that the line is projected up and behind the caster.

THE BACKCAST

As the rod nears the vertical position, accelerate and then make an abrupt stop at a point just slightly beyond the vertical. Stop the rod forcibly as the end of the fly line lifts off the water. As the rod approaches the vertical position, the wrist should make a decisive snap. This "wrist snap" should be crisp but not overblown. Correct wrist rotation will project the rod tip upward and slightly behind the caster. Excessive wrist rotation will plunge the tip way past the vertical position causing a rounded-off "igloo cast" behind you. Remember, don't paint the ceiling of an igloo. Try to imagine painting a line across a conventional ceiling at the end of the backcast. The paintbrush should draw a straight line across the ceiling and then flick paint off the brush at the end of the backcast. The wrist snap should *not* force the tip of the rod off of the conventional ceiling.

The wrist snap should pass the tip slightly over the butt of the rod. Once the tip passes over the butt of the rod, the casting loop is formed. Stopping crisply will help form narrow, well-defined loops.

Backcast Tips

Imagine the backcast as really an *up cast:* Try to propel the line upward more than backward. If you were to embed a marshmallow on the tip of the rod, you would flip the marshmallow off only at the end of the stroke and stop *right after* it pops off the rod tip. The line will travel in whatever direction the marshmallow is tossed. Tossing the imaginary marshmallow up and over your shoulder will elevate the line in an upward direction, allowing the front cast to unfurl downhill. It is, of course, much easier to cast a line downhill rather than uphill.

After a brief pause or stop on the backcast, the line will be fully extended behind you. Now it's time to start the front stroke. Don't wait too long. Allowing the line to fall below the rod tip will create problems for the front cast. The line should be parallel to the ground as you start the front cast. If the line is up and behind you, how do you know when to begin the front cast? Great question! Use an open stance and simply turn your head to see the backcast develop. This will help you to see when the line is completely stretched out and, more importantly, it will allow you to see where the rod has stopped. The

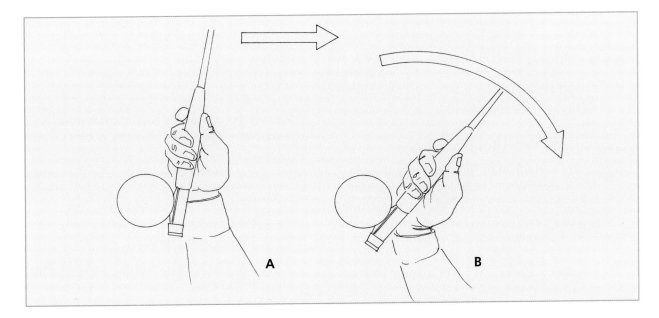

A: Correct use of the wrist at the finish of the backcast. Proper wrist rotation on the backcast will lead to correct rod position.
B: Do not break the wrist at the finish of the backcast. Breaking the wrist on the backcast is bad form and will lead to severe casting problems.

problem I see most often with beginners in our fishing schools is that they don't have any idea where they are stopping the rod at the completion of the backcast. Poor rod position can be cured by just turning your head and watching the development of the backcast.

THE FRONT CAST

The mechanics of the front cast are easy to execute, especially if the line has been correctly positioned with the backcast. The rod has come to a crisp stop, allowing the line to extend fully. Start the forward action slowly. The rod butt will lead the way, moving forward and at a slight angle downward. The rod should begin to bend so that the tip lags well behind the grip and hand. As the rod flexes, smoothly accelerate your cast and project the tip so that it stops abruptly at or about eye level.

The wrist plays a major role in the formation of the front cast. As you near the completion of the forward stroke, think of pushing the thumb into the cork grip and pulling back on the pinkie with a decisive wrist snap. Your elbow should remain close to the body as the

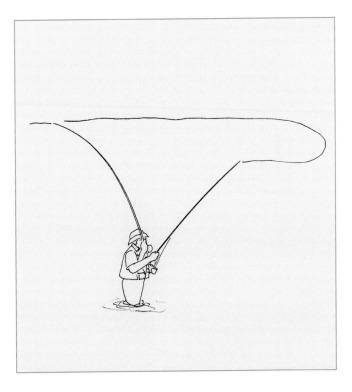

The Front Cast
1: Try to think of the front cast as pulling the line forward. Why? Although it is nearly impossible to push limp fly line so that it straightens out, it can be easily pulled forward.
2: Stop the rod tip abruptly at the finish of the forward stroke and the line will unfurl over the water.

rod tip is pushed out in front of you. Don't "throw" the rod as you would a baseball. Rather, project the tip out in front of you, stopping it at eye level. The rod tip will come to a halt and the line should unfurl uniformly over the water, landing softly.

Front Cast Tips

Try to think of the front cast as pulling the line forward. Why? While it's nearly impossible to push limp fly line so that it straightens out, it can be easily pulled forward.

Your elbow should remain close to your body, yet not be pressed into it. Years ago, fly casting was taught by practicing with a book tucked under the casting arm. The cast was supposed to be executed while the casting elbow held a book in place. This method is too restrictive, however. Although this technique may have been helpful with the old soft bamboo rods, it does not apply to today's modern graphite rods. The arm position should feel more like having a grapefruit tucked up in your armpit. The casting arm and elbow have much more freedom to move if you are holding up a grapefruit instead of a book. If your hand lunges too far forward on the front cast, however, the grapefruit will fall out. Your casting hand may reach out in front of you, but your elbow should remain close to the body.

After you have completed the forward stroke, lower the rod down to the water to begin another pickup. Repeat this process until loop size and line control are well within your grasp.

RECAP
(TIPS TO THINK ABOUT FOR THE PICK UP-AND-LAY DOWN CAST)

- **Tip #1:** Start the rod tip near the surface of the water to begin the pickup portion of your cast. This will cause the rod to load quickly, allowing for an early completion of the backcast.

- **Tip #2:** Open your stance and turn your head to see where the rod is stopping on the backcast.

- **Tip #3:** Try to think of the backcast as an up cast. The line will straighten out with less effort if it is cast upward on the backcast, then cast down slightly on the front cast. Put another way, it is easier to cast the line up a hill first, then pull it down off a hill on the front stroke.

- **Tip #4:** Do not over-rotate your wrist. Use the correct amount of forearm motion, then apply the wrist properly.

- **Tip #5:** Keep your elbow comfortably near your side while you execute the forward cast. Try to project the rod tip forward without throwing your hand with

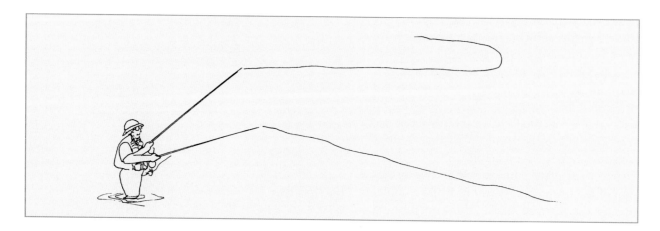

1: The line will unfurl in whichever direction you point the rod.
2: After you have completed the forward stroke, lower the rod to begin another pickup.

Legendary fishing guide Joe Bressler completing a forward cast on Idaho's South Fork of the Snake. Note the flex of the rod, the position of his hand, and the rod tip at eye level.

it. Then stop the rod abruptly, at about eye level.

Some other general points that you should keep in mind while casting: First, to make casting nearly effortless, the rod must bend. Fly casting requires very little strength if the rod bends properly. You can cast a fly line with a broomstick, but that's hard work and not very pretty. When you are having a combination of problems, you can often smooth out many of them by focusing on making the rod bend, without worrying unduly about where your wrist and forearm and elbow are pointing.

Second, it is the rod tip that casts the line, not the handle. If you can get your mind off holding the rod and focus on where the action is, you will be able to follow directions better and will understand what the rod is doing. Thinking "out near the tip" also helps keep a bend in the rod.

Third, never let the line drop below the rod tip on an overhead cast. This has practical applications, both for casting form and for safety. Any time the line falls below the tip on the backcast, you are robbing your cast of energy that has built up in the spring of the rod. In order to build up maximum energy, the line must be parallel to the ground and pulling the rod tip into a bend. On the forward cast, always keeping the line above the tip of the rod forces you to point the tip in front of you quickly, and prevents tailing loops. And if you always keep the line and leader above the rod tip, you'll never hit yourself with a fly.

Finally, try to maintain tension on the line with the rod tip. Jerky starts and stops that form slack between the rod tip and line introduce sloppiness. Maintaining constant tension with the line gives you the maximum energy from your casts and makes them smoother. It is the constant tension idea that introduces subtle drift or follow-through on a cast, and is a major distinction between a smooth caster and a mediocre thrasher.

CHAPTER FOUR

THE LINE HAND AND SHOOTING LINE

— TOM DECK —

THE LINE HAND

After the pick up-and-lay down cast, the next step in the Orvis Progressive Casting Method is the introduction of the line hand. To learn how to master the fundamentals, practice the casting motion by pinching the line against the grip with the first two fingers of your casting hand. Once you can control the basic motion, free the line from the cork grip and control the line with your left (opposite) hand. Fly fishing is a two-handed sport: The line hand is critical because it helps you develop line control and reduce slack while fishing.

Start by pulling off two arm lengths of extra line from the reel and let it hang freely. Hold the rod in your right (casting) hand and pinch the line between the thumb and forefinger of your left (noncasting) hand. Tend the fly line so there is no slack between the stripping guide and the line hand. The rest of the excess slack should form a long U-shape that will dangle near your knees.

The next step is simple: Just execute the basic pick up-and-lay down cast while holding the line near your belt buckle with the line hand. Change nothing in your casting motion. Maintain some tension on the line between your left hand and the stripping guide. If slack appears, there is a flaw in your casting stroke. Most likely the stopping points of your casting arc are incorrect or the timing of your power stroke is off.

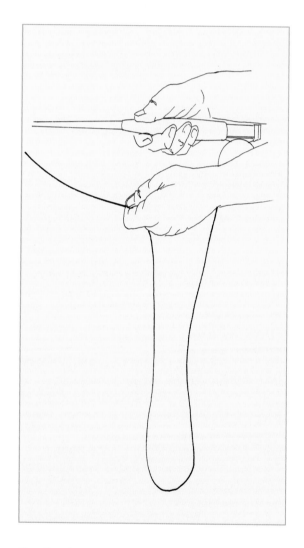

Line Hand
Once you have mastered the basic cast, release the fly line from your casting hand and hold it in your line hand.

Shooting Line
After the rod comes to a stop and a casting loop is formed, let go of the line with your line hand and it will sail through the guides. Timing is the key; don't let go too soon or hold on too long.

Don't let the line slip through your fingers as the rod is traveling between the forward and backcasts. If you let the line slip prematurely while the rod is in motion, the flex cannot be maintained and the pick up-and-lay down cast will falter.

Although you are freeing the line from the grip, the line will still be under some tension as you hold it with your left (noncasting) hand. This will produce additional flex in the rod, which in turn will increase your line speed. Practice the basic stroke in this fashion until the line can be laid out with sufficient line speed and control.

SHOOTING LINE

Once you have sufficient line speed and loop control, it is time to start shooting line at the finish of the pick up-and-lay down cast. Although it is a serviceable cast, the pick up-and-lay down cast does have its limitations. Many fishing situations will call for adding line

to increase the distance of your presentation. Shooting line at this stage of the progression is done on the forward cast only.

If you want to shoot line correctly on the front cast, *concentrate on the backcast.* Many of my students initially try to shoot line by concentrating exclusively on the forward stroke. They subsequently let their backcast fall apart. Remember, if the backcast is poor, the front cast will be poor. If the backcast lacks sufficient line speed or proper loop control, then shooting line becomes difficult.

Begin by feeding twenty to twenty-five feet of line out beyond the rod tip. Have about ten feet of extra line in reserve, enough so that it hangs near your feet or a little touches the ground. The slack line at your feet is the amount you will shoot at the finish of the forward stroke. Before you start, make sure there is no slack between your line hand and the first guide on the rod.

Shooting line is actually quite simple. The fundamentals of the pick up-and-lay down

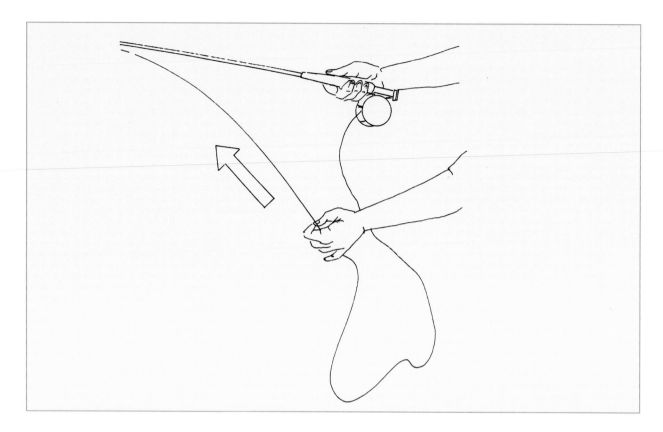

Form an "OK" sign as the line is released. This will allow you to control the line as it is presented, which will set you up for an effective retrieve.

cast remain unchanged. At the completion of the forward stroke, however, you release line and let it sail through the guides. The casting hand dictates the stroke but it's the timing of letting go with the line hand that determines how the well the line will shoot through the guides on the rod. If you let go of the line too soon during the forward motion, the flex in the rod will unload prematurely and the cast will lose energy. Conversely, if you hold the line too long at the finish, you will choke off the momentum of the line.

Timing is critical. You must let go of the line at the completion of the power stroke, at about the same time the rod comes to a stop. After the power is applied, quickly release the line as the rod tip comes to a halt. It helps to think of the order as stop and let go, not let go, then stop. This all happens so quickly that it will feel like you are releasing the line at the same time you stop the rod.

Note that you cannot let go of the line until the casting loop is formed. For shorter casts, loops are formed very quickly and the line is released just as the rod comes to a stop. On longer casts, the loops take longer to develop. Subsequently the line is held just a bit longer, allowing for the casting loop to form. Once you see the end of the fly line pass by your head on the front cast, let go with your line hand. Practice shooting line until you can make it fly at will. It is really fun to see line successfully shoot out over the water. Let it fly!

CONTROLLING AND RETRIEVING LINE

As you develop the ability to shoot line, learn to control it. Release the line by forming a circle with the thumb and index finger of your left hand and allow the line to run through it as shoots through the rod tip. Your line hand will

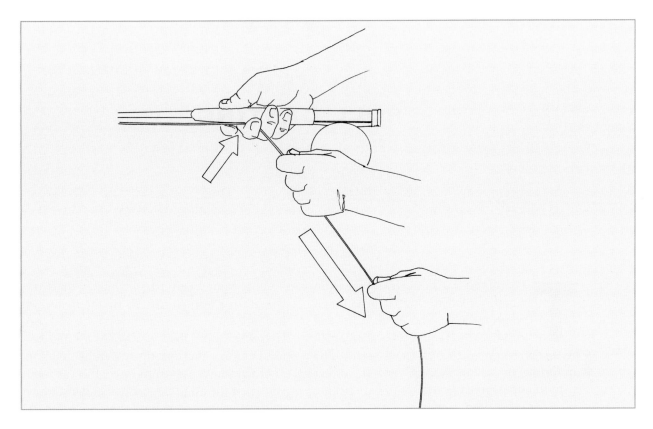

Retrieving Line
Hook the line behind the middle or forefinger of your rod hand and retrieve by pulling from behind that finger.

form an "OK" sign as if to say it is "OK" to let the line go. This will allow you to control the line as it is presented and sets you up for an effective retrieve.

Once the line has shot through the rod tip and has landed on the water, you will need to retrieve it so you can cast again. In fly fishing, you manipulate the fly by retrieving with your line hand, not with the reel, as in spin fishing. You can accurately control the speed and action of your flies by stripping in the line with your left (noncasting) hand.

Start with the rod tip low, near the water. Grab the line with your left hand and hang it over the forefinger or middle finger (or both) of your casting hand while holding the rod. Retrieve the line by pulling it in strips from *behind* your finger. Do not reach in front of the casting hand and replace the line in the middle finger for each strip.

CHAPTER FIVE

ROLL CASTING

— TOM DECK —

The roll cast is used to present the fly in situations where there is little or no room for a backcast. In fact, the roll cast does not require a backcast at all. As its name implies, the roll cast is executed by unfurling or rolling the line over the water with a simple forward cast. Say you are fishing the edge of a deep, tree-lined lake and can't wade out more than ten feet, but you need to reach fish that are a good thirty feet out from shore. Although a roll cast offers neither the accuracy, delivery, nor distance of the overhead cast, it will get your line out to the fish.

A requirement of the roll cast is that the end of the line be under tension as the cast is being made. Some of the fly line must remain on the water as the stroke is executed. It is best to practice this cast on a pond or some type of still water. If you try to roll cast on grass, the surface tension will not enable you to roll out the fly line.

Start with twenty to twenty-five feet of line extended beyond the tip of the rod. Pinch the line against the cork grip with one or two fingers of your casting hand. (It is best to learn this cast with just one hand at first.) Raise the rod slowly and slide the line on the water smoothly back toward you. There is no acceleration at the beginning of the roll cast so don't overdo it and jerk the line out of the water. Bring the line back to you with the rod tilted to the side, about ten degrees from the vertical. This will keep the line off to one side so it does not slam into the rod when you make the cast.

Raise your casting hand higher than you would for a normal cast. Bring the fly reel up to about ear level as you draw it back and cock your wrist more than you would for an overhead cast, so that the tip is well behind you. Try to break your wrist more on this cast. This will cause the tip to extend farther back, which will put some line behind you and your rod hand. (You can't make this cast without some line behind you.) The longer the roll cast, the more line you will need behind you. The line will form a large semicircle that extends from the tip of the rod to the water at your feet. The rest of the line should remain on the water in front of you. Make sure that the line comes to a complete stop before you try to roll it forward.

Start the roll cast with a break in your wrist so that the rod is tilted back at an angle that is around two-thirty on that same clock reference. Begin the roll cast by pulling down with the forearm so that the tip lags behind as the rod starts to bend. As you finish the cast, drive the tip forward by rotating your wrist and pushing on your thumb. Try to bend the rod in a smooth motion as you drive it forward. It should have a slow start with an acceleration to a complete stop, just like a normal forward cast. In fact, it's virtually the same forward motion.

End with the rod tip near eye level so that the line rolls out over the water. Don't push the rod tip down too low or the line will pile up on the water. Remember, the fly line will unroll in whichever direction the rod tip stops. Point it to the eye and see it fly!

TROUBLESHOOTING

1. **Problem:** After you start using the line hand, the cast will not completely straighten out.

   - **Cause:** The line hand is not providing tension as the cast is executed. As a result, line is being leaked into the casting motion and the bend in the rod is being prematurely unloaded.

   - **Solution:** Secure the line with the thumb and forefinger of the left hand and hold the line under tension for the duration of the casting motion. Make sure you don't change the shape or the size of the casting arc just because the line hand has been introduced. You should still be casting the same amount of line as when the line was locked against the grip.

2. **Problem:** The line will not effectively shoot through the rod at the completion of front cast.

   - **Cause #1:** You're releasing the line with improper timing. Holding on for too long after the cast has been made will choke off the line's momentum. Conversely, letting go of the line too early during the forward stroke will cause the bend in the rod to "unload" prematurely and there will be no energy left to shoot the line.

   - **Solution #1:** Let go of the line only at the finish of the forward cast. Try to release the line as the rod comes to a stop. Once you can see the end of the line pass overhead on the forward stroke, release the line and it should sail out through the guides. Don't let go and then cast— rather, cast, then let go.

   - **Cause #2:** The actual casting stroke may be below par, with a lack of line speed and loop control.

Tom Rosenbauer helping his daughter Brooke with a roll cast in a tight spot. Note the loop of line behind the rod.

   - **Solution #2:** Correctly shooting line requires narrow, well-defined casting loops. Develop proper shape to your casting loops before trying to shoot line.

3. **Problem:** The end of the line is hitting the water while you're false casting.

   - **Cause:** The stopping point of the rod tip is too low on the front cast. The size of the casting arc may also be too large for the amount of line being cast. This will lead to uncontrollable casting loops as you false cast, which will cause the line to slap on the water.

   - **Solution:** When presenting the line on the water, the rod tip should stop at or just below eye level. When attempting to false cast, stop the rod tip higher than eye level. This will allow the line to unfurl higher over the surface of the water.

     Try false casting with fifteen feet of line beyond the rod tip when you practice. It is very easy to control and false cast shorter amounts of line. Then, as you progress, add some line and expand the casting arc.

The amount of line you can handle when false casting varies with the size of the rod, the type of line, and your own casting ability. As a rule-of-thumb, never try to false cast more than thirty-five feet with a trout rod or fifty feet with a salt-water rod.

4. **Problem:** Tailing loops—the fly is hitting the rod tip or the line as it is being cast.

   • **Cause:** You are overpowering and "shocking" the rod through the casting motion. The bend or flex in the rod is harshly exerted and is not being controlled throughout the cast.

   • **Solution:** Smooth out your casting. Try not to jerk when starting the casting motion. Begin the stroke smoothly and apply power progressively throughout the casting stroke. Apply the power just before the rod comes to a halt. Each cast is a gradual speed-up to an abrupt stop.

Tip: Open up your casting loops and develop the control to adjust loop size at will. Slightly open loops are going to be better than tailing ones.

5. **Problem:** When roll casting, the line does not completely unfurl and the line piles up at the end of the cast.

   • **Cause:** The casting hand is not raised high enough and there is not enough line behind the rod to start the roll cast.

   • **Solution:** Raise your casting hand high (near head level) as you draw the line in. Holding your hand high will allow you to generate more momentum and rod bend as the roll cast is executed. Next, break your wrist slightly. This will push the tip farther back and put some line behind you and the rod. The more line behind you and the rod, the easier the roll cast will be. If some line is not behind the rod at the start of the roll cast, the line will not unfurl.

The Roll Cast
1A: To properly make a roll cast, make sure some line is behind you and that the end of the line is anchored in the water. Start the cast by pulling down on the rod with the forearm.
1B: The rod should be tilted to the side slightly, so that the cast can unfurl to the inside of the line on the water.

2A: Try to progressively flex the rod with wrist rotation near the finish of the stroke.
2B: As the rod unloads, stop the tip abruptly near eye level.

3A: As you finish the cast, the line will unroll because its end is anchored in the water.
3B: After the cast is made, lower the rod to begin another roll cast.

CHAPTER SIX

THE SINGLE HAUL AND DOUBLE HAUL

— TOM DECK —

Once you attempt to cast beyond forty or fifty feet, the casting hand alone cannot produce enough flex in a fly rod to present the line. **Hauling,** or pulling the line with precision as the rod moves through the paces, will produce additional tension as the line is working through the guides. This tension, in turn, will cause the rod to flex more, providing increased casting energy.

There are many advantages to mastering the magic of the double haul. Not only will it help you cast longer and farther, but it will also increase your line control and speed—which will improve your casts at any distance. For short casts, hauling can help to straighten out

longer leaders and control the slack line between the casting hand and guide surfaces. Learning to haul correctly makes fly casting easier with any length of line, and all accomplished fly casters should master its secrets.

THE SINGLE HAUL

Before jumping right into the intricate timing of the double haul, first learn to make a single haul on the backcast. This is the initial step in the double haul anyway, so it is a perfect starting point. You can also perform a single haul exclusively on the front cast, but for the purpose of learning, start by hauling only on the back stroke.

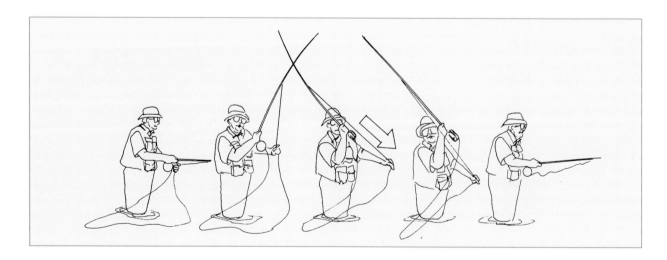

Single Haul on the Backcast
The haul is executed with the line hand at the same time the power is applied with the wrist snap of the casting hand.

Hauling will permit you to pick up and present more line than a conventional cast, so start with thirty-five to forty-five feet of line extended beyond the rod tip. Begin with the rod tip near the surface of the water. Reach up and grab the line within six inches of the stripping guide and have ten to fifteen feet of slack in reserve at your feet. Grabbing the line close to the first guide will reduce any chance for slack to form between the line hand and stripping guide at the start of the stroke. Slack is your worst enemy when you are learning to haul.

Next, start the casting motion by slowly raising the rod. Hold the line securely in your left (noncasting) hand throughout the cast. Raise the rod and the line hand together as you begin the cast. Once the rod approaches the vertical position, apply more power with a quick and decisive stroke by raising your casting hand to near head level and shoving the tip of the rod back to about the two o'clock position. As you drive the rod through the back stroke, pull on the line with the left hand at the same time. Timing is crucial, so haul with the left (line) hand exactly at the same time you power the rod. Try to maintain some tension with the line hand as you make the haul. Don't overdo it and pull too far as you haul. Instead of a long pull, make the haul a short, crisp tug. When you are learning to haul correctly, your hands should never separate more than two feet.

The haul should stop when the rod comes to a halt. Stop your stroke sharply so the bend in the rod unloads and delivers the line powerfully behind you. The combination of pulling on the line with a well-timed power stroke should allow you to pick up all the line on the water and cast it decisively up and behind you.

Finally, drive the rod forward with your casting hand and stop the tip at eye level. Let go of the line at the finish of the front cast and shoot it out over the water. Hauling correctly on the backcast will actually help improve your front stroke. You will be able to shoot more line effectively just by hauling properly on the backcast. Because a single haul puts

Guide Frank Catino completing a double haul in the Florida Keys. His line hand will drift back to the stripping guide as he shoots the line.

more energy and line speed into the backcast, it's often helpful to do this when you have the wind at your back. Tail winds can collapse your backcast and hauling compensates by helping you slice through the wind. You are handling more line, which makes this a longer cast so expand the casting arc. This will permit the rod and casting hand to travel through a longer stroke. Don't overextend, though: Your elbow should be near your side and bent slightly at the completion of the backcast. Try not to overwork yourself—make the rod flex and lay out the line for you.

Line Hand Drift
After a haul is made on the backcast, the line hand will drift back to the casting hand. This will reposition the line hand so that another haul can be made on the forward cast.

Recap: Tips to Think About for the Single Haul

- **Tip #1:** Start with the rod tip low. Hold the line so there is no slack between the first guide and the left hand.
- **Tip #2:** Raise the rod smoothly and begin to accelerate as the rod reaches the vertical position.
- **Tip #3:** Increase the bend of the rod by applying the power stroke and pull the on the line with the left hand at the same moment.
- **Tip #4:** Stop the rod sharply and allow the line to unfurl behind you.
- **Tip #5:** Make a forward cast and let the line go with your left (noncasting) hand as the rod comes to a stop. The line should fly out of the rod, drawing up the excess slack that was at your feet.

Practice the single haul on the backcast until you have complete control over the tension with your line hand. If you can haul with precise timing and no slack appears between the line hand and the guides, you are ready for the double haul.

THE DOUBLE HAUL

The double haul is really just two single hauls—one applied on the backcast and one on the front cast. The key to unlocking the timing of the double haul is to learn how to effectively reposition the line hand after making the first haul on the back stroke.

Again, start with more line out over the tip. Make a few normal overhead casts until you have thirty-five to forty-five feet of line in front of you. In this case, more line is better than less, so don't try to make it easier by practicing with thirty feet of line; it won't work. The added weight of the extra line helps to reposition the line hand after the first haul is made.

The Back Haul

Complete a single haul on the backcast. Before you attempt the front cast, reposition your left (line) hand so that a haul can be made on the front cast. After pulling on the line, your hands should be about twenty-four inches apart. Don't pull excessively on the back haul—that keeps the hands too far apart, making it harder to control slack in the line. It also makes it harder for the line hand to drift back to the reel for the second haul on the front cast.

At the completion of the backcast haul, the line hand drifts back to meet the reel in a quick bouncing move. The line that was pulled with the line hand on the backcast must be given back so that a haul can be made on the front stroke. The two hands should end up together, near your head.

Most students have trouble with this drift and repositioning of the line hand back to the reel. Imagine that the line between your left (line) hand and the first guide on the rod is actually a large rubber band. After you have hauled on the backcast, the line hand should bounce back to the reel due to the tension of the rubber cord. The line will not actually pull your hand back up to the reel. It is simply a quick "down-up" motion.

Haul on the Front Cast
The haul on the front cast is made at the same time the casting hand applies the power stroke. Practice repositioning the line hand even on the front haul, as this will help you control slack in the line.

The Front Haul

The two hands are together, back up near head level at the finish of the backcast. Both hands move forward together as the front cast begins. At the start of the front cast, imagine using the line to pull down on the rod, so that the butt is pointing out slightly in front of you. Make the rod bend progressively throughout the stroke. Near the finish of the cast, apply the power stroke with the wrist by pushing your thumb and pulling the pinkie. The front haul is executed simultaneously by pulling on the line with the left hand. Both hands work in unison: As your right hand applies the power to the rod with a wrist snap, your left hand pulls on the line at the same moment.

Once the haul is made, let the imaginary rubber band pull your left hand back to the reel. Channel any slack line at your feet through the first guide. After the front haul, don't let go of the line yet. Controlling the slack between the line hand and the first guide is key. Practice double hauling until you can haul and maintain line-hand tension on both the front and back hauls.

Once you have control of the line on both hauls, try shooting more line on the front cast after you make the forward haul. Simply release the line with your left hand immedi-

Shooting Line after the Forward Haul
Release line with your line hand right after the forward haul is made.

ately after the forward haul is made. The line will fly out impressively if your timing and technique are sound. With proper timing and careful coiling of slack line at your feet, you can learn to shoot thirty feet of line or more by using the double haul. To maintain control of this shooting line, many casters use a stripping basket. These devices keep the line from tangling on itself or your shoelaces.

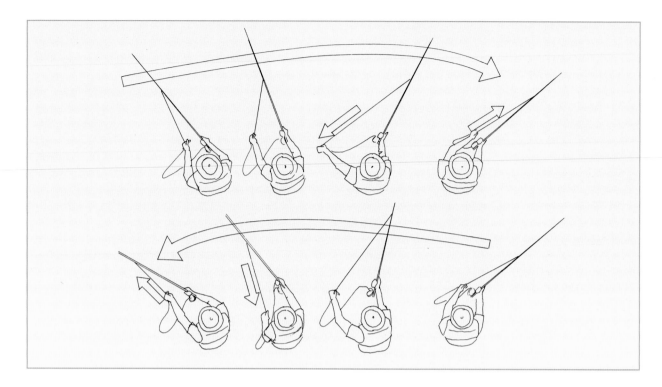

The double-haul practice drill on grass.

Practice Drill: The Horizontal Double Haul

Find a grass lawn to practice this drill. Lower the casting plane so that the rod is horizontal to the ground or so that you are casting completely side-arm.

Make a backcast with a haul and have the line hand follow back up to the reel. Let the line fall onto the grass after the cast is made.

Next, make a front cast with a haul and maintain line-hand tension so that the left hand bounces back to the reel. Separate the backcast from the front cast and let the line fall on the ground after each cast. Watch as your hands start together and pull apart, with the left (line) hand then drifting back to the reel. This drill will help you learn to reposition your left hand and control line-hand tension.

Casting Drift

All accomplished fly casters naturally develop what is called a drift at the finish of each cast. This drift move is really just a smooth follow-through at the finish of the cast. Drifting allows the casting arc to expand while still having an abrupt stopping point in the stroke. Incorporating a drifting move will allow you to cast longer lines more gracefully, with less effort.

For the most part, there is little or no follow-through when you are casting shorter distances. Longer casts require an expanded casting arc to accommodate more line traveling through the air, so a longer follow-through is used when casting longer lines. The rod tip is still brought to a crisp stop, and the drift helps the casting arc expand after the stop.

At the Orvis schools, we address rod drifting only when a student demonstrates that he or she can cast a longer line effectively and can control the size of the casting arc to correspond with the amount of line being handled. Most people develop this drifting move naturally, but it is helpful to make them aware of their follow-through. Consciously drifting the rod at the finish of the stroke allows you to make smoother, more elaborate casts.

1: Only a short drift is needed on short casts.

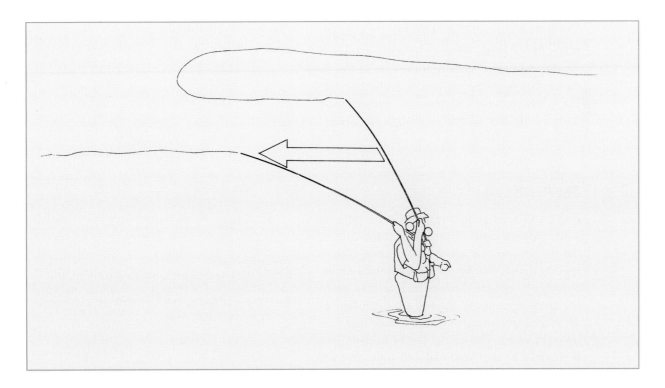

2: A longer drift is needed to help expand the casting arc on long casts.

CHAPTER SEVEN

PRESENTATION CASTS

— TOM DECK —

SLACK-LINE CASTS

Many situations call for the line to extend out perfectly toward the fish. Hitting the mark with your fly is the goal but as the fly moves through the water, the way it drifts or floats is often the real reason why a fish decides to take your offering. Most of a trout's diet floats naturally in the current, for example. A straight-line cast is ideal for presenting the fly to the target but will sometimes cause the fly to drag artificially through the water. To counter this, you often need to add some slack into the cast so the fly drifts naturally once it lands in the current. Slack-line casts will enhance your presentation with the fly rod, so add them to your casting repertoire.

The Reach Cast

Fishing in rivers and streams can be difficult when cross currents disturb the natural drift of the fly. The reach cast, or reach-mend cast, is used to deliver line across a stream with different current speeds. Before the line falls on to the swirling currents, the rod tip is pushed or flipped upstream so that some slack line falls onto the water. This allows the fly to drift drag free. Make an overhead cast and wait until the line completely unfurls in the air. Now swing the rod tip upcurrent and let some slack form near the rod tip as the line falls to the water. This will reposition the line across the stream

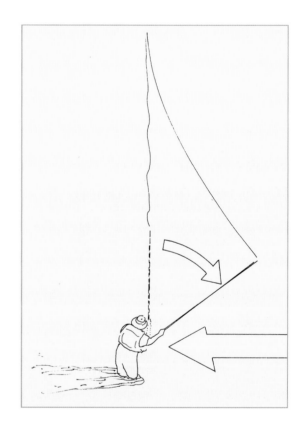

The Reach Cast
Before the line falls on to swirling currents, the rod tip is pushed or flipped upstream so that some slack line is added to the cast. This slack will allow the fly to drift drag free.

but the slack line will be above the fly. As the fly drifts downstream, the slack line will be in the faster current, allowing the fly to be undisturbed as it is presented to the fish. The reach cast permits longer, drag-free drifts that can produce fish when dealing with tricky cross-stream presentations.

The S-Cast

The S-cast is used to add slack into the line as it is presented to the water, allowing the fly to drift realistically in the current. As the cast is delivered, the rod tip is wiggled back and forth before the line falls onto the water. These S curves provide slack in the line as it drifts over multiple currents. The S-cast is easy to do but the trick is to add the S curves after you complete your normal forward cast. Finish the forward stroke, stop the rod tip at around eye level, then wiggle the rod tip side to side, putting some S curves in the line as it falls to the water. You can place a few big S curves or a bunch of smaller ones, depending on the situation. If you are fishing on a small trout stream with tiny micro-currents, a few small S curves are all you need to eliminate drag on your fly. On larger, more turbulent rivers, you may need to make more S curves with larger loops. The way you shake the rod tip at the end of the cast will determine the size and number of S curves you put in the line.

THE FLY-FIRST OR TUCK CAST

The fly-first cast is used in many fishing situations and is a way to present the fly on the water ahead of the line. This cast may be used to drive a subsurface fly into the water so that it sinks quickly. It can also be effective when you're fishing pocket water with dry flies. This cast lets you be very precise at dropping a dry fly tightly into the quiet water behind rocks or other obstructions. Because the fly lands on the water first, it will give you a few valuable moments of drag-free drift before the line lands on the water.

To present the fly first, your front cast needs to be slightly overpowered or accelerated to a high and aggressive stop. Make a normal high backcast, then drive the rod tip to an abrupt stop on the front cast. Stop the rod tip high

The S-Cast
To get a drag-free float over multiple currents, wriggle the rod tip back and forth. These S curves provide slack so the fly can drift drag free over multiple currents.

overhead, above eye level. The combination of overpowering the front stroke and stopping the tip higher will force the fly to hit the water ahead of the line.

THE CURVE CAST

The curve cast is really just a tuck or a fly-first cast turned on its side. The fly-first cast is executed vertically; the curve cast is the same motion, just angled more horizontally. Rather than overpowering the rod to a stop high overhead, lower the casting plane more to the side and cast the fly around a corner. The more you drop the cast on its side, the more the fly will swing around a curve. The key is to not let the rod tip lag around to a slow stop at finish. Drive the front stroke side-arm to a hard stop and cast the line around a corner. The line will

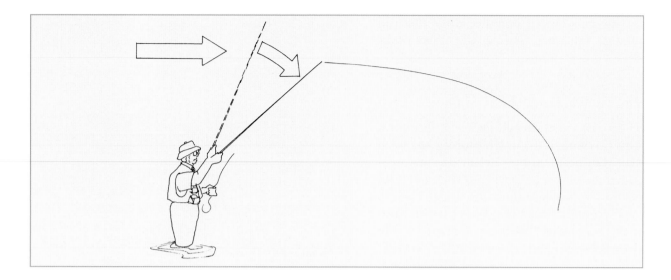

The Fly-First or Tuck Cast
The combination of slightly overpowering the front cast and stopping the rod tip at a higher point in the arc will force the fly to hit the water ahead of the line.

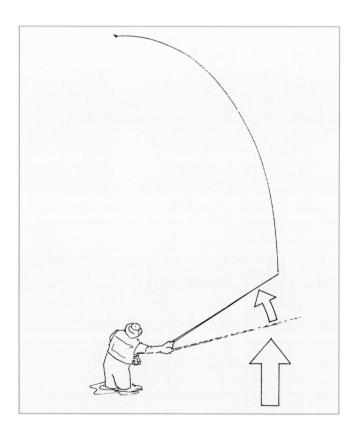

Curve Cast
A curve cast is really a tuck cast thrown side-arm. Lower your casting plane so you are almost casting side-arm. Energetically bring the rod to a stop and the extra line speed will sling the line around a corner.

go in whatever direction the tip points when it is accelerated to a stop.

This cast is very useful for presenting a fly under overhanging trees or branches, especially to hard-to-catch fish. As trout see more and more flies, they become increasingly leader-shy. The curve cast is popular because a fly can be cast upstream and curved around and over to a feeding fish. This way the line and leader do not drift over a fish's head.

THE PARACHUTE CAST

Downstream presentations can be very effective at fooling wise old trout. When you're casting downstream, the fish will see the fly first, not the leader or line. If you position yourself effectively upstream, a downstream presentation can make a difference when casting to leader-shy fish.

The parachute cast is most often used when casting downstream to feeding fish. If a straight-line cast is made downstream, the fly will drag as it hits the water. With the parachute cast, the rod tip is stopped at a high point in the arc, so the fly will land softly upstream, above the fish. As the fly touches the water, the rod tip is lowered at the same pace as the river's

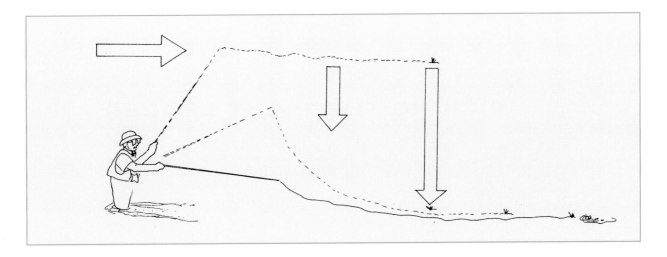

The Parachute Cast
On this cast, the rod tip stopped high overhead so the fly lands softly upstream, above the fish. As the fly touches the water, the rod is lowered so that the fly drifts at the same pace of the river's flow.

flow. This way, the fly drifts naturally downstream to the target. The Parachute Cast is an excellent way to present flies downstream and you won't miss strikes because there is very little slack in the line as the rod tip is lowered downriver. The key is to make sure that the rod is lowered at the same rate as the river's flow. If it is lowered too slowly, the fly will drag.

The **S**-cast is also used for downstream presentations but the slack created with this cast makes it hard to set the hook when the fish takes the fly. When using the parachute cast, the slack line can be controlled as the rod tip and line is lowered quietly to the fish.

TROUBLESHOOTING

1. **Problem:** When double hauling, slack forms between the line hand and the stripping guide after the back haul, and there is no line tension available to perform the forward haul.

   - **Cause:** The back or first haul is too aggressive and too much line has been pulled on the back haul. Pulling excessively on the back haul creates slack between the stripping guide and the line hand.

   - **Solution:** Make a short, crisp back haul so that there is less line to take up on the repositioning of the line hand for the forward haul. Don't rip the line out on the back haul so that your hands are pulled wildly apart. Your hands should never be more than twenty-four to thirty inches apart when attempting to double haul.

Tip: When attempting to learn the double haul, it is easier with heavier line weights. Smaller, delicate trout rods (4-weight or less) are difficult because the lines are so light that it is hard to maintain line tension while double hauling. Instead, try the double haul with a 7- or 8-weight. Better yet, try a shooting head! These heavier lines will suck up the slack effectively on the back haul, making it easier to reposition the line hand back to the reel before the forward haul.

2. **Problem:** Tailing loops form when double hauling.

   - **Cause:** The timing of the hauls is off. The line is being pulled or hauled prematurely during the casting stroke. The haul is being made before the casting stroke is executed, in other words.

   - **Solution:** The hauls need to be smoothly timed with the power stroke. Make a short, crisp tug on the line as the power stroke is applied.

CHAPTER EIGHT

PICKING THE RIGHT LEADER

— TOM ROSENBAUER —

Most people have no trouble accepting the fact that a leader removes the fly from the vicinity of the heavy, opaque fly line, which can spook a fish or at the very least make it suspicious. We usually want the fly line to land at least six or seven feet away from the fly and thus the suspected lie of a fish, so leaders must be tapered in some way. Why? Because a six-foot level piece of 4X tippet tied to a No. 12 dry fly will land in a big pile after the cast is completed. As we'll see shortly, this big pile is not always unwelcome—but not when it lands right next to the fly line!

A well-developed loop at the end of a forward cast is accelerating briskly. A leader that is too stiff and short, without a taper to absorb energy along its length, would slam your fly into the water. Conversely, a leader that is too limber and long will prevent your fly from ever reaching its intended target. Somewhere in between a long thin leader and a short stiff one is a reasonable compromise. All leader tapers incorporate a stiff, heavy butt section (the part that attaches to your fly line) and a midsection that forms a transition between the heavy butt and the fine end where you tie your fly—the tippet. The tippet is usually level and at least twenty inches long. The exact formula varies depending on the materials used to make the leader, but the most common taper is 40 percent butt, 30 percent mid, and 30 percent tippet. The taper can be made by joining sections of level material with many knots or it can be

of one continuous piece of extruded material without a single knot. The taper can even be constructed by making the butt and mid sections of one kind of material and the tippet of another, as in poly and braided leaders.

One final thought on leaders: It is not always enough to drive a fly with precision into a spot the size of a dime sixty feet away. A stiff, tapered leader can do that easily. You need, however, a more natural presentation in order to attract fish. Once your fly hits the water it should appear to be unconnected to anything, especially in stream fishing, and the farther your fly is from the stiffer part of the leader (which means a long, flexible tippet), the better. So there is nearly always a delicate balance between accuracy in the air and flexibility on the water. In our eagerness to cast the fly just where we want, the flexibility part is often ignored.

TYPES OF LEADERS

As in many areas of fly fishing, there's a bewildering array of options when the time comes to pick a leader. Don't let it bother you. Fly fishing is a subjective, individualized passion, and although there is a never a right or wrong way to do something, there is usually a simple solution that takes care of 95 percent of the conditions you'll encounter on the water. If you don't want to bother with the intricacies of leader designs, just buy a nine-foot 4X knotless leader with a loop on the butt end (most of them come this way) and be done with it.

KNOTTED LEADERS

If you want to learn about leader design and practice your knots, I'd recommend that you start by tying your own knotted leaders. Do this and you'll learn how leaders are tapered, you'll learn how to tie a wicked Barrel Knot, and you'll save money in the process. Whether knotted or knotless, pre-made leaders cost about three bucks each. Knotted leaders will cost you less than fifty cents each if you make them yourself.

Knotted leaders are made according to formulas like the one below, which specifies the length of each section. You'll notice how the leader tapers down from heavy to light, and that the heavy butt section and tippet section are longer than the transition sections in between. When you sit down to tie your own leaders, you'll need a yardstick (which is easier to use than a tape measure), a pair of snips or sharp scissors, and good light. Tie a Perfection Loop in the butt section material, then measure the butt section, adding perhaps an inch for the end of the knot that will be snipped off. Don't worry if any of your sections are an inch or so longer than the formula once you're finished, as leader taper is not that precise a science.

The Perfection Loop is not the easiest knot to tie but it is preferred for putting a loop in the heavy butt section because it is neat and compact—an important consideration when you're working with nylon that's .021 or .023 in diameter. You can tie a Surgeon's Loop (simply a double or triple overhand loop) in the butt of your leader but in addition to being a bulky knot, the Surgeon's Loop ends up cocked in relation to the rest of the leader. The Perfection Loop always ends up perfectly in line with the leader.

After you've tied a loop in the end of the .021 section, measure out twenty-nine inches (the twenty-eight inches plus the extra inch you'll cut off). Cut a sixteen-inch section of .019 (fourteen inches plus an inch at either end, since you'll be tying a knot at both ends). Tie a three-turn Barrel Knot between the two sections. Now cut the .017 piece and repeat the process, knotting it to the .019 piece.

NINE-FOOT 4X ORVIS KNOTTED LEADER FORMULA

LENGTH	DIAMETER
36"	.021"
16"	.019"
12"	.017"
6"	.015"
6"	.013"
6"	.011"
6"	.009"
20"	.007"

If you look at the formula, you'll notice that no two adjacent sections differ by more than .002. There are a couple of reasons for this. One is that the transfer of casting energy moves down the leader more smoothly if there are no abrupt changes in diameter. The other is that the Barrel Knot, the neatest and cleanest knot ever developed for nylon, loses strength when you jump more than .002 between sections. You can make a knotted leader with fewer sections (and knots!) using Surgeon's Knots, but the resulting leader would not have the delicacy needed for most trout fishing. Bass and saltwater leaders are often made this way because delicacy is not quite so important.

When you're casting, you'll notice that knotted leaders feel different than knotless leaders. Not better, not worse—just different. Some anglers believe that the compound taper you can get with a knotted leader (in other words, not a constant or smooth taper but a heavy butt, then a quick jump to the tippet using short pieces of material) is better than the smoother taper dictated by the machines that extrude and stretch knotless leaders. Others feel that the mass added by the knots helps unfurl the leader at the end of the cast.

It's also easier to modify a knotted leader on the water, at least when you're starting out. If you refer back to that nine-foot 4X leader formula, you'll notice the tippet section (the piece

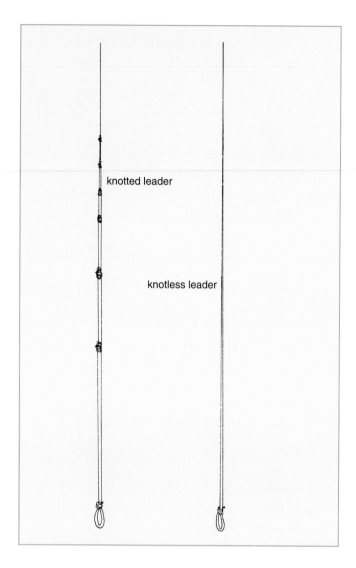

knotted leader

knotless leader

Tapered leaders: a knotted leader (left) and a knotless leader (right). The stiffer butt section loops onto the fly-line loop; the fine end (tippet) is the flexible part where the fly is tied.

where it goes. With a knotless leader, you can't see exactly where your tippet ends, and unless you carry a micrometer with you (don't laugh—some people do), it's hard to be certain where the new piece goes.

With a knotted leader, you tie a new piece of .006 tippet material to the six-inch piece of .007 material and you're back in business. Eventually, the six-inch piece of .007 stuff will also get too short and you'll have to replace that section, too. The intermediate transition sections are really there as connectors, though, so as long as they are long enough to tie a knot in, they're okay. When I tie my own leaders, I always make the last four six-inch sections about seven inches long, so I can get more mileage out of them.

Knotted leaders do have drawbacks, however. I think the weight of the knots makes a knotted leader land a touch harder on the water, an important consideration in shallow water where trout are spooky. The knots can also catch on debris such as aquatic weeds, sticks, and cottonwood fluff on the surface. And once the knots are loaded up with even a tiny amount of debris, the leader performs miserably. There is also the strength issue, but it's not as bad as you think. If you assume that a knot between two pieces of material gives you about 90 percent of the breaking strength of the weaker piece, so long as the knots in the heavier material are tied properly, the only link you have to worry about is the knot that joins your tippet to the rest of the leader. Let's say your tippet is two-pound test, and it's joined to a piece of three-pound test, which is joined to a piece of four-pound. The link between your tippet and the first section breaks at about 1.8 pounds ($2 \times .9$). The next knot up the line tests at 2.7 pounds. In other words, your tippet knot will always break before any of the other knots (assuming all are tied correctly).

KNOTLESS LEADERS

Knotless leaders are made by extruding hot nylon and subjecting the pliable material to a complicated series of rolling and stretching

of .006 nylon) starts at twenty inches. But every time you tie on a new fly—or lose one in the trees—you will lose anywhere from a half-inch to an inch of material between the knot and whatever you trim off.

After a half-dozen fly changes, the tippet is now only fourteen inches long. At this point it becomes so short that the fly slams into the water. The fly also becomes a less credible imitation in moving water, because the shorter tippet does not allow it to move as freely in the currents. So you need to tie on a new tippet, and with a knotted leader, you know exactly operations. The leader is heated and cooled a number of times along the way. The process is computer-controlled, requiring a fifty-yard run of machines and not simply an extrusion, as many anglers think. Early knotless leaders were often stretched to the point where the properties of the nylon were changed, almost always to their detriment, and it was impossible to construct a knotless leader with a butt over about .019 in diameter. Since most experts recommend a leader with at least a .021 butt for proper performance, early knotless leaders were clearly a compromise. Since about 1990, knotless leaders, particularly the ones coming out of Japan, have improved considerably in butt diameters, taper, and quality control. Most fly fishers now consider them as good as any other type of leader.

The obvious disadvantage of knotless leaders is that, at first glance, they seem to be disposable. Every time you tie on a new fly the leader gets shorter but it also gets stiffer. Because the diameter of your tippet section can be the most important part of your tackle, it's important to know when the piece to which you're tying your fly is too heavy.

Knotless leaders are manufactured with a level tippet that is somewhere between two and three feet long, depending on taper and length. Where the tippet ends and the intermediate transition section begins is never a clear division because there's no knot or even an abrupt change in diameter to tell you. So what do you do after you change flies ten times and feel that your tippet is too thick? Throw away the leader and spend three bucks for another one?

For flexibility and convenience as well as economy, you'll want to carry an assortment of tippet spools and gradually turn your knotless leader into a semi-knotless leader. Let's say you are using that nine-foot 4X leader and that you've tied and removed a dozen flies, so you have lost at least a foot of tippet material. That's too short—take my word for it for the time being.

Somewhere up along that leader the material widens into .008 or 3X, the next size up from your 4X. You can find this spot with a

A knotless leader won't gather weeds or other debris when you're playing a fish.

micrometer or one of the less expensive feeler gauges made for measuring tippet diameter. You don't have to get that fancy, however. Pull spools of 3X and 4X tippet material out of your fishing vest and hold a piece of 3X alongside your leader, sliding it up along the leader until you get to the point where the diameters look the same. Cut your leader here and tie on a new piece of 4X, anywhere from two to five feet long. We'll get into the particulars on how long it should be shortly.

Eventually, you'll be able to eyeball the diameter of your leader and won't even have to bother with this sliding business.

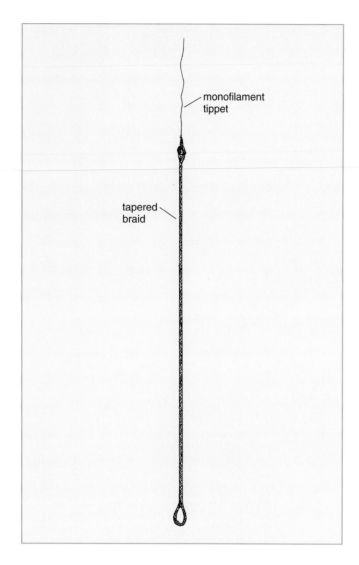

monofilament tippet

tapered braid

A braided leader, showing the permanent loop where the solid monofilament tippet is attached (loop to loop).

BRAIDED LEADERS

Braided leaders are more correctly called braided-butt leaders since the tippet end is made from standard solid monofilament. You might also see them called furled leaders. In contrast to knotted and knotless leaders, in which all parts are made from solid monofilament, braided leaders incorporate a butt section made from many tiny filaments, each much smaller than an individual piece of tippet material. Tapers are made by gradually eliminating fibers from the braid as the leader gets closer to the tippet end. At the fine end of

the braided section is a permanent loop, to which you attach looped tippet sections. You can either buy packs of looped tippet sections or make them yourself. Store-bought tippets sometimes come with a Bimini Twist in one end, which is a saltwater knot used to double the end of a section of line. It's a knot with 100-percent strength, which makes it unique, and if you use the doubled section to tie a knot, you maintain 100 percent of the weaker section's strength. The reason it's used for trout tippets is that it gives the tippet section a nice taper and makes it turn over better.

You can see the obvious convenience of a braided-butt leader. When your tippet gets too short, you just remove it and attach a new one with a loop-to-loop connection: no tying any of those nasty knots! Of course, there is no reason you can't put a permanent loop onto the end of a piece of solid monofilament other than the fact that loops are a little bulkier in solid mono than in braid.

Braided leaders have other advantages. Because they are more flexible than solid leaders in the butt section, yet still have the mass and momentum to uncurl, they mimic the casting loop of supple fly line. Because there is no hinged effect between the supple fly line and still leader butt, you preserve the energy of your casting loop. What this gives you is the ability to easily straighten out a five-foot tippet; with some practice you'll be able to straighten a tippet up to double that length. And the longer your tippet, the more realistic your presentation, because the heavier part of the leader is farther from the fish.

The flexible butt section of a braided leader has another advantage, too. Once the leader hits the water, the conflicting currents pulling at it are less likely to move the fly unnaturally, because its flexibility will bend and absorb the energy of the currents. With a stiffer leader, any current movements at the butt section are more likely to be telegraphed right to the fly—resulting in the unnatural movement of the fly, or drag.

Yet another advantage of braided leaders, a more subjective one, is that some people just like the way they cast and feel they are much easier to turn over. There is absolutely nothing wrong with choosing a leader this way; try one and see how you like it.

Braided leaders do have some disadvantages. The biggest objection to them is that the hollow braid holds water, and that you throw spray onto the water when you false cast over a fish. This is not a problem in broken or dirty water but might spook the fish in clear shallow water. Most of the spray can be eliminated by rubbing a small amount of paste fly dressing into the braid which will keep it from absorbing water. Some braided leaders on the market come pre-treated with a permanent dry silicone treatment.

Because of their flexibility, braided leaders don't work well with big air-resistant flies, with weight on the leader, or with strike indicators. If you think part of your day might involve streamer fishing or casting in pocket water with split shot on the leader and a strike indicator, you might want to start out using a solid leader, unless you feel like changing leaders in the middle of the day. This is not to say you can't fish this stuff with braided leaders but most anglers reserve braided leaders for fishing with dry flies and nymphs No. 12 and smaller.

POLY LEADERS

Poly leaders are made by coating a monofilament core with clear, flexible polyethylene. Bigger in diameter than regular monofilament leaders, they have a lower specific gravity and the pure polyethylene ones float. There is a loop in the polyethylene on the end that loops to your fly line; at the other end the nylon core extends from the end of the polyethylene coating and forms a loop to which you can attach a looped tippet section. As with braided leaders, you can make your own or buy tippets with Bimini Twists.

The advantage of poly leaders over braided leaders is that they can't hold water so they need no dressing and won't throw any water spray. Because they have more mass than other leaders, poly leaders will really punch a fly with a short tippet, and when you need delicacy they will straighten a tippet up to eight feet

A braided leader will give you a more natural drift in situations where drag is tricky and a long tippet is needed.

long—which is needed when fish are spooky, because the heavy butt section hits the water pretty hard.

These leaders are best when you need to punch a fly into the wind and when delicacy is secondary. Such situations might occur when you are fishing streamers or weighted nymphs in streams, or when you are fishing stillwater in a wind, where the mass of the leader will help straighten the tippet and the splash of the heavy butt section hitting the water will be masked by waves.

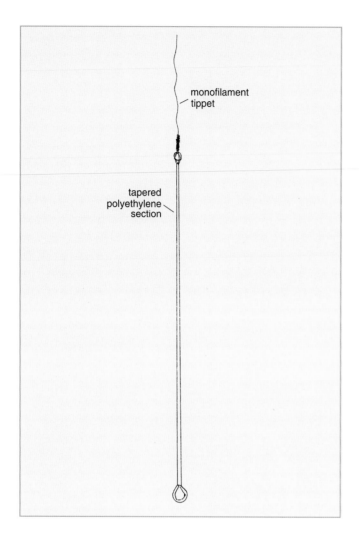

A poly leader, with a larger diameter than regular monofilament. Although the butt section is heavier, a pure polyethylene leader will float. Poly leaders shed water and don't throw any spray.

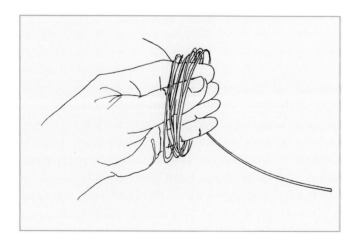

By uncoiling and recoiling a leader this way, you'll avoid tangles.

SINKING LEADERS AND MINI LEAD HEADS

Some braided leaders incorporate tungsten slurry into the braid, which produces a fast-sinking leader. Use these the same way you would use an ordinary braided leader, at least as far as attachments are concerned. These leaders hit the water hard, however, and should only be used in fast and/or deep water with a short tippet. They are a quick alternative to a sinking or sink-tip fly line when you only need to get a wet fly or streamer a few feet below the surface of the water.

Mini Lead Heads are short pieces of sinking line with loops on both ends. They can be looped to the end of a braided leader or right at the end of the fly line. They offer virtually no delicacy but neither does a sink-tip line. These are easier to carry in a fishing vest than another fly line and a spare spool for your reel.

TAKING A LEADER OUT OF THE PACKAGE

This may seem like superfluous advice but I remember that when I started out fly fishing I would invariably tangle a leader when taking it out of a package. Here's how to avoid problems: Take the coiled leader out of the package and insert one hand into the middle of the coils. Find the heavy end, which usually has a loop on it, and work this end out from under the rest of the leader. You'll have to pass it under the coils a half dozen times or so, until you see that it is not wrapped over the rest of the coils. Now slowly pull the heavy end of the leader, letting the coils pay off your hand until the entire leader is free.

To put a leader away, simply reverse the process. Start wrapping the tippet end of the leader around the fingers of one hand until you get to about six inches from the end. Wrap the heavy end of the leader around the coils four or five times. You can now remove the leader from your fingers and it will stay in a nice neat package.

CHAPTER NINE

ATTACHING A FLY TO THE TIPPET

— TOM ROSENBAUER —

CLINCH KNOT

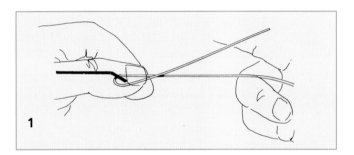

This is the traditional knot for tying monofilament to any loop. It is most often used to tie the tippet to the eye of the fly, but it is sometimes used with dropper flies to either connect the dropper to the bend of the hook or to the standing part of the leader itself, above a knot. It is strong and reliable but must be tied carefully. When using PVDF material or when tying a tippet to a fly where the diameter of the tippet is much smaller than the wire diameter of the eye, I recommend either the Orvis Knot or the Twice-Through-the-Eye Clinch or Trilene Knot. Both of these knots are superior to the Improved Clinch Knot, a version of the Clinch Knot that is not worth learning.

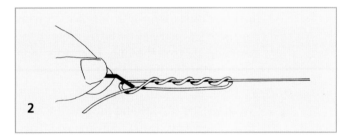

1. Pass the tippet through the eye of the hook. It doesn't matter whether you come from above or below. Place the thumb and forefinger of your left hand in front of the eye to keep a loop open. Cradle the standing part of the line in the last two fingers of your right hand.

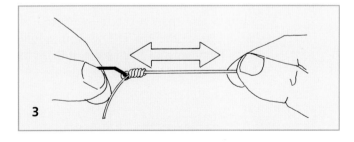

2. Wind the tag end around the standing part of the line by using the thumb and forefinger of your right hand to do most of the work. Use the third finger of your left hand to help pass the tag end around the standing part. All of this sounds complicated and you may develop your own method, but by using your fingers precisely as shown, this knot becomes very easy. Use five complete turns for monofilament in diameters from .007" to .017". Use three turns for shock tippets, because you will never get the coils to tighten in the heavy stuff and three turns seem to hold well. In material smaller than .007" in diameter I use seven turns, because the smaller stuff seems to slip more easily.

3. Pass the tag end through the loop you have held open in front of the eye. Lubricate the knot with saliva and draw it tight with a quick pull on the fly and the standing part of the tippet. Let go of the tag end when tightening this knot. Trim the tag end very close to the knot.

TWICE-THROUGH-THE-EYE CLINCH KNOT OR TRILENE KNOT

I use this knot mainly for bigger flies. Although this is my favorite for tying saltwater flies to a regular tippet (not a shock tippet), it's also great when fishing big nymphs, streamers, or bass flies. The knot is trickier to tie and tighter than the Clinch Knot.

1. Start this knot the same way as you would start a Clinch Knot, but after you have brought the tippet through the hook eye, keep coming around and pass the tippet through the hook eye a second time, in the same direction as the first pass. This will form a double loop in front of the eye as you start to make your turns around the standing part of the line. Keep this loop open with the thumb and forefinger of your left hand.

2. Wind the tag end around the standing part *five times only.* Bring the tag end back through the double loop in front of the eye.

3. Moisten and tighten carefully. Instead of letting go of the tag end as you would when tightening a Clinch Knot, it helps to hold the tag end tightly against the fly.

A Trilene Knot (modified Clinch Knot-twice through the eye.)

ORVIS KNOT

This is a small, strong knot that is hard to tie incorrectly once learned. It is superb for all fresh-water applications, and for tying saltwater flies to the tippet when you are not using a shock tippet.

1. Give yourself plenty of tippet for this one. Pass the tippet through the eye of the fly from the bottom and form a loop by bringing the tag end over the standing part of the tippet on the *far* side.

2. Form a second loop, farther away from the fly, by bringing the tag end all the way around the standing part, then passing the tag end through the first loop from the *far* side.

3. Fold the tag end over and take two turns around the loop just formed (the second loop). Make sure these turns start at the *far* side of this second loop.

4. Lubricate the knot. Tighten the second loop against the standing part by pulling on the fly and the tag end. Then let go of the tag end and pull on the fly and the standing part until the knot snugs neatly against the eye. Trim the tag end close to the fly.

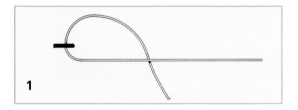

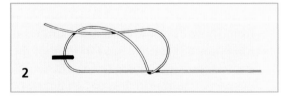

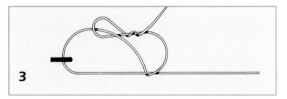

CHAPTER TEN

TYING LEADER MATERIAL TOGETHER

— TOM ROSENBAUER —

SURGEON'S KNOT

This is one of the easiest knots to tie. It is also one of the strongest and unlike the Barrel Knot, it can be used to join sections that are as much as .0040 different in diameter. Its only disadvantage is its bulk; in sections heavier than .0120 the Barrel Knot is much neater and smaller.

1. Overlap the tag ends of the two strands you are joining by four to six inches. The section not attached to the rest of your leader and the line (in most cases a new tippet) should start in your left hand.

2. Form a loop in the overlapped strand and pinch the junction of the loop with the thumb and forefinger of your right hand.

3. Using your left hand, wrap the standing part of the tippet (or smaller piece) and the tag end of the bigger piece through the loop three times. Treat them as a single piece; they'll stay together easier if you wet them with saliva. Many sources recommend using only two turns but lab tests have shown us that the Triple Surgeon's Knot is marginally stronger and no harder to make with a third turn.

4. Tighten this knot by holding both short and long ends on each side and pulling quickly and tightly. Make sure all strands are snug, then trim the tag ends as close to the knot as possible.

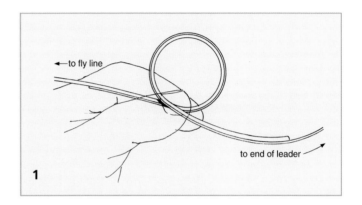

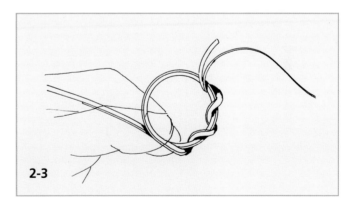

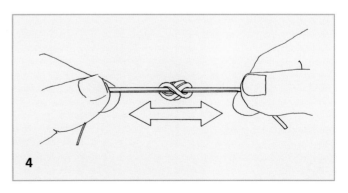

BARREL OR BLOOD KNOT

This knot is used to make knotted leaders. The knot is neat and clean, and nearly as strong as the Surgeon's Knot when tied carefully. The sections joined should differ by no more than .0020 in diameter. (In other words, you can join 2X to 4X but not 1X to 4X.)

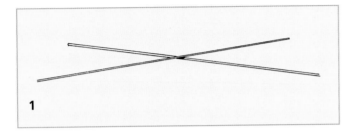

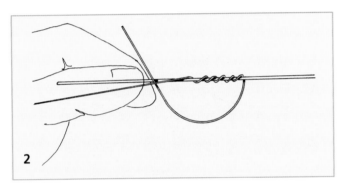

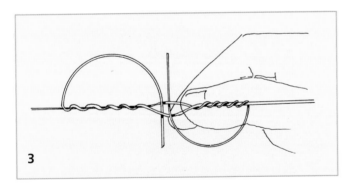

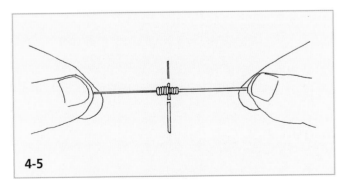

1. Cross the two strands of monofilament, forming an X. This knot is easier to tie if there are five to six inches of tag end on each side of the X.

2. Cradling the standing end of each strand in the last two fingers of each hand, start by winding the tag end of one strand around the standing part of the other strand, working away from the X. Use your thumb and forefinger to make these turns. Keep the loop formed at the X open by pinching it with the thumb and forefinger of the hand you are not using to wind. In this knot, unlike the Surgeon's Knot, it doesn't matter which hand holds the heavier strand, and the smaller end does not have to pass through the knot; if you already have a fly tied onto your tippet, this knot is easier.

3. Use three turns on each side with monofilament bigger than .0170 in diameter. With material from .0150 to .0100 in diameter, use five turns; and for material .0090 in diameter and smaller, use a full seven turns. Pass the end you have just been winding through the loop at the X. Now pinch the loop with the thumb and forefinger you have just been using to wind. Try to keep the loop open, because the tag end from the other side will have to pass back through this loop. Repeat the process on the other side, making sure you wind the same number of turns on both sides. Pass the second tag end back through the same loop as the first tag end, from the opposite side of the loop.

4. Make sure that the tag ends stick out from the loop enough so that they don't slip out when you tighten the knot. Don't pull on these tag ends when tightening the knot. Moisten the knot and pull on both standing parts quickly. The barrels on both sides of the knot should form neat coils; if not, cut the strands and start over.

5. Trim the tag ends close to the knot.

ORVIS TIPPET KNOT

A variation of the Orvis tippet-to-fly knot, developed by Orvis CEO Perk Perkins, can be used to join two pieces of tippet; as in the Surgeon's Knot, the tippets can be up to .0040 different in diameter. This is a very strong knot, with close to 100 percent of the break strength of the weaker strand, but like the Surgeon's Knot, it is bulkier than the Barrel Knot and is best used with larger diameters. If you can tie a Surgeon's Knot, this one is only slightly more difficult.

1. Line up both strands with about eight inches of overlap. Form a loop by bringing the tippet end (and the short end of the heavier piece along with it) around in front of the crossover.

2. Bring these pieces around the back and up, forming an open loop. At this point it helps to pinch the second, open loop.

3. Coming around the front of the first loop, close the second loop by bringing the tippet (and the short end of the heavier piece) through the first loop.

4. Keep going around in the same direction for a second turn.

5. Moisten the knot and tighten it by holding both pairs of long and short ends and then pulling them against each other at the same time. Trim the tag ends as closely as possible.

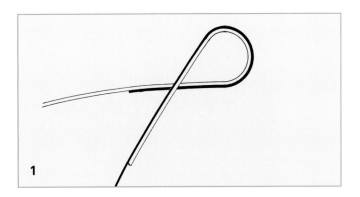

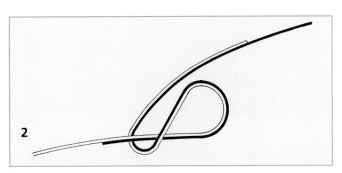

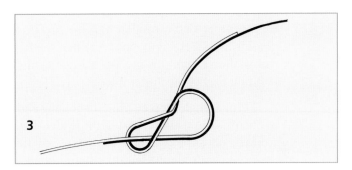

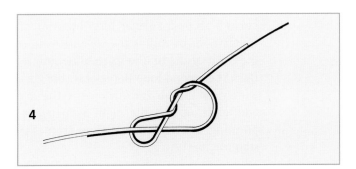

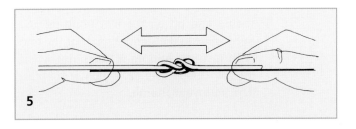

CHAPTER ELEVEN

TYING LOOPS IN MONOFILAMENT

— TOM ROSENBAUER —

PERFECTION LOOP

This knot makes a neat, small loop, ideal for putting a loop in the end of a leader. The Perfection Loop lies perfectly in line with the standing part of the line and as far as we know, it is the only loop knot that can make this claim. It is difficult to tie at first so follow the instructions carefully. The secret is to make sure that the tag end is always pointing at a right angle to the standing part of the leader.

1. Form a single loop by bringing the tag end behind the standing part of the leader. The tag end should be pointing toward the right, at a right angle to the standing part of the line.

2. Form a second, smaller loop in front of the first one by rolling the tag end around the front of the first loop, then behind it. Push the second loop flat against the first with your thumb and make sure the tag end ends up on the right side again, pointing at a right angle away from the standing part.

3. Take the tag end and fold it to the opposite side, passing it between the two loops. It should end up on the left, pointing at a right angle to the standing part of the line. Push it to the bottom of the point where the two loops overlap. Pinch it in place here with your thumb.

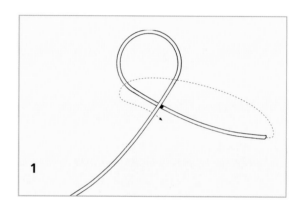

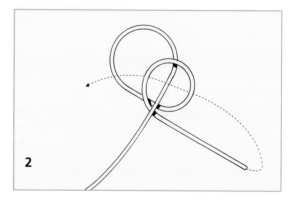

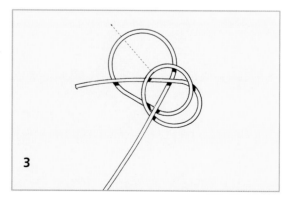

4. Reach behind the first loop and pull the second smaller loop through it. Make sure the tag end stays put on the left at a right angle to the standing part. Tighten the knot by pulling the second loop straight in line with the standing part of the leader. Do not hold the tag end or put pressure on it.

5. Tighten the knot fully and inspect it. The tag end should still be pointing at a right angle to the standing part of the leader and the loop itself should be in line with the standing part. If not, cut the knot and try again. Trim the tag end when you are satisfied the knot is tied properly.

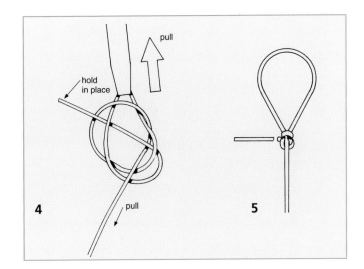

SURGEON'S LOOP

The Surgeon's Loop is simply a double overhand knot, one that's very strong but not as neat as a Perfection Loop. It is most often used to form a loop in a trout-sized tippet (for instance, when making a tippet section for a braided-butt leader) or for making a loop in a tippet that has been doubled with a Bimini Twist. Its bulk does not matter in these smaller sizes and because tippet material is not as stiff as butt material, you can't tell that the loop is not in line with the standing part.

1. Make a loop and overlap the tag end with the standing part of the leader for about five inches. Pinch the material close to the top of the loop and near the bottom of the overlap.

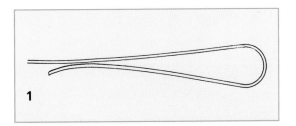

2. Tie a loose overhand knot in the doubled section and pass the single loop through the double loop you have just formed. Don't tighten.

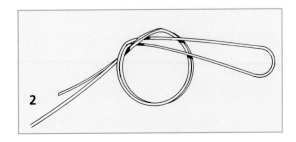

3. Make another turn of the single loop through the doubled loop. In other words, make a double overhand knot in the doubled section.

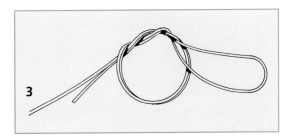

4. Moisten the knot. Tighten it by pulling the loop away from both the tag end and the standing part of the line. Make sure you pull equally on the standing part and the tag end of this knot, unlike the Perfection Loop. Trim the tag end closely.

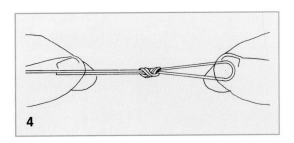

PART II
TROUT

CHAPTER TWELVE

HOW TROUT FEED

— TOM ROSENBAUER —

Trout are shy and careful cold-blooded creatures. In contrast to brightly colored bluegills—fish that feed right under your boat and investigate everything that plops into the water near them—trout are well camouflaged, fussy about what they eat, and will bolt for cover at the slightest disturbance. Think of bluegills as chickadees and trout as woodcock. A chickadee will feed on your windowsill, never try to hide, and can be tame enough to eat out of your hand. Woodcock creep around in heavy brush probing for worms, freeze at the first sign of your presence, and take flight when they think you've spotted them.

Trout evolved over tens of thousands of years to feed in moving water. They are perfectly adapted to preying upon insects: Their streamlined shape allows them to tip up into the current and spear a mayfly nymph from the conveyor belt of moving water that brings them a constant food supply. Their eyesight is sharp enough to spot a tiny midge no bigger than a pinhead when it is still two feet away. Their metabolism is highest when aquatic insects are most active. They can change the color of their bodies to adapt to different stream bottoms; a trout that moves from a dark granite bottom to marble bedrock, for example, will lighten several shades in a few hours. This ability to remain camouflaged allows them to prey on their food supply without being preyed upon (except by anglers) and thus is critical to their survival.

Trout are also adapted to still water, revealing their oceanic origins prior to the retreat of the last Ice Age. In slow pools or lakes they swim about searching for prey, and although they prefer food that does not try to escape, when needed they can run down a minnow with blinding speed.

Trout are efficient feeding machines, although they may seem lazy when looked at with an anthropomorphic eye. Over many thousands of years, their tiny brains have evolved into amazing pea-sized computers that can instantly gauge the net energy benefit to be gained from rising through three feet of water to chase a fleeing insect, as opposed to plucking a nymph drifting six inches away. Energy used is always balanced metabolically with energy obtained, to the point where—perhaps through taste—a trout can instantly judge that eating a mayfly will get them more net calories than chasing a water strider.

DRIFT FEEDING

From the time they are hatched from eggs until they are about fourteen inches long, trout in moving water do nearly all of their feeding by plucking insects and crustaceans from the current. As trout become larger, they may become foragers and prowl for bigger food such as minnows and crayfish. But if insect food is abundant, trout will continue to feed from the drift no matter how large they become. It's an efficient way of getting a lot of food with little

Trout feed efficiently in currents, wasting little energy.

expenditure of energy. The current supplies a constant flow of food and all a trout has to do is make sure that what it plucks from the current is worth the effort.

By trial-and-error, a trout takes up a station on the bottom of a river that lets it stay in place with little effort but is close enough to a flow of water that supplies food. The flow of currents over a riverbed is hardly constant: Pockets of slow and fast water are formed by turbulence and the rougher the stream bottom, the more good places there will be for trout to feed. A typical lie would be behind a rock, where a trout can rest in the slow water behind the rock and dart to the faster current on either side. A spot that's nearly as good but not as apparent is the space in front of a rock, where the current piles up and forms a cushion of slow water immediately in front of the rock. Other desirable spots are places where water rushes over a depression in the stream bottom or places where fast current smashes into slower water and forms what is called a seam.

A trout feeds in the drift by tipping its fins and letting the current push it to a series of spots where it can intersect food. You don't see much movement of the trout's streamlined body because its control surfaces (much like those of a 747 taking off) use the current in such an efficient manner. A trout taking food from the surface lets the current push it up and back slightly. The fish then tips its fins so the current pushes it back to the bottom; a small wiggle of its body brings it back upstream to its original position. In the same manner, when a trout sees a piece of underwater food off to either side, it uses the current to push it in that direction.

Dr. Robert Bachman, one of the top trout biologists in the country, received his Ph.D. by spending five thousand hours in an observation tower studying the feeding behavior of wild brown trout. Because he could recognize each trout by its unique spot pattern, he could determine how much time a trout spent in each position on the bottom of Spruce Creek in Pennsylvania. He noticed that some trout preferred the same position on the creek bottom more than 90 percent of the time, and would feed from this one position *year after year*, not only throughout the season. Others had three or four preferred spots and would move from one to the other throughout the day. When frightened, each trout had a favorite hiding spot. The shadow of an approaching fisherman or a merganser over the water would send each trout fleeing for a logjam or under a flat rock.

Bachman also observed that trout feeding went on all day when water temperatures were between fifty-five and sixty-five degrees Fahrenheit (F.), a range that is optimum for trout. And, unless there was a heavy hatch, trout fed both on underwater nymphs and insects trapped in the surface film, without much preference for floating or drifting food.

Bachman also observed that hatchery fish don't always act like wild trout. They seem to lack the ability to gauge the bioenergetics (potential energy costs versus benefits) of a situation, perhaps because they were bred in concrete tanks with little current. A hatchery trout often darts from one place to another, seldom taking up one feeding position, and thus wastes energy. This is one reason hatchery fish rarely survive more than a few months: They literally starve to death, even when surrounded by abundant food.

In slower water and only when insect food drifting in the surface film is abundant, a trout will hover just below the surface and feed in a regular manner. This is called *sipping*.

AMBUSHING

When some trout reach a length of about fourteen inches, they somehow "discover" that more energy can be obtained by ambushing the occasional baitfish or crayfish than bothering with little bugs. This happens more frequently with brown trout than with other species. Browns, in particular, become nocturnal or forage heavily when a stream gets dirty after a rain, probably because their prey become disoriented and can be captured with less effort. Radio-implant studies on the Ausable River in Michigan have shown that brown trout will roam *over a mile* at night prowling for food.

After dark, large trout that stay hidden under logjams or undercut banks during the day come out and cruise slow, shallow water in search of prey. Small fish that stay in the shallows during the day, partly because they can't handle the heavier current, also tend to stay in the shallows at night. Although this keeps them out of reach of large trout in the daytime, it makes them vulnerable at night, when they can't see predators coming until it is too late. Crayfish also come out from under rocks at night to forage the river bottom for carrion and aquatic plants. Trout can see quite well in low light and also use their lateral line (which senses vibrations) and their hearing to locate prey.

SELECTIVITY

A trout learns to distinguish food from litter when it's young. The next time the fishing is slow, bend down and look into the water. You'll see all kinds of stuff on the surface—cottonwood fluff, sticks, bits of vegetation, perhaps some insects. Unless there is a heavy hatch of insects, most of the surface litter is junk in terms of food value. Somehow, through taste or perhaps texture, a trout learns to distinguish food from garbage. We're not so different; one reason people become obese these days is because of the availability of fatty foods. Physically, we're still part prehistoric forager and something in our chemistry tells us to ingest these calorie-packed bundles because we don't know when we'll get our next meal.

Trout seldom experiment with their diet. They prefer to stick to safe and predictable food. Suppose there is a heavy hatch of a particular species of No. 14 cream-colored mayfly every day for two weeks. A hungry trout samples one: Its system tells it that the calories obtained are sufficient so the trout looks for more No. 14 cream mayflies. The trout develops a "search image" for the size, shape, color, and behavior of this mayfly. It doesn't perceive a bigger brown caddisfly as threatening or even bad-tasting—it simply ignores the other bugs, just as it ignores sticks and stones drifting past. But occasionally a trout will experiment: If the mayfly hatch is dwindling, the trout is hungry, and that caddisfly makes a twitching movement, the trout now recognizes the caddisfly as something alive and samples it. The trout thus develops a "search image" for the caddisfly at the same time. Fish do seem to have rudimentary memories, so the trout may take a cream mayfly in a few days, even if it hasn't seen one in a while.

Many times there will be half a dozen different kinds of insects on the water and although a trout might seem to prefer one type over the others, it will be looking for all the insects it recognizes as food at the same time. On the other hand, even though you see a variety of insects on the water, the trout you are fishing for might be seeing only little olive mayflies, because the insects that are drifting over its feeding spot are of only one type. So you try a brown caddisfly imitation and the trout ignores your fly. This is not a casual statement: The trout really does *ignore your fly*. Unless the fly drags in the current, the trout does not sense any danger associated with your imitation insect. It simply ignores your fly, as it does all the other inedible junk in and on the water.

You will see times when trout don't appear to be selective at all and will take any fly thrown in their direction. This usually happens when there are lots of different bugs on the water or if you are fishing a stream that does not offer much food and the trout have to take every lifelike tidbit that drifts by in order to survive. Fish in every stream, particularly those in these sterile streams, do make mistakes; they sometimes attempt to eat twigs and rocks. As Bachman says, "Every time a trout takes my nymph, he screwed up!"

You can fish only a No. 14 Adams for the rest of your life and catch lots of trout. You might do this and concentrate on developing your skills in casting, reading the water, and approaching trout without spooking them. But there will be times when trout will ignore your fly and you will have to be satisfied with a nice day on the water. If you carry a wide variety of fly patterns appropriate to your waters, and if you study the life history and behavior of the foods trout eat, you'll catch more fish—providing your flycasting presentation is lifelike.

HATCHES AND DRIFT

A great hatch, one that brings every trout in the river to the surface, is the event of a lifetime. This kind of hatch does not happen as often as you might think. Most of the time a hatch dribbles insects off the river in twos and threes instead of hundreds, and although there might be a hatch of five insects going on at once, the trout seem to ignore the bugs—at least on the surface. Why are insect hatches so important?

In order to survive, aquatic insects must stay hidden from both predators and the current by living under rocks, in aquatic vegetation, or (in the case of caddisflies) secured to the bottom in ballasts of sticks and stones. Once a day, however, many of these insects release their hold on the bottom and drift freely in the current. This happens after dark and is a method of re-colonizing the lower parts of rivers, because most insects fly upstream to lay their eggs. Trout do feed on these drifting insects, especially early in the morning, at the end of the drift, when there is enough light to allow the fish to see the insects. But most of this drift happens overnight when the fish can't see the insects.

Besides *nocturnal drift*, the other instance when insects are abundant is during a *catastrophic drift*. This happens when a rise of water increases the current flow and insects get washed loose. Trout feed heavily at the beginning of a water rise for this reason. Catastrophic drift can also happen during daily water fluctuations below dams, or even when a stream bottom is disturbed by a wading fisherman. In some rivers, notably the San Juan in New Mexico, the upper Yellowstone in Yellowstone Park, and the South Platte in Colorado, big trout will often follow wading fishermen like puppies, feeding on the insects they kick up. The trout get so close that you can't even cast to them and when you try to shoo them away with your foot they come right back. This has lead to a despicable practice known as shuffling, where the bottom of the river is purposely kicked around to attract trout. This can harm the bottom of the river; moreover, it's unsporting—don't do it.

Aquatic insects stay hidden on the bottom most of the time but are available to trout during periods of drift or when they are hatching.

THE EFFECTS OF TEMPERATURE

Both trout and 99.9 percent of the foods they eat are cold-blooded (apart from the occasional mouse, lemming, or baby muskrat that a giant old trout might sample while feeding opportunistically). The metabolism of the fish has evolved so that it is at its maximum efficiency when its primary prey is available for capture. During the winter, when water temperatures range from near freezing to forty-five degrees F., a trout is mostly inactive. At that time of year most insects are also buried in mud or are inactive under rocks and gravel in the streambed.

In the spring, as water temperatures warm to fifty degrees F., insects begin to hatch and thus are more vulnerable to capture by drift-feeding trout. But at fifty degrees, a trout's metabolism is still relatively logy and the fish does not need to eat all day. It is not a coincidence that in early spring, insect hatches occur only during the warmest part of the day. Trout time their feeding accordingly. By May, insects hatch throughout the daylight hours. When water temperatures are in the low sixties, a trout's metabolism is in high gear and perfectly attuned to transforming insect and crustacean flesh into fat, protein, and bone.

If water temperatures rise above seventy degrees F. in the summer, both insect hatches and trout feeding dwindle. A trout's metabolic rate continues to increase and its body utilizes oxygen at an increasing rate. Now, because warm water cannot hold as much oxygen as cold water can, the trout must become dormant. If the fish did not slow down, its energy demands would outstrip its supply of oxygen so quickly that it would die. In fall, as water temperatures decrease, trout begin to feed heavily again, until the water gets too cold in early winter.

The temperature of the water, plus photoperiod, or day length, affects the hatching of insects. Each insect species has a particular time of season and temperature when it hatches and mates. Although most of the insects that hatch will get eaten, a small part of the population will survive to meet and mate, so the species will survive. Some insect species will hatch for just a few days each season; others may hatch for as long as a month. A few insect species are multi-brooded and have two or three hatch periods during the year. Just as you see trillium blossoms only in early spring, wild phlox in late spring, and asters in August, insect hatches are regular and predictable. Knowing the hatching seasons aids greatly in identification.

The chart following gives you a general idea of the types of prey a trout is most likely to be eating at any given time of year.

TROUT FEEDING HABITS

MONTHS	FOOD MOST LIKELY TO BE EATEN	TYPICAL DAYTIME WATER TEMP.	TROUT FEEDING BEHAVIOR
Dec.–Mar.	Midge larvae, minnows, stonefly nymphs, leeches, crustations like sowbugs or scuds	35°–40°F	Very little movement, mostly in bottoms of slow pools. Fish will not chase their prey more than a few inches.
Mar.–Apr.	Mayfly nymphs and adults, stonefly nymphs, minnows and crustaceans, midge larvae and adults	40°–50°F	Trout will become slightly more active at the upper end of this temperature range and may feed on the surface in the middle of the day.
May–June (May–Aug. in cooler western and far northern rivers.)	Mostly larger emerging and adult mayflies, caddis flies, and stoneflies. Minnows and crustaceans will also be taken.	55°–70°F	Trout are very active all day long. Fish will actively chase insect larvae and make splashing rises. Trout will also drift-feed below the surface and "sip" mating insects that have fallen inert onto the water surface.
July–Aug.	Ants, beetles, grasshoppers, and other land-bred insects become much more important as aquatic insects dwindle. Mayflies, caddisflies, and stoneflies are mostly tiny—smaller than No. 16. Large fish will prowl for crayfish and minnows.	55°–75°F	Feeding is more concentrated in early morning, late evening, and after dark. Most feeding is more sedate; rises will be more of the quiet "sipping" variety.
Sept.–Nov.	Both tiny and large mayflies, caddisflies, and stoneflies. Minnows are eaten by large fish on spawning migrations. Midges and crustaceans once again become important, as hatches of aquatic insects become even more sparse.	50°–60°F	Feeding is erratic—it can be very active one day and almost dormant the next, depending on weather and geography. Best hatches and fishing are once again in the middle of the day.

CHAPTER THIRTEEN

A BRIEF LIFE HISTORY OF AQUATIC INSECTS

— TOM ROSENBAUER —

Some trout foods, such as crustaceans and minnows, are active and available to trout all season. But most insects, both aquatic and terrestrial, are dormant during the colder months. Insects are consequently more vulnerable to trout during the warmer months, when hatching from larvae into adults or when returning to the water to lay their eggs. Let's take a closer look at the life cycle of aquatic insects.

LARVAE

Larval aquatic insects are the wingless stages that live under water. Most of these live for about eleven months under rocks, in submerged weeds, or buried in the sand and gravel. Trout don't often grub food off the bottom unless it is easy for them to obtain: If cased caddis larvae are abundant, for example, trout might scrape them off rocks on the river bottom—but that is the exception rather than the rule. Larvae are easier for a trout to capture when they are migrating daily in the nocturnal drift or when floods or water fluctuations below dams dislodge them.

Some larvae are also captured and eaten more easily than others. Burrowing mayfly nymphs make tubes in the sand and a trout doesn't really get a crack at the nymphs until they emerge to hatch into adults. Flat, wide mayfly nymphs cling tightly to the undersides of rocks and seldom venture to the currentwashed side of the stones. Other mayfly nymphs swim

through aquatic vegetation and sometimes get washed away and eaten. Midge larvae seem to drift more often than other insect larvae, and even though they are tiny, in some trout streams they are so abundant that they are the primary source of trout food. Freeliving caddis larvae—the ones that don't build cases—roam the bottom of the river where they often get carried away by the current.

EMERGING ADULTS

In most rivers, emerging adult insects are the most important source of trout food. A few days or weeks prior to hatching, aquatic insect larvae get restless and begin to migrate into the shallows in preparation for hatching. For instance, the larva or nymph of the March Brown mayfly, a big brown one, hatches in mid-May on eastern rivers (the old name "March Brown" comes from a similar-looking English mayfly that *does* hatch in March). A week prior to hatching, the shallows are full of these big nymphs which earlier in the spring lived under flat rocks in the middle of the river. As the nymphs migrate to the shallows they sometimes lose their grip on the bottom and become part of the drift. Trout learn to recognize them as food and a big brown imitation nymph will catch trout weeks before you see any hatching adults.

The day a March Brown mayfly hatches, the exoskeleton of the nymph begins to fill with gases that buoy the insect toward the surface.

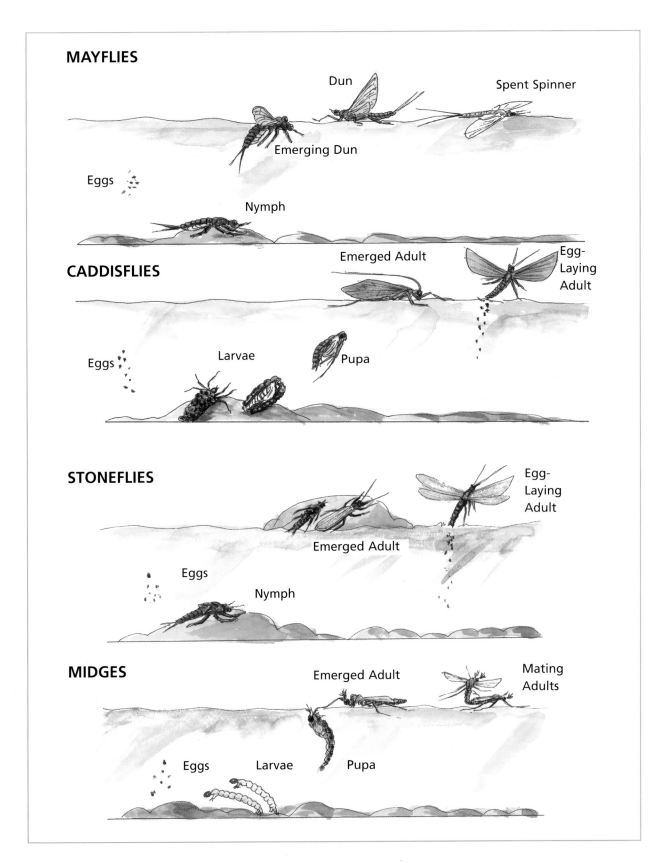

MAYFLIES

Dun

Spent Spinner

Emerging Dun

Eggs

Nymph

CADDISFLIES

Emerged Adult

Egg-Laying Adult

Eggs

Larvae

Pupa

STONEFLIES

Egg-Laying Adult

Emerged Adult

Eggs

Nymph

MIDGES

Emerged Adult

Mating Adults

Eggs

Larvae

Pupa

Life cycles of the most important orders of aquatic insects.

A mayfly is most vulnerable when it is emerging from its shuck in the film.

An insect may drift helplessly in the current for a few feet or, in some cases, for over a mile before it reaches the surface, splits its skin, and hatches into an adult. Trout are on the lookout for these nymphs and will eat them—close to the bottom when the nymphs begin to drift and closer to the surface as they hatch. This is a helpless stage for the insect: It can't get back to the bottom and most species cannot swim. Trout usually key into the prey they can capture with the least expenditure of energy and a drifting nymph is perfect.

Mayfly and stonefly nymphs rise to the surface while they are in the same larval stage they were in while living under water. Caddisflies and midges, however, like butterflies and other insects that undergo complete metamorphosis, form a *pupal stage,* which looks unlike either the larva or the adult and is an important part of the life cycle for imitations.

Once the nymph reaches the surface, it has trouble penetrating the surface tension of the film on the water. The insect will push and wiggle against the surface barrier, at the same time the winged adult tries to wriggle out of its larval skin. (Have you ever seen a movie of a monarch butterfly emerging from its cocoon?) Again, this is an easy meal for a trout, which senses the emerging insect's helplessness. Most fish you see rising at the height of a hatch will be eating emerging insects in the surface film

rather than plucking the adults that have emerged and are twitching on the surface, drying their wings.

Why do trout do this? Because the adult winged insects are able to leave the surface of the water abruptly and an experienced trout soon learns that a winged adult is not a sure meal. A trout that keeps rushing to the surface, only to be rewarded with a mouth full of air, is not going to get much to eat and may not live long. This is why you see small trout leaping for insects while the older survivors "sip" emerging insects just below the surface. Those youngsters haven't learned to be careful and sedate.

Some insects also crawl out of the water onto rocks to hatch and don't ride the currents as adults unless they get blown into the water. Most stoneflies and craneflies hatch this way as do a few species of mayflies and caddisflies.

Before the 1970s, most dry flies were imitations of a fully winged adult insect resting on the surface just prior to flying away. This makes sense because that stage of an insect's life is most visible to us. But our imitations don't always sit on the water as if they were ready to take off, and when they slump into the water, they make fine imitations of emerging insects. It seems that we fool ourselves as often as we fool the trout!

There are times when trout will eat fully winged adults on the surface. Most species hatch in riffles at the head of a pool, and in a big river such as New York's Delaware, where pools are nearly a mile long, trout in the tail end of a slow pool don't see many emerging insects. Any insects drifting on the surface have usually emerged long before they have reached the far end of the pool. Insect wings don't dry well in cold or wet weather, however, so during a rainstorm, species that might ordinarily take flight immediately may drift for many yards before doing so.

EGG-LAYING ADULTS

After an insect hatches and flies away, it heads for a nearby tree or bush to rest. The adult insects are hard to see after they do this

A mating flight of mayfly spinners can be seen by looking into the sun.

because they rest on the undersides of leaves to avoid being desiccated by the sun. (Drying up is as big a threat to their survival as trout or cedar waxwings.) Mayflies have a unique life stage because they are not sexually mature when they hatch as winged adults. The immature winged adult is called a *subimago* by scientists and a dun by fly fishers. These subimagos molt within a day or two into egglaying adults which are called *imagos* or *spinners*.

Most other insect species rest during the day and either return to lay their eggs or migrate in early morning or late evening. They copulate in midair or on the water surface. The females then lay their fertilized eggs by dropping them from above the water, dipping their abdomens into the water, or by crawling under water along the shore. Females and males both eventually fall to the water and die. The entire process of mating, laying eggs, and falling

spent to the water takes anywhere from several minutes to several hours. Large mating swarms of aquatic insects can often be seen hovering over the water for hours before they actually hit the surface. This gives you time to plan your attack.

Fishing to spent versions of adult insects is not well understood; some fly fishers even ignore this aspect of fly fishing. It often stimulates, however, trout to huge feeding frenzies and produces some of the best dryfly fishing of the season. Timing your dryfly fishing to imitate spent adults includes not only the more famous mayfly spinner falls but also the lesser-known mating flights of midges, caddisflies, and stoneflies.

MATCHING THE HATCH

When fishing for bass or bluegills, the idea is to lure a fish into thinking your fly or lure is

A Green Drake mayfly dun beside an extended body artificial.

just something to eat. Fly fishing for a drift-feeding trout requires convincing the fish that your fly is a *specific* kind of food. The better your fraud, the better your chances of catching a trout. What's most important? Should you fish a gray No. 18 caddis imitation if you are sure the fish are taking mayflies and you don't have any mayfly imitations in the right size and color? Most authorities will tell you *size* is most important, followed by *shape,* followed by *color.* An important factor that we often ignore, is the *attitude* and *behavior* of the fly *on or in the water.* In fact, I would rank that second in importance, between size and shape.

The process of matching the hatch is pretty simple if you have a large selection of flies. It only becomes difficult when you have a slim assortment of flies and need to decide which compromises you should make. You see a fly on the water, and you have seen a trout eat one of these flies, so you open your fly box and choose the one that's closest to the natural prey item. Make your selection in the following order and you should be in business:

1. *The size of the fly.* There is no need to measure the natural. Capture one if you can and place it on the lid of your fly box. If you cannot capture one, choose a fly that appears to be at least one size smaller than the ones you see on the water and two sizes

bigger than the ones you see in the air. Looks can be deceiving.

2. *The attitude and behavior of the fly on or in the water.* You can determine this by watching the insects hatch, by knowing something of their life history, or by observing the behavior of the trout. Check the insect's attitude on the surface: Is it flush with the surface film or riding high on the water? If you can determine this, you can choose either a highfloating fly or one that just barely hangs in the film. Check the natural's behavior: Is the insect fluttering across the surface or riding the currents sedately? If the insect is a nymph, is it drifting calmly with the currents or actively wiggling in the water column? With subsurface flies, you can get away with moving the imitation yourself. With flies on the surface, trying to make the fly twitch like a natural is a dangerous process because we invariably move the fly too much and cause drag. Although there are techniques to make a fly move, they require special flies, treating the leader, and positioning the fly precisely on the water. It's much more reliable to simulate movement by choosing a fly with lots of hackle which causes an apparent illusion of movement, at least to the trout.

3. *The shape of the fly.* Is it a mayfly, caddisfly, or stonefly? Are the wings upright or sloped along the body? Is the natural long and skinny or short and squat?

4. *Color.* Trout can see colors quite well but their perception of color depends on lighting conditions and other factors beyond our understanding. A discussion of whether color makes a difference or not could fill an entire book. Experience shows that the most important factor is at least choosing the correct shade—if a trout is taking creamcolored flies, it often will reject a black one in favor of a tan or yellow one. Color is probably more important in subsurface flies than in highfloating dry flies.

CHAPTER FOURTEEN

A QUICK GUIDE TO INSECT IDENTIFICATION

— TOM ROSENBAUER —

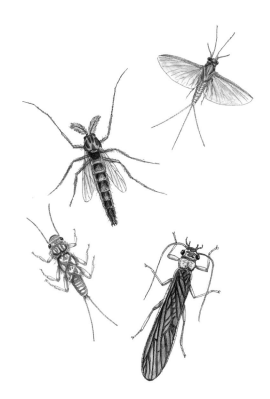

The most accurate way to identify or "key out" insects is with a binomial key, a type of "decision tree" in which you have two options for each anatomical characteristic, which in turn lead to choices between pairs of other characteristics. This is the way identifications are narrowed down in traditional entomology texts. I have found, however, that people who are not familiar with scientific procedures have trouble with this approach to insect identification. They prefer quick and easy charts. Look at the insect you are trying to identify—if it matches all of the characteristics in the chart below, you can be 90 percent sure of its identification.

To choose a reasonable imitation of a natural that will allow you to catch trout, identifying insects on the stream as members of the correct scientific order—mayfly, caddis, stonefly, or midge—is probably as far as you need to go. If the trout are rising in midafternoon and you see a pinkish-gray insect hatching at three o'clock, you can pick a fly from your box without knowing the species and still catch plenty of fish.

The ability, however, to key an index to genus and species can tell you this bug is the mayfly *Ephemerella subvaria,* known to fly fishers as the Hendrickson. Now you can take advantage of some practical fishing tips.

Your fishing entomology text tells you that this particular mayfly forms big mating flights in the evening and that the insects fall to the water just after the sun sets, bringing large

trout to the surface. Although you had a dinner date and were going to leave the water at five p.m., instead you stay until dark and have the best dry-fly fishing of your life. You also have relationship difficulties for a few days.

The following charts will help you identify the kind of insects you will commonly see trout eating. (I have limited these charts to the most important groups of aquatic insects and will assume that you can tell a grasshopper from a beetle.) The first chart will help you identify insect larvae that you will encounter by turning over rocks or by placing a small aquarium net in the water.

INSECT	GENERAL APPEARANCE	TAILS	BODY
Mayfly Nymph	Size: 1/8 to 1½ inches long. Color: tan, brown, cream, or olive. Shape: Anything from very skinny to broad and flattened. Found in all types of water.	As long as the body of the insect and thin. 2 or 3 are present.	Feathery gills on abdomen may be very apparent or almost invisible. Never has gills under thorax. Distinct wing pads on top of thorax.
Caddis Larva	Size: ¼ to 2 inches long. Color: Dull shade of cream, brown, olive, tan, yellow, or bright green. Most larvae form cases made from stones, sticks, or other vegetation. General shape is caterpillar-like. Found in all types of water.	None. A pair of tiny hooks are often present instead of tails.	Abdomen very fleshy and without gills. No wing pads present. Free-living caddisflies (ones that do not build cases) can be easily confused with aquatic beetle larvae but examination with a hand lens shows that beetle larvae have distinct pincers around the mouth.
Caddis Pupa	Size: ¼ to 1¼ inches long. Distinct curved shape. Color: dull. Found drifting in all types of water.	None.	Long trailing antennae. Emerging wings very apparent and held close to body.
Stonefly Nymph	Size: ½ to 2¼ inches long. Mostly flattened shape, but some smaller ones are round and skinny. Color: brown, black, tan, or yellow. Nearly always found in fast water.	Always 2, shorter than body length.	Gills located under thorax. Distinct antennae. Distinct wing pads. Legs robust, each leg always ends in 2 claws.

INSECT	GENERAL APPEARANCE	TAILS	BODY
Midge Larva	Resemble tiny maggots. Size: ½ to ⅜ inches long. Color: tan, brown, black, bright green, or red. Found in slow water.	None but a pair of tiny vestigial legs is visible/present at end of abdomen.	Eyes tiny. One pair of tiny prolegs at head.
Midge Pupa	Curved shape with distinct segmented abdomen. Dull colors. Size: ½ to ⅜ inches long. Found in slow water.	None but small feathery gills can often be seen at end of abdomen.	Wing pads tucked close to body. Distinct feathery gills branching off the front of the head. No long trailing antennae.

INSECT	APPEARANCE AT REST	APPEARANCE IN THE AIR	BEHAVIOR
Mayfly Dun (subimago)	Resembles a tiny sailboat. Wings always erect. Wings are speckled or translucent. Bodies full and opaque. Color: varies from dark brown to bright pink.	Look like tiny butterflies. Usually a distinct, cross-shaped profile. Only one pair of wings apparent.	Flutter or remain at rest on water. Stately, slow fliers. Usually fly upstream.
Mayfly Spinner (imago, or adult)	Wings may be erect or prone on the surface of the water (in "spent" adults). Wings always transparent, sometimes with slight speckles. Bodies very skinny. Difficult to see on water when spent without close observation of the surface. Colors: Similar to those of duns.	Tails very distinct and longer than those of dun. Females can be seen with egg sacks. Only one pair of wings apparent.	Fast, agile fliers. Often seen in large mating swarms above the surface of the water. Will also form mating swarms over wet roads and shiny cars.

INSECT	APPEARANCE AT REST	APPEARANCE IN THE AIR	BEHAVIOR
Caddis Adult	Wings are tent-shaped and held low over body. Long, distinct antennae. No tails. Colors: generally dull tan, brown, black, gray.	Look like small moths when they fly. Only one pair of wings apparent.	Very active when hatching. Emerging adults often flutter and skitter across the water when hatching; they usually do not rest on water after hatching. Quick fliers once they hatch. Usually fly up-stream. Mating swarms fly upstream in long, continuous columns.
Stonefly Adult	Wings always held flat over body. Adults look like nymphs with wings. Most hatch on rocks at the edge of streams, unlike other aquatic insects.	2 pairs of very apparent wings. Heavy body usually seen hanging below wings in flight.	Slow, clumsy fliers. Will fly up or downstream. Only seen on the water when blown onto the surface after hatching or when returning to the water for mating flights. Females can be seen dipping into the water during mating flights.
Midge Adult 	Resemble small mosquitoes: Long, spindly legs and feathery antennae. Distinct soft, "fuzzy" look. Wings held tight to body when at rest. Color: Usually black, gray, or cream.	Look like gnats or mosquitoes in the air.	Often skitter across the surface when hatching. Quick and agile fliers. Mating swarms form large groups just above the surface of the water. Individuals often clump together in twos or threes.

CHAPTER FIFTEEN

HOW DO YOU TELL WHAT THEY'RE TAKING?

— TOM ROSENBAUER —

Just knowing there are cream mayflies on the water or gray caddisflies in the air or grasshoppers on the bank does not guarantee successful fishing, no matter how perfect your presentation. Catching trout consistently depends on a combination of proper presentation and a reasonable guess at *what the trout are eating.* Identifying the bug is only half the battle: For instance, even though the water is covered with adult mayflies, most of the trout may still be taking the nymphs under the surface. Or trout might pass up big juicy mayflies to sip mouthfuls of tiny midge pupae. You can learn a lot by observing how trout feed.

UNDER THE WATER

It's tough to tell what trout are feeding on when they are feeding under water. This is true in fast or deep water, dirty water, or in most rivers. Trout are well camouflaged, they seldom flash on their sides when feeding under water (when you see this, it's usually suckers or whitefish), and they feed in places that make observation difficult. If you can see a trout, so can an osprey or heron.

You usually can't see trout feeding below the surface when you are wading in a river but if you can creep carefully up to a deep bank or peer warily off the side of a bridge, you may be able to spot them. You can also spot trout feeding below the surface in late-season low water and in the rich shallows of spring creeks and tailwater streams. Watch the fish carefully: A big school of fish is either a school of suckers, shad, or minnows, or else a bunch of trout that have been spooked and are hiding in the deepest water they can find. Trout don't normally school—any time you see them close together something is wrong.

A fish by itself or at least a few feet from another one might be feeding. A fish that is motionless for up to five minutes is resting, spooked, or just plain not eating. You have no clues. A fish that darts from side to side without tipping upward is eating some type of larvae or crustaceans close to the bottom. A fish that tips up for food is eating emerging insects, particularly if the fish occasionally breaks the surface in a swirl.

Generally, the larger the insect, the farther a trout will move to intercept it. Trout will move two feet for a No. 8 Green Drake nymph but will seldom move more than six inches for a midge larva. Some larvae, like those of damselflies, a few species of mayflies, and some caddisflies, can swim quite fast. Trout will run down and capture these insects with a long pursuit instead of just making a quick dart to one side.

If you see a big swirl—one that looks as if a trout just made a quick ninety-degree turn—that often indicates a trout that is chasing minnows. If you see this after dark in the moonlight, at first light, or if the water has just risen with a sudden rainstorm, you can be even more certain.

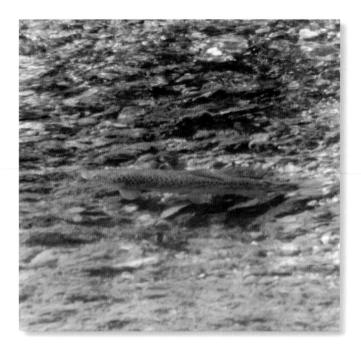

Unless you are a careful observer, you won't have many clues when trout are feeding under water.

Although trout rarely grub right on the bottom of rivers, generally letting the current bring the food to them instead, once in a while you'll see trout bottom-feed in an unusual manner. Sometimes trout will work their snouts under rocks to pry caddisfly cases from the bottom. I once saw a trout root a big crayfish out from under a flat rock. And in spring creeks, trout sometimes shake weeds the way a puppy shakes a rag, then drop back to gulp the scuds and sowbugs they have shaken loose.

By watching a trout feed under water, you can make an educated guess as to the size of their food, whether it swims or not, and where it is drifting in the water column. All of these observations can help you narrow down the right fly pattern.

Turning over rocks on the bottom of the river or grabbing a handful of submerged vegetation and spreading it out on the shore can help you figure out what the fish may be eating. Crustaceans such as scuds and sowbugs never hatch so unless you look under the surface, you'll never see them. When looking for insects under rocks, pick flat rocks in shallow

water with a fast to moderate current. Most insects hatch in the riffles, and the species that are about to hatch (and are more available to the fish) will often migrate to the shallows before hatching.

ON THE SURFACE

A hatch of aquatic insects, even one that seems to cover the water surface, does not always guarantee rising trout. Trout may be eating tiny or spent insects when all you see are big ones. This can frustrate you unless you stop, relax, and observe both the trout and the surface of the water. If you see trout rising, watch the water for about five minutes before you jump in. Watch the slow backwaters along the bank for insects. You can even see nymphs drifting below the surface if the water is clear enough and you look carefully. If you can't see anything along the banks, wade out to a place where trout aren't rising so you won't spoil the water by frightening them, then bend down close to the water and wait. Close all your pockets and take off your hat before you bend down really close to the water. Look now, and you can often see tiny mayflies or spent insects that were invisible from the bank.

Once you have spotted the insects riding the surface, try to figure out which ones the trout are taking. The luckiest situation is when trout are eating the juicy mayflies with big sailboat wings that you see twitching on the surface. Right—fat chance. It's seldom so easy.

You often can't see anything disappear into the mouth of a trout when it is rising. So if the trout isn't eating a big insect with upright wings, your other choices are tiny insects on the surface, spent insects in the surface film, or emerging insects just below the surface.

It's fairly easy to tell when a trout is taking an insect below the surface. When a trout takes an insect within inches of the surface, the momentum of its rise to feed takes the fish through the film, or at least the swirl the feeding trout makes carries through to the surface. Sometimes subsurface feeding can produce a hefty splash. But if you look carefully, you won't see any big bubbles. When a trout takes an insect from the surface it also takes in air, expelling the air from its gills as it swallows. In general, the bigger the splash accompanying the rise, the more likely it is that the fish fed just below the surface.

Your clue to a trout eating insects on the surface is either big bubbles trailing the rise form or seeing the trout's snout poke through the film. The snout may also be followed slowly by the dorsal fin and even a wiggle of the tail. A violent, noisy rise can mean either a trout going after an insect twitching across the surface or that it is a big one. A sedate rise with most of the head and dorsal fin breaching the surface like a miniature porpoise often means the trout is eating a spent insect such as a mayfly spinner or ovipositing (egg-laying) caddis. A quiet rise that is more concentric and just shows the snout of the fish is usually the end of a tiny mayfly or midge.

Insects in the air may not be what the trout are eating.

IN THE AIR

The first insects we notice when walking toward a trout stream are the ones in the air—especially if they are trying to bite us. They may be helpful but they can also be misleading. Slow-moving insects that rise from the water's surface and quickly head for streamside brush are insects that have just hatched and are good clues for fly selection. Insects hovering over the water and dipping on its surface are laying eggs. They will soon fall to the surface as spent adults and are also worth a close look. Flying insects that move upstream in a rush, however, like commuters leaving a subway terminal, may only be migrating. If so, they might not touch the surface of the water *for days*. These huge insect flights, most often seen with caddisflies and midges, can be frustrating—so many insects and not one available to the trout!

Trout can't eat insects that are in the air. (Actually, that's not entirely true—small trout sometimes leap into the air for insects hovering above the water.) You might see massive clouds of mayfly spinners above the water, but they could be mating and perhaps not a single

one has touched the water yet. The trout could be rising but they might be rising to an entirely different insect—one that's hatching at or near the surface. So insects in the air are only a clue, not the answer.

The best way to spot insects in the air is to look into the sun. You can miss a cloud of tiny mayflies unless you see sunlight reflecting off their wings. Another way to spot them is to look against a dark-colored bank or tree. Look just above the water first but then keep looking up. Spinners of the Eastern Green Drake can form mating flights one hundred feet above the water. If you spot them early, you can watch them gradually descend to the water and be prepared with the right fly when they finally land on the surface, usually just at dark.

Insects are attracted to shiny surfaces and apparently get fooled into thinking wet pavement or car windshields are water. I live about one hundred yards from a trout stream yet I can tell when mayfly spinners are active by watching them dip above my windshield in the driveway.

CHAPTER SIXTEEN

ANGLE AND ATTITUDE OF APPROACH

— TOM ROSENBAUER —

HOW MUCH OF YOU CAN A TROUT SEE?

Trout face into the current. It's the only way they *can* face because of the way they're built, with bullet-shaped heads in front and a flexible body and tail behind. They feed most often by lying in place, waiting for the current to bring them food. Trout have a blind spot immediately behind them. Unless you splash your line down right on top of them, create ripples on the surface by moving too fast, or make a lot of noise while wading, you can approach them quietly from behind. Be careful in big pools that might have reverse eddies in them because although you might be facing *upstream*, the fish may be facing *into* the current but downstream.

Trout facing upstream have a blind spot immediately downstream and can only see out of the water in a circular window.

Because of the way water bends light rays, trout can see more of the outside world when lying in a deep pool than they can when lying in shallow water. There are complex formulas and drawings that theorize on just how much a trout can see at various depths. Don't worry about them. Just be aware that a trout in three feet of water can see you from farther away than one lying in a foot of water. You can often keep your body below a trout's window of sight by crouching or kneeling. And by getting into the water and wading close to a trout, rather than approaching one on the bank, you can keep your profile lower.

Your position relative to the sun can make a big difference on bright days. Trout don't have the ability to squint so they don't see objects well when looking into the sun. If the sun is behind your back, a trout will have a difficult time spotting you unless you let your shadow fall over a trout's lie or you are silhouetted against the sky. Trees or bushes behind you will help break up your profile. It follows that if you are facing the sun and are illuminated in bright light, a trout will be able to spot you more easily. If you have to approach a trout this way, keep your profile low and your movements slow.

Fly lines flashing in the sun can also spook trout. Use a side cast to keep the line below their line of sight. False cast off to the side of a feeding fish and then change direction on your last cast to get the fly in place. Either that, or make your false casts deliberately short, shoot-

In small streams, the direct upstream approach is your best option.

ing enough line on the last cast to put just your tippet over a trout's head.

SHOULD I FISH UPSTREAM OR DOWN?

Most anglers prefer to move upstream as they fish. Unless someone is wading just ahead, you'll be coming up behind trout, where they can't see you as well. The bigger the stream, the less important this becomes because once you get directly across from a fish that's forty or fifty feet away it won't be able to see you or if it does, you won't appear to be a threat. Still, since most wading fly casters fish dry flies and nymphs, and both of these methods are best used in an upstream or upstream-and-across direction, it's easier to wade upstream as you fish. If you wade downstream and then turn around the way you came to fish, you are fishing over water that you have just walked through!

When fishing streamers or wet flies on a swing, it is often easier to work downstream. With these methods you try to cover as much water as possible, so working downstream, wad-ing with the current, tires you less and again lets you present your fly over water you have not yet waded.

On big rivers, with pools that stretch fifty yards or more from bank to bank, sometimes you'll just wade into a pool and fish directly across-current, without moving more than a few yards upstream or downstream. When you're done fishing a spot or a pod of rising fish, you will disturb the water less (and tire yourself less) if you wade back the way you came, walk the bank until you find another spot, and then wade out into the pool. Wading up and down a big pool spoils the water for you and anyone else in the area.

HOW FAST SHOULD I MOVE?

In food-rich streams, full of insect life and fish that don't spook easily, you can hook fish all day long without moving more than a few feet. New Mexico's San Juan, Colorado's South Platte, or the spring creeks of Mon-tana's Paradise Valley are just a few of these delightful waters. On the other hand, more than six casts in each tiny pool in a small

In small mountain streams, you should approach each pool cautiously but not waste much time in each place.

mountain stream with a sparse food supply and spooky trout are probably a waste of time. Small stream trout usually grab anything that looks remotely edible. If they don't take your fly, you've spooked them or the pool is empty, so you can move on. When fishing a small stream, it's not unusual to cover a half mile of water in an hour.

Most streams will fall in between these extremes. How fast you move should depend on what kind of fly you are using, whether you see trout feeding or not, and whether you feel like moving or not. There are no right or wrong answers. When fishing a streamer fly you should move all the time, never throwing more than two casts to the same spot. If a trout doesn't snatch a streamer on the first pass it will ignore subsequent casts, no matter how hard you flog the water. If you are fishing a dry fly "blind" (that is, not fishing to visibly rising fish), more than a dozen casts in the same foot-square spot are a waste. If you see trout rising to insects, you can stay in one spot, changing flies, tippet sizes, and casting angles until you catch them or spook them. One summer I fished for a single large brown trout on the River Test in England for more than an hour,

gave up, came back an hour later, and finally hooked the fish after another hour of changing flies and casting angles.

The other instance where moving is not necessary is when you are fishing a nymph, you are sure the trout are feeding, and you are sure there are many fish in front of you. This often happens in clear spring creeks or tailwaters where you can see trout feeding under the surface. Trout in these clear, rich streams may ignore your nymph for two hundred casts because something was not quite right with the drift, then inhale the fly on cast number two hundred and one.

If you don't see fish under the water or feeding on the surface, you have to guess how long you should spend in one spot. A typical time for fishing a pool fifty feet wide by one hundred feet long might be a half hour. In this time you'd try to hit all the likely spots you are going to learn about in a few pages. You might change flies three or four times. If you haven't caught a fish or had a strike in thirty minutes, it's probably time to move on. Perhaps someone was in this pool earlier and spooked the trout or maybe more trout are feeding a few pools upstream.

CHAPTER SEVENTEEN

EFFECTS OF RIVER CONDITIONS ON APPROACH AND PRESENTATION

— TOM ROSENBAUER —

FISHING TINY BROOKS AND BIG RIVERS

Most of what I have said so far applies to "average" trout streams, from twenty to one hundred feet wide. In small brooks and huge rivers you might need to adjust your tactics. In small brooks, it's almost imperative that you fish directly upstream: You can't fish directly across because the stream channel is too narrow, and if you fish directly downstream, trout will be able to see your every move. Trout in small waters are very spooky, given the shallow water and the ease with which predators can grab them.

In small streams, limiting factors to trout abundance are depth and protection. There is no secret to where you'll find them—in the deepest pools and places where logs or rocks give them cover. Unless you find a particularly deep pool where water is more than three feet, most pools and pockets can be fished with a dozen casts at most. After that, you've either caught all the fish or you've spooked them, as trout in tiny brooks are seldom selective and are always looking for food. Move quickly between pools but approach each new pool with extreme caution, keeping your profile low by crouching. Stay at least fifteen feet below the tail of the pool, and observe before proceeding. Where is the best place in the pool, where depth offers security and current brings the most food?

Don't overlook the tail of a pool in a small stream. Fish here are spooky and you often won't see them because by the time you've made a cast they have already bolted for cover. The best approach is to stay well back from the tail and throw your first few casts so that only half your leader lands in the pool. Try to throw the rest of your leader and line over rocks below the pool so that your fly does not drag instantly; if there are no convenient rocks, throw slack by making a parachute cast. You *will* hang up on rocks and logs at the tail of the pool. Your dilemma now is whether to break off your fly or sneak up to the tail and unsnag it. That depends on how good the pool looks.

Once you've covered the tail, move up a bit and make a few casts in the middle of the pool. Don't waste much time here unless there are some nice rocks or a deep slot. Most of the trout you find in bathtub-sized pools will either be in the tail or the head of the pool. Cover the head thoroughly, throwing right into the foam at the lip, and don't forget the seams at either side of the head.

The best way to fish a small stream, particularly if the water is less than two feet deep, is with a dry fly. Trout in small streams don't have far to go to rise to the surface, and you can bet they'll see your dry every time. As long as the water temperature is above fifty degrees Fahrenheit (F.), a dry fly can be as effective as a worm in the right hands. Another advantage to

As long as the water temperature is above fifty degrees F., a dry fly, cast straight upstream, is the most deadly way to fish small streams.

fishing a dry is that you can put your fly up against tight spots or tiny pockets and have it become effective instantly.

Nymphs require a bit of drift to sink and if a trout grabs your nymph as soon as it hits the water, you may not see your floating line or strike indicator twitch. I like to reserve nymphs for deeper pools, after I've tried a few casts with a dry, or when water temperatures are below fifty degrees F. A strike indicator helps but you'll rarely need to add any weight to your leader. Don't forget to set your indicator at about twice the depth of the water—which will be considerably shallower than you set an indicator in most rivers.

Small streamers, such as Nos. 10 and 12, can also work in small streams. The best place for streamers is in the larger pools, especially those at the bases of small waterfalls where trout may be reluctant to come up for a dry or can't see it because of the white water on the surface. Cast your streamer right up into the foam, let it sink

briefly, then strip it back in steady pulls right to your feet.

Trout will be everywhere you think they should be in small brooks. But in huge rivers, one hundred yards wide with pools up to a quarter-mile long, you may have trouble finding them. There is no way you can effectively fish a giant pool on Montana's Missouri or New York's Delaware without narrowing down the playing field. Giant pools are usually slow so you need to find the places where the current is swift enough to bring a steady quantity of food, which means you should concentrate in the head and the tail. Sometimes you'll find a jumble of rocks in the middle of a pool where the concentrated flow will hold some trout. In these large pools, the deep bank is typically more productive than the shallow one, especially if the bank is rough and broken with rocks or little bays and points.

One of the best ways to find trout in large pools is to observe them with binoculars. The slow current encourages surface feeding and because the trout might be a long way from a riffle, most of the food they see may be crippled emergers or spent spinners. Watch for cruisers. Although trout in most waters stay in one spot when feeding, if a pool is big enough and the water is slow, they will cruise looking for food because the current does not bring it to them fast enough. It's as if they get impatient waiting for the next morsel. They'll develop a pattern when cruising and if you watch long enough, you'll be able to predict where a trout will feed and place yourself in a position to intercept it. Trout will almost always cruise upstream, then turn around and swim back to where they started, repeating the process over and over again. I once watched a large brown trout in the Connecticut River on the Vermont–New Hampshire border cruise from the tail of a two hundred-yard-long pool to the head and then swim all the way back to repeat the process. At first I thought there were a number of fish in the pool and I kept moving upstream to get into position. Then I noticed that all the fish moved their heads with a peculiar sideways motion when rising and that there was never more than one fish feeding at one time. I tried to keep up with this single cruising trout without disturbing the water but when I finally thought I had caught up with him at the head, I turned around and saw he was already back at the tail! Then I waited and tried to intercept him when he returned but he refused my fly on his second pass. I finally gave up on him after playing the game for an hour. It was fun, though.

TEMPERATURE

Water temperature affects the way you approach a stream, the time of day you should fish, and how you present a fly. Approach is simple: In cold water below fifty degrees F., trout will be found in the deeper pools, in slow water, and will not be as spooky as when they're more active. As water warms above fifty degrees F., they'll become more active, will slide into shallower water to feed, and will be more alert and easier to frighten.

Watch for cruising trout in giant pools.

In water below that magic fifty degrees F. number, the best fishing will be in the middle of the day from eleven a.m. until about three p.m. This is when water is warmest and both trout and insects are more active. Between fifty and fifty-five degrees F., trout will be active from midmorning until the sun leaves the water. At water temperatures from fifty-five to sixty-five degrees F., trout will be active from dawn until dusk and well into the darkness if insects are still on the water. From sixty-five to seventy degrees F., water temperatures become uncomfortable but tolerable for trout, and the best fishing will be from dawn until midmorning because the water has cooled down to a minimum overnight. It's often thought that evening fishing is best in midsummer, and although you'll see some fish feeding right at dark when insects are on the water, remember that the warmest water will be in the evening. Night fishing becomes effective in this temperature range and streamers fished on a slow swing in the tails of shallow pools can be deadly. For some reason, humid nights with a new moon seem to produce the best action after dark.

Trout will feed sparingly above seventy degrees F. but it's not really ethical to fish for them at this time. Playing a trout in seventy-five degrees F. water will exhaust it and the fish

Nick Lyons suspects there is a hidden spring entering this pool on New York's Willowemoc because of the steep rock banks on the far side.

will become oxygen-starved from exertion (water this warm cannot hold much dissolved oxygen). Most trout caught in water at their upper range will die after being released, even if carefully revived.

When most of a river is above seventy degrees F., you can often find cold-water refuges where trout will be active and healthy. In many streams, trout move into the headwaters and tributary streams, closer to springs, and where dense shade keeps sun off the water. Steep cliffs often have subterranean springs seeping into a river so pools along steep banks may offer cooler water than other sections. If you listen carefully, you can sometimes hear the tinkle of spring water as it enters a river along a brushy bank, unseen by the casual angler. Carry a thermometer and search for water below sixty-five degrees F.

Water temperature is important when deciding how to present a fly. In water below fifty degrees F., you'll see few fish rising and a dry fly fished "blind" will be pretty useless. Nymphs and streamers are your smart options. Nymphs should be fished right next to the bottom, completely dead drift, in slower water. If you are not hanging your fly on the bottom once every dozen casts, you are not getting deep enough. Trout will move reluctantly for a fly, so precise casting into deeper slots is essential; if your fly is a foot too far on either side of

a trout, it will probably be ignored. Streamers should also be fished deep. Cast upstream, let the fly sink, and strip line until you feel resistance. Then let the fly drift a foot or so before stripping again. This makes your fly flutter like a wounded baitfish in the current and since it does not appear to be going anywhere in a hurry, a trout may think it's an easy target.

In water between fifty and fifty-five degrees F., trout start to warm up. They'll respond to a hatch but fishing blind with a dry fly is still not a safe bet. Nymphs should still be fished dead drift but trout might move up more in the water column so you may not have to get your fly right on the bottom. You can pick up the pace on your streamer retrieve, too.

You'll be in hog heaven with water temperatures from fifty-five to sixty-five degree F. You can fish a dry fly with success even if you see no rises or insects on the water. A nymph fished dead drift is still most effective but trout will be "on the grab" and will move several feet for the fly. They'll also respond to a wet fly or nymph that is swung in the current, especially if mayflies or caddisflies are hatching. You can fish a streamer upstream, across stream, or straight downstream. Strip like mad. Trout can capture a streamer moving faster than you can strip and in this prime temperature range a fast strip often works best, as the trout grab the fly from reflex without getting a good look at it.

Water temperatures between sixty-five and seventy degrees F. will usually be found only in midsummer after most aquatic insects have hatched. Mayfly larvae left on the streambed will be tiny ones and terrestrial insects take up the slack because of the paucity of hatches. Presentation should be cautious, and you should use light tippets and long leaders. You may see tiny mayflies and caddisflies (No. 20 and smaller) in the morning and evening, thus small dries or nymphs will be most effective. Ant, beetle, and grasshopper flies are good choices during the day. These dries and nymphs should be fished dead drift. You'll have better luck in bubbly riffles where the oxygen content is higher, than you will in the stagnant water of slow pools.

If you fish nymphs slowly and deeply enough, you can take trout all winter long.

At the height of the season, when water temperatures are perfect and flow is not too high or too low, trout can be caught almost anywhere using any method.

Streamers won't work well during the day but sometimes are quite effective at first light. Stick to patterns on the small side—No. 8 and smaller—when the water is this warm. If you can find pocket water with lots of turbulence, you might be able to tease strikes from trout on streamers until midmorning.

WATER LEVEL AND CLARITY

You can tell when a river's water is higher than normal by looking at the banks. A river in flood has narrow banks and some of the streamside brush will be under water. At times like this it can be futile to try to fish fast water or spots in the middle. Fish out there won't rise to a dry fly and you may not be able to get your nymph deep or slow enough to look natural. What's left? Try the water right along the banks, in the tails of pools, and at the head of shallow riffles where the current is slow and shallow enough

for trout to capture insects. Trout will move into these places on high water, spots that might be dry enough to pitch a tent under normal water conditions. Another place to look for them is in side channels that might be just a trickle in low water. The velocity of the current will be greatly reduced in these channels. I've had many a fishing trip saved by poking around behind islands when the water in a river looked too high for good fishing.

High, clear water is not too bad but high, dirty water limits your options even further. Don't give up yet. Fish that have moved into shallow water can still be caught on dry flies if the water clarity is a foot or more. Because dirty water carries a lot of debris with it, though, nymph fishing can be difficult. It seems like the fish give up trying to discern food from junk when there's too much inedible stuff in the flow. Sometimes a wet fly or nymph swung in slower currents will draw

During high water, you might have to stick to streamers.

strikes as the motion of the fly contrary to the current tells the fish your fly is something other than trash.

Streamers really come into their own in dirty water. In fact, huge trout that seldom feed during the day can be approached and caught on a fly because they lose their normal caution. Minnows and crayfish get pushed around, disoriented, and swept into deeper water, and trout respond to this with a vengeance. Streamers are big enough to be spotted by trout in dirty water and a bright pattern, something with white or yellow in it, can often draw strikes in water that seems too dirty for fly fishing. If you happen to be on the river during a quick rise of water after a rainstorm, the first hour after the water gets dirty can provide some amazing streamer fishing.

Low, clear water, where current flow is restricted to a narrow thread, presents other challenges and opportunities. In big rivers,

trout that might be difficult to reach, even with your longest cast, can be approached (but with caution). It's also easier to read the water during low flows because water that has enough current to provide food is limited to places where you see the line of bubbles and debris weaving its way through a pool. Fish that were spread out over hundreds of feet during higher flows may now be confined to a narrow slot.

Low flows also offer better dry-fly fishing. At higher velocities, trout are reluctant to move toward the surface because it's too much work and they get pushed out of position by the current. As the current slows, however, trout can hover just below the surface, sipping insects from the film with little effort. Typically, this calls for a cautious, straight upstream approach and a small fly. A beetle, ant, or midge pattern will often do the trick.

It's often possible to see trout in low water, a luxury you don't have in most rivers because

During low water periods, dry-fly fishing and nymphing to visible trout make this challenging time exciting as well.

the trout are too deep and well-camouflaged to locate. But when the sun is overhead during low water, you will be able to see some of them. Fishing for a trout you can see in shallow water with a small nymph is one of the greatest thrills in fly fishing. You must approach the fish from directly downstream or you'll spook it. And you must use a long leader, at least a twelve-footer, and remove any weight and strike indicators from the leader. Pitch a lightly weighted nymph ahead of the fish. A good rule of thumb is to lead the fish by double its depth; in other words, if a trout is lying in a foot of water, lead it by two. You may see your leader twitch as the fish takes the fly but most anglers watch the fish instead of the leader. If the fish moves to the side or seems to dart after something when your fly is even with its position, make one quick strip of line. If the trout hasn't eaten your fly, it might think that the bug has suddenly put on speed; if it has, then you're in

business! Striking by raising the rod tip will usually spook the fish.

FOOD-RICH VERSUS FOOD-POOR STREAMS

Knowing the relative density of trout and the abundance of food in a river can shortcut a lot of trial and error in approach and presentation. Brown trout in a sterile mountain stream can appear to be different animals than their counterparts in a rich tailwater river. You may know something about the richness of the river you're fishing already, from reading about it or talking to other people on the river. But even if it's an unknown stream in a Wisconsin cornfield, there are ways you can eyeball a river to get some clues.

Rich streams look soupy. They often have some type of aquatic vegetation, either rooted to the bottom, along the banks, or clinging to rocks. The water may be clear but the bottom will probably not look clean because of all the organic matter. Stable rivers (typically tailwater rivers and spring creeks) seldom flood and don't have wide gravel banks. Instead, vegetation grows right down to the water's edge because it is not uprooted by frequent periods of high, fast water. This stability encourages trout and insect growth. Streams in lowlands are typically richer than mountain streams because they pick up nutrients as they flow.

Food-poor streams look clean or tea-stained. Streams with clean rocks and clear water don't have an abundance of organic matter. Nor do tea-stained rivers because this tinge comes from acidic soils, usually heavy in conifers. Acidic streams, with a pH of less than 7.0, are limited in insect life and almost devoid of crustaceans because the dissolved calcium needed to grow a crustacean's shell is very low in acidic streams. Wide gravel or rock banks indicate strong water fluctuations during the season, which further reduce a river's productivity.

Examples of food-rich streams include most of the West's famous tailwaters, such as Montana's Bighorn, Madison, and Missouri rivers; New Mexico's San Juan; Colorado's South Platte; Utah's Green; and California's Pit. The White River in Arkansas is a food-rich tailwater, as is New York's Delaware. All of the famous spring creeks, from Hat Creek in California to Montana's Paradise Valley creeks to Pennsylvania's Letort and Falling Springs are rich in food. It's harder to give you famous examples of food-poor streams because by nature they don't produce huge fish or large numbers of them and are thus not as popular. New York's Ausable, Wisconsin's Brule, Montana's Kootenai, and nearly all small mountain streams fall into the food-poor category. Many rivers, like Vermont's Battenkill, New York's Beaverkill, Pennsylvania's Kettle Creek, and Wyoming's Snake, fall into a middle-of-the-road category for which predictions are tough.

Trout in food-rich streams will be more selective about what they eat. They may eat during spurts of insect abundance rather than all day long and won't grab every piece of food that drifts past. Your fishing day might consist of hours of slow periods followed by intense

Stable banks and rich vegetation tell you this is a rich stream and that it probably holds big fish.

In a rich steam, fishing to risers is smarter than trying to blind-fish with a dry fly.

Wide rocky banks, clear water, and no submerged vegetation tell you that the trout in this river probably won't be too picky about fly patterns.

and many trout can be packed into one place, all feeding at once.

Where trout have an abundance of food, they are not as easy to frighten. Apparently the stimulus of getting as much food as possible overrides their caution. In some of these rich streams trout will even follow anglers through riffles, feeding right at their feet on insects kicked up during wading. Thus, you can confidently fish a pool that another angler has just left, and if you spook a rising fish, sit on the bank for a few minutes because it will probably resume feeding. Also, keep in mind that on popular rivers, where trout are used to seeing anglers all day, the fish can actually get conditioned to your presence and not view you as a threat.

In food-poor streams, on the other hand, trout don't see large quantities of any one insect. They are seldom selective except during the rare hatch. They feed eagerly all day long, as long as the water temperature is between fifty and sixty-five degrees F. You can fish nearly any kind of fly with success, including dry flies, even if no rises are seen. Flies as large as a No. 10 can be effective even if none of the insects you see are that large. Wet flies swung in the current, and even twitched or dragging dry flies, can be effective. Your strategy here should be to catch a trout's attention.

Trout in these streams will only be in prime spots—places where slow water meets the main current, heads and tails of pools, right next to rocks and logs, and along deep banks. There is not enough drifting food to support them in slower backwaters. Each spot may only have one or two fish in it, and the fish will either grab your fly or spook. Move often and don't waste much time in each pool.

Trout here will be more easily frightened. They are not preoccupied with feeding and are constantly on the alert. Even though you should not spend much time in each pool, don't rush up and down the banks. If you spook a trout, forget it, as that fish might not feed again for hours. For the same reason, try to avoid fishing water that has been occupied recently by another angler because this water will be spoiled for longer than even the most patient angler is willing to wait.

feeding activity. They won't move far for their food so casting accuracy is more important. Blind fishing a dry fly is seldom productive except during the summer when grasshoppers, beetles, and ants can be effective in the middle of the day. If you don't see any hatches, a nymph fished dead drift will be your most reliable method. Streamers work best at dawn and dusk but can also be effective tossed right up against a deep bank.

Trout can be found anywhere in food-rich streams. Reading the water in this kind of river is tough because each river seems to have its idiosyncrasy when it comes to what kind of water fish prefer. They can often be found in almost-stagnant backwaters because food is abundant even there and it's easier for them to capture food in the slow currents. Fish all types of water and look for rises in unexpected places. Once you find some fish, stay there and fish thoroughly because they often form pods

CHAPTER EIGHTEEN

FISHING TO HATCHES

— TOM ROSENBAUER —

FINDING RISING FISH

Finding the Right Water

Trout aren't found everywhere in a river and even when present they may not rise. You've probably stood on the bank of a river watching scores of insects floating by, wondering at the lack of rises. Why? First, water may be too cold or too hot for trout to feed actively. Under forty-five and over seventy-five degrees Fahrenheit (F.), trout seldom feed at all, although in some rivers where trout get acclimated to extreme temperatures, you can find them feeding down to about forty-five and up to seventy-eight degrees F. But you'll see most surface activity when the water is between fifty-five and sixty-five degrees F. This is also the temperature range in which aquatic insects are most active.

Just as important as temperature is current velocity. Fishermen seldom pay as much attention to velocity, perhaps because it is not as easy to measure and, unlike temperature, velocity can vary at a magnitude of as much as ten in just a few feet of river.

Trout prefer to lie in water that runs about one foot per second (FPS). This is about the speed of a slow walk. To get an idea of what current speeds are, throw a stick in the river and see how long it takes to move about a foot downstream—or even measure off ten feet, time the stick with a stopwatch, and divide by ten.

Trout won't lie in water that's too slow because it does not wash enough oxygen past

their gills and because a slow current does not bring food to them fast enough. They can't lie in water that's too fast because they expend more energy staying in position than they gain by feeding. The ideal place in a river is where a current of 1 FPS adjoins a current that runs 3 or 4 FPS. A trout can dart into the faster water for the constant food it supplies and slip back into the more comfortable slow water with scarcely a wiggle of its tail.

Trout won't move more than a few feet from this comfort range to capture prey; it's too energy inefficient, and besides, they can't see an insect from more than a few feet away unless they are in very deep water. A trout may be lying on the bottom among rocks that break the current and be able to see insects three feet above it drifting on the surface. The surface velocity, however, might be at 5 FPS, just too much current for a trout to handle. This fish will feed below the surface where it's easier to capture prey because it does not have to move as far to feed.

Studies show that once the rate of prey capture falls below 3.5 objects per minute, a trout lose interest in feeding and look elsewhere. At some point during a hatch, the number of insects on the surface far outnumber those drifting down below and trout switch to plucking insects from the film—but only if they don't have to work too hard to do it.

You often see a frustrating result of too much surface velocity during early season hatches. A pool is carpeted with juicy mayflies

Fishing into the slack water on the inside seam of a fast run produced a nice fish for this angler.

yet you see no rises. The trout are lethargic from cold water temperatures and even though they may see insects on the surface, they just won't make the effort to fight the flow. Later in the season, when water temperatures are at optimum range and the current slows, the same trout will feed on the surface whenever there are enough bugs on top. Also, shallower water later in the season means trout can lie on the bottom and only have to move six inches instead of two feet to get to the surface, meaning they will be more likely to feed on top. In some perfect locations, the current speed at the surface is only 1 FPS, and here trout will hover just under the film, feeding for hours at a time without returning to the bottom. This is called *sipping* and it only happens when you get the harmonious combination of dense insects and optimum current flow throughout the water column.

Seasonal Changes

Anticipating where trout will feed on the surface is one skill that separates the novice from experienced anglers. A neophyte will see insects on the water and stand in one place, waiting for the trout to react. A more experienced angler will say, "Wow, lots of bugs but they'll never rise in this fast current. I'll go find a place where the fish can tuck behind a rock or find some slow current along the bank." Especially in early season, there may be only one spot the size of a bathtub in a mile of water where trout feed during a hatch. Common early season hotspots are tails of pools, in the middle of a pool where the main current runs along a bank but slows behind projecting logs or rocks, or at the whirlpool on either side of the head of a pool. The best spot of all is where a mostly straight, deep bank curves inward, forming a little bay that is protected from the current and collects insects.

Once water temperatures begin to warm into the fifties and water velocity drops (early May in most parts of the country; mid-June in high mountain rivers) trout may be found rising almost anywhere. They'll be in those early season places but will move closer to fast water. Trout will be spotted rising in fast, broken water in front of and behind rocks, along seams where fast water meets slow, in the shelf where fast water dumps into a pool, and especially in places where shallow riffles adjoin deep water. Riffles produce most of the aquatic insects that hatch this time of year and are also the places most species of mayflies, caddisflies, and stoneflies return to lay their eggs. Some trout will stay close to the riffles all the time. Other fish may pack into the shallows during a hatch. The South Fork of the Snake River is famous for big cutthroats that gradually move shallower in a riffle as a hatch progresses. By the height of the hatch, scores of fish compete to see who gets farther (and shallower) upstream in the riffle, acting more like hogs at a feeding trough than noble trout.

Late season brings warmer water, lower dissolved oxygen levels (warm water holds less oxygen than cold water), and slower flows. Here, the challenge may be to find places deep enough to hold trout and with enough current to bring them food. It's almost the opposite of the early season because in high water in April you look for trout as far from the main current as possible. In August, look for the bubble line that betrays the main current flow. The current threads will bring more food and slightly more oxygen. Much of the water may be at 1 FPS and under, so you may find trout sipping and holding just under the surface in almost any type of water. Always look where fast water deepens slightly, like at the head of a pool or just downstream of a riffle. Trout may be concentrated here because the dissolved oxygen level is slightly higher in the bubbly water.

Cover or Current?

A word about cover and dry-fly fishing: All trout need a place to hide when danger threatens and the perfect spot for a trout is 1 FPS water with a fast riffle to provide food on one side with cover on the other. But the places that offer the best cover—deep rocky holes, logjams, tangles of willow roots—are not usually the best places to feed on insects. Trout choose places to feed based mostly on water hydraulics and food supply. As long as there is a refuge to which they can bolt when threatened, fish will feed on surprisingly open, exposed places in a river. Even large fish.

One of my favorite banks on the West Branch of the Delaware always holds the biggest rising trout in a very discrete spot and I can go back to this place year after year, knowing the best fish will always be there. Surprisingly, the spot is just on top of a flat rock that juts out on a point along the bank, in about nine inches of water. I've watched trout here for hours and the point funnels all the food along the bank into one narrow lane. Because the trout is in such shallow water, it can just raise its snout to feed without wasting effort.

TYPES OF RISES AND HOW TO SPOT THEM

You've already solved half the puzzle in finding rising fish—narrowing down the water types. Now you just look for splashes in the water, tie on the right fly, and catch a big fish, right? Sometimes. The form a rise takes can tell you how far a trout came for the fly and something about what kind of insect the fish ate.

Splashy Rises

Rises can be categorized into two broad groups, splashy and sedate. A splashy rise means that a trout built up some momentum to take the insect. Rises that throw spray often betray a fish rushing from deep water to spear an insect on the surface. Splashy rises are also created when a trout chases a fast-emerging

Sedate rises like this one are hard to spot but the fish under it is often easier to catch than one making a splashy rise.

caddisfly to the surface, catching the insect just below the surface. Even though the fish stops its forward progress six inches or even a foot below the surface, the pressure wave it creates when turning back to the bottom forms a surface disturbance that looks very much like a rise. Sit in a bathtub, cup your hand, and a grab an imaginary object six inches under the surface. You'll see why a trout chasing caddis pupae appears to be feeding on the surface.

One way to judge a splashy rise is to watch the rise form for bubbles. Big bubbles mean a trout has inhaled some air when taking the insect from the surface, expelling the air from its gills as it dives to chew its meal. Just a swirl without bubbles tells you to fish an emerger instead of a dry. Sometimes the sound of a rise will betray the fish. A big swirl that produces a *psshhyyt* sound often means a subsurface rise. A deeper *chunk* sound is more likely to be a true surface rise. A *splish* sound that throws thin ribbons of spray is a small trout that could not control its exuberance. This enthusiasm betrays their position and they quickly learn to curb the impulse—or they get eaten.

Trout in fast currents always make some kind of splash because they have to dash and grab. When they put on the brakes to return to their positions, the resulting disturbance always throws some water. Notice I said fast *current*, not fast *water*. Trout tucked in the slow

current behind a rock with fast water all around can make deceptively dainty rises and you'll miss them if you merely scan fast water for splashy rises.

Two sometimes-reliable rules-of-thumb are that splashy rises indicate a bigger insect or betray an insect that is fluttering on the surface. The second is far more reliable as I've seen trout make quite a splash over No. 20 caddisflies skittering across the surface. Trout know that a mayfly standing on its tiptoes and fluttering on the surface is about to fly away; if they don't move quickly, they'll miss out. This is not total gospel as I've also seen big trout sip in No. 8 green drake duns in flat water with barely a ripple.

Before we talk about the more sedate rises, I'll mention something that seems patently obvious but is ignored by many anglers: *Insects have to be on the surface or just below it to create rises.* Flies in the air won't do you any good yet you'll be amazed at the fishermen you hear complaining about fish not responding to a hatch when it's really a flight of migrating caddisflies that never touch the surface. When trout do begin rising, find some steadily feeding fish and watch the place where they rise. Did you see an insect disappear in the rise? Watch a few times. If you see many rises but the fish ignore all the juicy mayflies floating over their heads, they are either eating just under the surface or are eating small or spent flies that you can't see. And as you'll see, if the flies are small or spent, the rises will probably be more sedate so a splashy riser that ignores surface insects is a prime candidate for a nymph or emerger.

Sedate Rises

I'll take a sedate riser over a splashy riser any time. In fact, in a pool full of rising trout, I'll look for the one fish that has a confident, quiet rise. I can be more sure that it is feeding on the surface and there is a good chance it's a bigger trout. Sedately rising trout are said to dimple, sip, porpoise, bob, boil, gulp, and many other appropriate descriptions. There are head rises, simple rises, satisfaction rises, and compound rises. You are supposed to be able to tell what the trout are eating by pigeonholing their feeding behavior into a certain bucket. I've spent over thirty-five years watching rising trout (it is my absolute favorite part of trout fishing) and I'll be damned if I can tell the difference between a trout rising to a tiny No. 22 dun or a No.16 spinner.

I will tell you some things to look for without having to memorize all those rise forms. But first, a few words about quiet rises. They will invariably be in moderate to slow current, which is also the preferred feeding place for most large trout; they've earned the right to feed in the easy places, pushing the smaller, less aggressive fish into fast water where they waste energy holding in place. Sedate rises can be to any kind of insect but they are most often seen when trout are eating insects No. 18 and smaller, eating emerging insects of all kinds, and eating spent caddisflies or mayflies. A trout feeding in this manner is always close to the surface, regardless of water depth, because a fish that rises up from the bottom to take a single insect always carries some momentum.

If fish are sipping, your first task is to see what they're inhaling. Sounds dumb but if you can spot an insect on the water and actually see a trout eat one, you don't have to worry about any more observation. It's often difficult to see what a steadily feeding trout is taking, even from thirty feet away. One way is to find a trout feeding close to a brushy bank and creeping up close behind the fish. Another way is to carry a small pair of binoculars or a monocular in your fishing vest. If you can see what trout are eating, you'll never have to worry about identifying their food by trying to figure out rise forms.

If you can't see what the fish are taking, put an insect net or a small aquarium net in the water to see if you can capture insects that are lying flush in the film or just below the surface. If that doesn't provide clues, watch the fish at the exact moment of feeding, not the ring behind them—the ring behind the rise that lasts for a few seconds is helpful in spotting them but nearly all rings look the same once the fish has risen. Don't forget: A rising trout will always lie upstream of the rise. When a trout moves to an insect, it glides backward from an inch to several feet following the insect, tips its fins so that its snout is pushed into the film, then tips its fins back down and swims back upstream to its original spot (unless the fish is cruising, which I'll discuss later). If you cast your fly right on a rise, you take the chance of casting into a trout's blind spot.

Look for a trout's head, dorsal fin (the one along the top of the back), or tail. Seeing a trout's head emerge from the water like a submarine surfacing is one of the most exciting rises because this fish is feeding steadily, is very confident, and is feeding on the surface or in the film. In fact, you often hear fishermen talk about "looking for heads," which usually means stalking big trout feeding in shallow water along the banks that less observant anglers never even see. In heavy hatches of tiny Tricos, olives, or midges on rich tailwaters like the Missouri or Bighorn, you often see twenty or more trout packed into a small eddy, each fish feeding about once a second with just their black heads poking into the film.

If you see the head of a trout followed by its dorsal fin and perhaps its tail, it is still feeding on the surface, and rather than tiny insects, the food of choice in this instance may be larger spinners or spent caddis. Look for bubbles emerging from the rise, the clue that the fish is eating on top. If you don't see a head or bubbles, and just see the dorsal fin breaking the surface, there's a good chance this fish is eating emerging flies drifting just under the surface.

Spotting sedate rises from a distance is one of the greatest skills a fly fisher can develop. I can't begin to count the number of times I've had terrific dry-fly fishing while drift boats and other anglers saunter right past feeding fish. All I had to do was spend ten minutes staring at the water.

Watching a Trout's Rhythm

The most annoying fish is one that rises once and then never comes up again or does not feed again for ten or fifteen minutes. You seldom catch these trout. Usually, these rises are splashy and the trout is following an emerging insect from the bottom. It's a good idea to switch to a nymph or try to cast your dry to the rise immediately after it occurs, because sometimes the trout will hesitate below the surface a few seconds before sinking back to the bottom. This is especially true if you see an insect pop out of the rise form—the fish missed its target and may still be looking for another morsel.

Before casting to a feeding trout, try to watch the fish rise at least three times. This gives you a chance to figure out what insect the fish is taking, whether it is rising in a rhythmic manner, and whether it is changing position or staying put between rises. It also lets you determine if there are other trout rising in the same area, as sometimes you'll see a fish rise forty feet away and make a cast to it, only to drop your line over a couple of fish that were only twenty feet from you. It's always easier and better to catch the closest rising fish first: Your cast will be more accurate, there is less chance that the fly will drag, and often, if you can hook the closest fish and lead it away from the other risers when you play it, you'll have a chance at other trout in the area.

Let's say you've spotted a trout and it is rising with a regular tempo, once every ten seconds. It doesn't take a genius to figure out that the best approach is to wait for nine seconds after the next rise and make sure your fly is floating over its head at the ten-second mark. In a case like this, the hatch is probably very heavy and those ten-second pauses are when the fish returns to its position and swallows its prey. If the fish does not take your fly, the most important information you glean might be over the next couple of minutes, so pay attention: Let's say that the ten-second riser does not take your fly but instead rises at fifteen seconds, then goes back to ten seconds again. There's a good chance the fish looked at your fly and it didn't like your pattern or there was some drag on the fly or it got spooked by the leader. If you notice that a trout's rhythm changes every time you pitch your fly, something is wrong. Rest the fish and don't cast for a few minutes. Carefully change positions to eliminate some drag, change your fly, or lengthen your tippet.

Often, faced with a pool full of rising fish, I've gone fishless during the entire hatch, only to figure out later on that, coincidentally, every trout I cast over stopped feeding. There were so many fish that I'd just move on to the next until I had gone through the entire pool. At first I thought the trout were being selective but the real reason was that I kept spooking those fish. It was like moving through a pool and snuffing out candles, one by one.

A trout may rise frequently but erratically, with no apparent cadence. The second rise might be five seconds later and the next rise after that not for a full minute. First, try to get a fly to the fish after it rises each time, similar to the erratic riser mentioned above. If that doesn't work, try getting as many drag-free floats as you can to the fish, casting repeatedly until you either spook it or get bored and look for another target. The real fun ones are fish that rise twice in very quick succession, followed by a pause. If you get your fly in position at the right time, you'll have two chances at getting a strike.

When trout rise to insects on gusty days, about 80 percent of the time you'll notice they stop rising when the wind riffles the surface. It's not just that you can't see the rises when wind disturbs the water; the trout really do stop rising, probably because they can't see their prey well. On days when the wind picks up and keeps blowing, trout may put a halt to surface feeding for the rest of the day. Gusty winds alternated by calm spells, however, are actually a big advantage to the dry-fly fisher. Find a rising fish and get your range set up by casting off to the side. Don't forget that when the wind stops, you'll have to adjust your cast slightly. Just as the water settles down, pitch your fly above the trout so that it's the first thing he sees in a calm patch. It's guaranteed: That trout has been waiting for an opportunity and should pounce on your fly.

VISIBLE TROUT, DIFFICULT FISH, AND CRUISERS

One of the most challenging, exciting, and educational experiences in fly fishing is casting to a visible fish with a dry. If you get close enough, you'll be able to see the trout's every reaction to the naturals and to your fly. You typically see this in tailwaters or spring creeks where the water is clear and shallow, and there is enough food to keep trout eating even though they probably sense your presence. The first thing you'll notice is that the feeding trout will move to places where they can suspend close to the surface. They'll move into shallow water because they can rest in the layer of slow current on the streambed yet have a short distance to rise through the water column. You'll often see them in the tails of pools or on top of weed beds. A motionless trout is probably spooked or just not eating; look for the ones that sway back and forth and make quick darts to the surface or off to the side.

Difficult Risers

When they rise, you may see a trout actually follow a juicy natural and turn away without feeding. This is when you know it's going to be a difficult day! With artificials, there's also a very stereotyped refusal of imitations. A trout will move toward your fly, follow it back with the current, and then return to the bottom without eating. The second time it notices your fly, it will begin to slide up under it but then slide back to the bottom. You can almost hear the fish saying, "Uh, uh, I've seen that one before and I don't want it." You might get a couple more wiggles out of the fish but after a few casts the trout will ignore your fly completely. Time to change flies or find another fish. Imagine the times this has happened when you couldn't see the fish!

What can you do when you know with complete certainty that fish are feeding on No. 18 pale morning duns, yet a trout has just done this with No. 18 Pale Morning Parachute? Trout can tell the difference between different fly patterns. Luckily, they don't often care but if a trout has refused your fly because it didn't look quite right or it dragged in front of the fish, it might take another pattern with a slightly different look. For important hatches,

On big pools like this, trout will often stop rising when the wind ruffles the surface. Wait for a calm spell and then quickly pitch your fly to a fish.

smart fly fishers will carry several imitations of the same insect, because a trout that has refused a Pale Morning Parachute might rise confidently to a hackled thorax version of the same mayfly in the exact same size and color. For instance, I'm not happy in April in Montana unless I have three different *Baetis* mayfly emergers, four different duns, and one spinner (the fish don't seem to be as picky about the spinner stage).

If you know your fly is not dragging, the fish are not spooked, and you only have one decent imitation of the bug *de jour,* all is not lost. First, you might try a smaller version of the same fly or even a smaller fly that is close to the insect the trout is eating. Trout seem to be less wary of a fly that is smaller than the natural. The other option is to take a pair of scissors and trim your fly. Suggestions here include trimming hackle off the bottom of a fly that is full and bushy, picking out the body of a fly with the point of another hook to make it fuzzier, or cutting the wings short to make a regular dry fly look like an emerger. As long as you don't spook a riser there is always something you can try. I once worked over one brown trout on the West Branch of the Delaware for at least two hours and twenty fly changes. When I finally hooked the fourteen-incher, it was one of the most memorable trout of my life.

Large brown trout like this will often cruise slow pools.

Compound Hatches

Seldom will you see just one insect on the water during a hatch. Favorable water temperatures and light levels stimulate many different insects to hatch at once. There may be mayflies and caddis flies hatching while mayfly spinners and adult caddis are falling to the water spent after mating and laying their eggs. Trout will sometimes eat a variety of insects; other times they will key into just one species at one stage of its life. How can you sort this out? First, of course, try to see what the fish are eating. That's not as easy as it sounds, however, when trout are sixty feet away or they rise as evening light drifts away. Next, look on the water. Put a net into the current to see what insects are drifting unseen in the film; this is often the only way to detect small mayfly spinners, midges, or spent caddis. Look in the air above the water for spinners, mating stoneflies, or mating caddis. Seeing these flies in the air does not always mean they are on the water but spinners might be falling into a riffle a hundred yards upstream and flushing by you unseen.

Behavioral studies of trout have shown that they prefer the largest prey of reasonable abundance. Apparently not all trout have read these studies. You'll often see them pass over large mayfly duns and feed on small spinners a quarter the size and calories of the bigger bugs.

They also just seem to prefer certain insects over others, perhaps because of the taste. Most trout are hard-pressed to pass up an ant or a spent caddis fly. Johnny Gomez, the noted San Juan River guide, once told me he catches trout twelve months a year on small brown foam ants, even in the middle of January!

If I can offer you any rule of thumb for complex hatches, it would be to find the most helpless insect of fair abundance. To illustrate, I remember spending an entire afternoon fishing and observing a small section of a pool on the Delaware River. The water was covered with big No. 10 March brown mayfly duns, No. 14 Hendrickson duns, midges, No. 18 black stoneflies, No. 18 rusty spinners, and No. 16 spent caddis. Despite their juicy look and seductive fluttering, not a single trout rose to the mayfly duns (probably too difficult to capture because they would twitch and then become airborne quickly). They ignored the midges (too small?). Not one even looked at the black stoneflies (skimming across the surface, I imagine they would be difficult prey). Trout regularly rose to the most abundant fly, the rusty spinners. The spinners were also lying prone in the film, not going anywhere and an easy meal. What was surprising, though, was the fondness of the trout for the less abundant spent caddis; the fish would move a foot or more for every spent caddis they saw. Since the spinners were just as helpless as the caddis, I can only guess that the trout preferred the taste of the caddis flies.

Cruisers

You'll often see large trout cruising in slow water. During a sparse hatch, their capture rate may fall below that magic 3.5 objects per minute, and the current may be even slower than their preferred 1 FPS. The fish just seem to get impatient, and rather than waiting for the current to bring them food, they cruise slowly upstream. It's usually a slow upward progression to a certain point with an occasional rise. The fish then swims downstream and begins the course again at the same starting point. Faced with sipping trout in a slow pool, try to determine if any of them are cruising since you don't want to wade into the return track of one of the cruisers or you'll spook it. Sometimes a fish will have a distinctive rise form that helps you identify it and track its progress through the pool. If there seem to be a number of erratic risers in a pool, notice if you ever see more than one fish rise at the same time. Just a few cruising fish in a pool can make you think there are a dozen of them.

The best tactic for cruisers, after you figure out a pattern, is to place yourself a comfortable casting distance downstream of the lower limit of a trout's pattern. Watch for the occasional rise in a downstream direction as the fish returns. You may also spot a bulge or swirl in the water as the trout slides into its starting point. Pitch your fly just above where you think the fish may be hovering. If it doesn't take and starts to cruise upstream, resist the temptation to follow the fish; wading may disturb it, and if it decides to return to the starting point prematurely, it may bump into you and swim away in fright.

Sometimes your casting may move a cruising trout upstream for good, so then you have no option but to follow and try to figure out its new pattern. I once chased a giant cruiser on the upper Connecticut River over one hundred yards up through a long pool. He kept moving up, I'd cast, the trout would reposition itself fifty feet upstream and continue rising. I'd move up, the fish would move up—until finally the fish dead-ended in a shallow riffle. I saw it swim arrogantly past me on its way downstream where I'm sure it started the process over again. That trout got the better of me, and I decided to leave the pool.

PROSPECTING WITH A DRY WHEN THERE IS NO HATCH

When and Where

Dry flies can be fun and productive when there is no hatch. Under some conditions it takes a heavy hatch to bring trout to the surface, although there are times when they'll pluck food from the surface with no *apparent* hatch.

Trout in small streams are inclined to take a well-presented dry fly all day long.

Notice I said no apparent hatch. In fast riffles, trout may be feeding on hatching insects but you miss them because their rises are hidden by the frothy water. When you watch a dry fly with white wings in fast water, you are concentrating on a very small piece of water and will notice a rise or just a dark head that surrounds your fly.

Trout in shallow water may truly rise to a dry fly when there are few insects on the water and no rises at all. This happens more often in shallow water because little effort is needed to rise a few inches to take a bug on the surface, where in two feet of water it's a longer journey to the surface. Trout in small streams, where all the fish are in shallow water, are particularly inclined to take a dry fly all day long throughout the season. In some of the small mountain streams I fish in Vermont, I won't see three rises in a season yet I'll catch hundreds of trout on dry flies.

Your success in prospecting with a dry depends on food supply, water velocity, and water temperature. In rich tailwaters, there is so much food that trout eat all day long; if they aren't feeding on the surface they are probably eating nymphs. In sterile mountain streams, however, where they don't see much food, anything that looks edible will be taken without hesitation, regardless of whether it's on the

The white wings on this dry fly helped the angler spot the rise when this nice brook trout ate the fly.

surface or in the water column. Fish in very fast water, unless it's less than a foot deep, are reluctant to come to the surface for a single isolated fly because it wastes too much energy. And trout at forty-five degrees F. are running in low gear. The same fish at sixty degrees is far more interested in eating and is thus a target for a well-placed dry.

Trout get more interested in random surface food as the season progresses. Water gets lower and warmer, and much of the fly life that was available under the surface has already hatched out for the season. Terrestrials, which by nature are random and not part of a predictable hatch, become more important, so trout look toward the surface for anything that drops into the water.

Water with some surface disturbance is easier than smooth water to prospect with a dry fly. Because you are not fishing to a discrete target when prospecting, you have to drop your fly into every likely spot. In a flat pool, these spots are hard to find, and the likelihood is that you'll drop your line on top of a spooky trout. In fast water, a trout may not even notice the slap of a line a few feet away. Additionally, trout will be in those discrete places offering

protection from the current. Since you can identify those places by observing the current, you can fire your dry into the exact place a trout should be lying: In front of and behind rocks, where riffles drop off into deep water, and places along the bank where rocks and logs create refuges.

A careful approach and avoiding drag are just as necessary when blind fishing as during a hatch. Just imagine a trout in a likely spot and make a half-dozen casts. If you don't raise a fish, move on to the next juicy place. You should be moving almost constantly. If you don't rise a trout in thirty minutes of fishing, try a different type of water; if you've been fishing shallow riffles, keep moving until you find water about two feet deep along a bank.

What kind of flies should you use when prospecting? Anything reasonable as long as you can see it. Because rises may be subtle and you need to see if your fly is in the right place and whether or not it is dragging, patterns with light-colored wings, parachute flies, Wulffs, and terrestrials with bright pieces of yarn or red spots of paint on top are all good choices. Pay attention to the few flies you see along the river. Caddisflies in the brush tell you to try something with a caddis shape. Mayflies trapped in spider webs suggest you try something with upright wings in the same size and color you see in the webs. The clatter of grasshopper wings in the sagebrush as you walk to the river is a good clue to try a hopper imitation even if you don't see any trout rising.

Whether you're casting over a pool of trout rising to a hatch of blue-winged olives or trying to pluck a nice rainbow from a fast riffle with a Parachute Adams, dry-fly fishing offers new and different puzzles every hour of every day on the river. Once you understand the basics introduced here, the best way to learn more is to get out there and immerse yourself in the world above and below the surface. I wish you many fun and productive hours on the water.

CHAPTER NINETEEN

DRY-FLY TECHNIQUES

— TOM ROSENBAUER —

DRAG AND WHY IT'S SO BAD

We've touched on drag but have not thoroughly described it. Drag is any time the fly is pulled in a direction contrary to the current in which it is sitting. Granted, insects flutter and skid across the surface but the movement a natural insect makes with its flimsy legs and wings is nearly impossible to imitate with the mass of a leader butt, fly line, and a stationary rod held by a human. Drag is not just the motorboat wake you see behind a fly. Drag can seem insignificant from forty feet away but if you were a trout underneath the fly and saw it move contrary to the current, you'd ignore it—or even dive for cover.

Imagine a fifty-foot cast straight across a river in current that looks perfectly uniform. Unseen by you, there are a half-dozen different velocities in that current. Distance from the bank, depth of water, and unseen rocks on the bottom all create friction with the current. If you could paint each current speed a different color, you'd see what looks like a bunch of ribbons blowing in the wind, and just like the ribbons, these current tongues will actually sway back and forth. Because the line and leader have more mass than the fly, they'll tug it along as they move at different speeds.

Drag is the main reason a steadily rising trout refuses a fly. Getting a drag-free float is far more important than having an exact match of the fly-of-the-moment, even at the

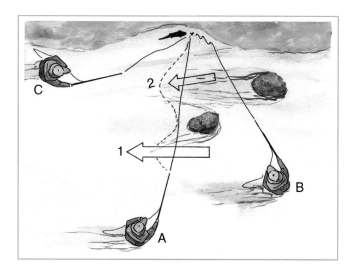

Drag and conflicting currents: The fisherman at A, with a standard upstream-and-across presentation, will have his line pulled downstream quickly at points 1 and 2, yanking the fly away from the trout. By wading upstream to B and casting downstream, with a Reach Cast, Slack Line Cast, or a combination of the two, he will get a much better presentation. If he can get across the river and fish directly upstream from C, he might get the best drift of all.

height of a hatch. If you can approach a trout without spooking it, choose a fly that is remotely close to what's on the water, and have a perfect drag-free float, you can catch every fish you see. Drag can be reduced or eliminated in three ways: With a long, slack tippet; with special casts; and with the angle at which you cast to a feeding fish. We've discussed how a long, fine tippet can help so let's move on to special casts.

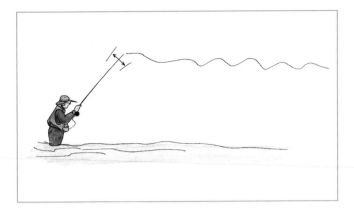

A simple Slack Line Cast can be made by wiggling the rod back and forth as it straightens in front of you.

An overpowered forward cast will snap back and create waves in the line and leader.

With a Parachute Cast, you aim high. The tip of the rod remains pointed up, then the entire rod drops down at the same angle. The line and leader will drop into a big pile.

SPECIAL CASTS

Slack Line Casts

Despite thirty-five years of fly fishing, I still don't consider myself an adept caster and the thought of tricky casts makes my palms sweat. The Slack Line Cast is really not a cast, but a variety of ways of making a controlled bad cast. *That* I can do. There are several ways to introduce slack into a cast and all of these methods can be used with a regular forward cast or with one of the specialty casts that follow. Remember: Because the squiggles you introduce will take up some distance, you'll have to cast enough line to overshoot the fish. How much to overshoot takes practice and I suggest you spend some time on the lawn before you try this with live ammunition.

One of the easiest ways to cast slack is to wiggle the rod back and forth just after the power stroke on the forward cast. This cast is commonly known as an **S**-Cast, and is very easy to do. Start wiggling as the rod passes the eleven o'clock position and continue on your follow-through. You can put coils in the line closer to the fly if you wiggle quickly at first and then follow with a smooth follow-through. Coils will form closer to you if you wait until the fly almost touches the water before wiggling. Shooting some line as you do this will help you get more slack and will smooth out your presentation.

One of my favorite slack-line deliveries is merely an overpowered forward cast that stops high. Stop the rod at ten o'clock after an abrupt power stroke—the line will straighten in midair, snap back against the rod and reel, and fall to the water in coils. This presentation is especially useful with a very long tipped (over three feet) and works best on casts over forty feet.

Yet a third way to cast slack is to make an under-powered forward cast. With this method, instead of a crisp power stroke on the forward cast, act like you forgot how to make a forward cast and stop the power stroke at eleven o'clock without a follow through, keeping your rod pointed about forty-five degrees above the horizontal. The line will still go in front of you but will land in loose coils and the leader will pile up. I find this cast to be most useful on shorter casts under forty feet.

By putting some extra body English into an under-powered cast, you can execute what's called a Parachute Cast, which is very useful for short casts where drag problems are extreme. Instead of stopping the rod at eleven o'clock, straighten your arm skyward at an angle of about seventy-five degrees from the horizontal so most of your casting energy goes up instead of forward and out. Follow through by dropping the rod straight down as the line falls to the water. The line and leader will land in one nasty pile but with some practice you can get the fly and leader just forward of the pile of line.

Reach Cast

The Reach Cast is perhaps the most useful cast in dry-fly fishing, especially when fishing across-stream. It's like a combination of a Curve Cast and Slack Line Cast. Imagine a trout rising in slow water close to the far bank. You're wading in the middle of the river because it's the only way you can get close enough to the fish but there's thirty feet of fast water between you and the trout. Even with a Slack Line Cast, the fly drags almost as soon as it hits the water. The current is running from right to left as you look across the river, and you wade about five feet upstream of the trout's position, but still thirty feet away.

Make a straight overhead cast to the trout but plan it as if you were going to overpower the cast for a slack-line presentation—so don't forget to add five or six feet of extra line to the distance between you and the trout. Overpower and aim high, as you would for a Slack Line Cast, and just as the line straightens above the water, reach out and upstream with the rod tip as far as you can. Your arm should be fully extended at the end of the cast. You'll throw a big arc with the concave end pointing downstream and the fly will land three or four feet upstream of the fish. With any luck, your fly will pass over the trout, drag free, before the line and leader. To get a better float, drop your rod tip

Slack Line Casts can help in tricky currents.

parallel to the surface after you reach and follow the line downstream with the rod. This cast can give you a drag-free float of many feet where a standard cast might give you a few inches.

Mending and Skidding the Fly Into Position

Mending, or flipping an arc of line upstream or downstream to keep fly, line, and leader moving at the same speed, should be avoided if possible. Because the fly is connected to the rod via the line and leader, unless there is much slack in your line, moving the line will move the fly. The only way to avoid this is to let fly line slip from your hand as you mend. This is not an easy process; unless you are very careful or very lucky, the friction of the line in the rod guides will make the line tug against the fly.

Mends should be done in the air, before the line hits the water, by using the Reach Cast. Tight brush, however, can prevent a good Reach Cast or a downstream wind may blow it back into a straight line. Mend if you must but always think ahead and mend before drag sets in. Anticipate drag; once it sets in, it's nearly impossible to eliminate.

One handy way to mend the line or to reposition a Reach Cast that has gone astray is to skid the fly into position. You have to be slightly upstream of a rising fish and I would

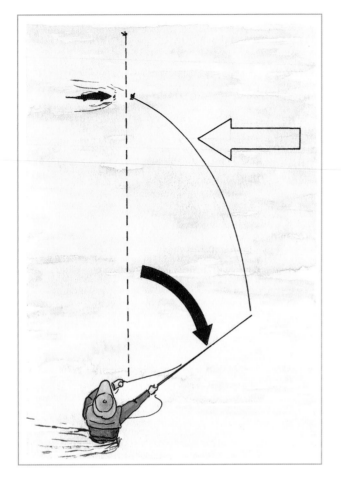

With the Reach Cast, you "reach" your fly rod upstream just before the line hits the water.

The Curve Cast from above. Make a sidearmed cast (1), stop the cast abruptly (2), and bounce the rod back slightly to make the cast curve around an object.

not advise skidding a fly into position unless it is at least three feet above a rising trout, otherwise you'll only frighten the fish. To do this, cast beyond and well upstream of a rising fish. Just after the fly lands, move your rod tip upstream and across your body so that the fly skids across the surface. When the fly is directly upstream of the fish, make a quick mend, then drop the tip of the rod for a drag-free drift. You'll need a fly that floats very well and stays on top. When done with finesse, it can put a fly directly above a rising trout and show the fish your fly before the leader.

Curve Cast

The Curve Cast will hook the cast to one side and can be used for the same situations where

you'd use a Reach Cast. It doesn't give you as much slack insurance, however, and it's less reliable than a Reach because it's more difficult to execute. The Curve Cast is, however, better than the Reach Cast for upstream presentations. For instance, suppose you think there is a trout near a big rock just upstream of your position. You could simply drape the fly line over the rock, letting the tippet and fly land in the water. But drag would set in very quickly. With a Curve Cast, you can hook the line to the side, and with uniform current, the fly will pass in front of the rock, along its edge, and even well below the rock, where drag finally takes over.

Here's how to do it (assuming you cast right-handed).

From just behind the rock, step off to its right side a bit so you can see your fly as it drifts in front of the rock. Make a forty-five degree sidearm cast (halfway between an overhead cast and one that's parallel to the water). False cast a few times with enough line to overshoot the target by two or three feet. On your delivery cast, after the power stroke, bounce the tip back slightly as the line straightens above the water. The line will snap back and form a curve. With some practice you'll be able to curve your line all the way in front of a rock or logjam. What you just followed was a right-hand curve. A left-hand curve is much trickier because you have to make a slanted cross-body cast.

The Moving Dry Fly

Although it seems like most of your time on the river will be spent avoiding drag, there are times when just a touch of controlled drag followed by a dead drift can be useful. You're trying to imitate the fluttering of a delicate insect on the water but like trying to pluck a single pin with a bowling ball, most of the time the equipment and the user are just to clumsy for the task. Moving a fly is done for two reasons: Either to imitate the fluttering movements of a specific insect during a hatch (typically caddis flies, stoneflies, or large mayflies), or to draw attention to your fly by otherwise blasé fish.

Don't just blast away, twitching the fly. If you just pull on the fly using the rod tip, the fly will move and then drag immediately. The best way is with an upstream Curve or Reach Cast. The Curve offers slightly better control because you want an upstream hook but you also want to be instantly in touch with your fly. In the late Leonard Wright's famous "Sudden Inch" technique, you move the fly an inch upstream by moving the rod tip an inch upstream, then follow the line with the rod so the fly drifts naturally. The point is to twitch the fly above a feeding trout so it notices something fluttering and then sips what it thinks is a helpless insect.

A more overt and exciting technique calls for more movement. It's called "Skating a Caddis" by today's anglers but thirty years ago

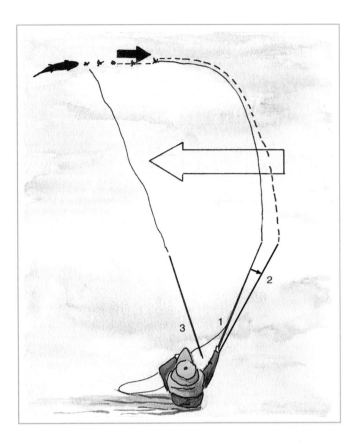

The Sudden Inch. Make an upstream Curve or Reach Cast to position 1, then move the rod an inch upstream at 2, then drop the rod tip and let the fly drift drag free over the fish at 3.

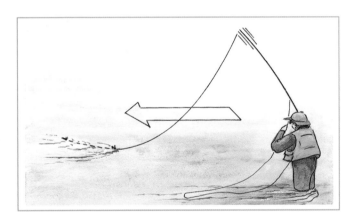

Skating a fly. Cast across-and-down, raise the tip of the rod, and strip line while twitching the rod.

it was called "Fishing a Spider" because the fly used was a tiny hook with stiff, oversized hackles that skimmed across the surface. I haven't seen spiders for sale in many years. They were exciting to fish but 90 percent of the time you

A dry fly can be anchored by a subsurface nymph and then twitched or dapped on the surface.

couldn't hook a fish that took one—either due to the hooking qualities of the fly or because trout refused it at the last moment. Skating a caddis results in more solid hookups.

Skating a fly involves some preparation. First, the fly must be light, with a delicate body and bushy hackle. An Elk-Hair Caddis will work if well hackled; any standard hackled dry fly will also work but they work better if you trim the ends of the hackles. The blunt ends hold the fly above the water better. The idea is to get a fly that will skim across the surface without leaving a big wake. Next, grease your entire leader with dry-fly paste or line dressing so it skims across the surface. A leader that drags a fly under will also hinder its skating performance.

Cast across and downstream with a normal straight-line cast. As soon as the fly hits the water, raise your rod tip to about eleven o'clock, raise your arm, and strip line while wiggling the rod like you've just woken up from a three-day bender. (You probably never have—neither have I—but just extrapolate from the worst morning-after you can remember). After you skate the fly for three or four feet, suddenly drop the tip of the rod and follow the line downstream. This gives you a very active fly to get the attention of a fish, then a drag-free float in case they're suspicious. Rises to a skating fly are usually explosive and it pays to use a tippet size one diameter larger than normal.

Skating a fly does not work well on riffled water because the broken surface pulls the fly

under. It also does not work well in slow water, where the fish are more easily spooked and get a better look at what you are doing. The best place is in the tail of a pool where the water is fast but smooth.

I've been experimenting with one additional way of using a moving dry fly for two seasons. Tie a bushy caddis or stonefly imitation on a shorter and heavier tippet than you'd normally use—for a No. 16, a two-foot-long tippet of 4X or 5X is about right. To the bend of the dry-fly hook, tie another two-foot section of the same tippet, and tie a fairly large weighted nymph to the end (a No. 12 nymph for a No. 16 dry is about right). Cast upstream and across, and after the flies land, raise your rod tip until the dry is suspended just above the surface, anchored in place by the weighted nymph. As the flies drift down toward you, dip the dry fly onto the surface, raise it back into the air, and keep dipping it as it floats even with you and downstream of your position. It's a modification of the dapping technique used by loch fishermen in Scotland. This is the only way I know of fishing an active dry fly upstream and it covers a lot of water. The fly is active on the surface yet because it is in the air most of the time, it doesn't have the chance to drag. This technique, unlike the Sudden Inch and Skating Caddis, works best in broken water.

Proper Use of the Basic False Cast

False casting is necessary and useful for drying a fly, for gauging your range, and for working out distance. Most people false cast too much, with too much line, and directly over a feeding trout's head. In most situations, three false casts should be enough. Line in the air can easily spook trout, especially on sunny days, and the leader and fly will throw spray on the surface which also frightens nervous fish. The best presentation is to pick up your fly with a roll-cast, false cast off to one side slightly short of your target, then point your tip toward a feeding fish on the last cast. Shooting five or six feet of line on this last cast will help smooth out your presentation and get the distance you need without having to hold the extra line in the air and waving it in front of your quarry's nose. It's always better to err on the short side rather than making too long a cast. A cast that falls short will land behind a fish's feeding station and you can let it drift out of danger and pick up for a slightly longer cast. A cast that is too long and puts the leader butt or the line on top of a fish will probably send it bolting for the nearest log or undercut bank.

ANGLES FOR DRIFT AND APPROACH

One of the best arrows in the quiver of a dry-fly fisher is the ability to change positions. A move of a few feet can give you a drag-free float in a tricky spot and moving to one side or another can also put you in a trout's blind spot so it does not see you. For instance, suppose you approach from behind a trout, knowing its blind spot is a fifty-degree cone behind its head. Because this cone gets smaller the closer you get to a fish, it's always a balancing act: Should I risk a longer cast, knowing I'll be less accurate, or should I wade closer, knowing that the fish might spot me and stop feeding? You also know that a trout rising in shallow water can see little of the world above the surface but one that is lying in deep water has a pretty good view of your movements if you are not in its blind spot. Can I approach this fish from the side? Should I kneel down to keep my profile low? There's never an easy answer, and water depth, surface disturbance, drag-causing currents, and the behavior of the fish help gauge your angle of approach.

Straight Up

A straight-upstream cast, directly behind a trout, has big advantages. The obvious one is that barring a sloppy cast or water disturbance caused by sloppy wading, you can get closer to a trout from directly behind. Another big plus is that you are invariably in current of the same speed as the feeding fish so drag is seldom a problem. And because drag is not a problem you can make a simple

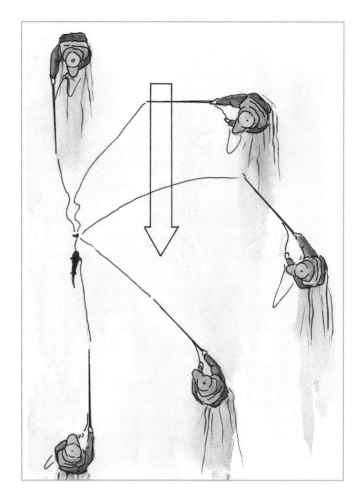

Casting angles relative to the current. Straight upstream with just the tippet landing on top of the fish. Quartering upstream helps to keep the fly line away from a trout. A straight cross-stream presentation usually requires a Reach Cast to avoid drag. Quartering downstream is good for a fish in slack water against the far bank, but probably requires a Reach Cast and some slack line. Straight downstream is usually used only when there is no other option, and you must throw lots of slack.

straight-line cast without having to go through the vagaries of a Curve Cast or the contortions of a Reach Cast. The big disadvantage of an upstream cast is that your leader will always drift over the trout before the fly. I don't mind this and to get around my leader spooking the trout, I use long tippets so that only very fine leader material drifts over a fish's head.

In some small streams, the only approach is directly upstream, as brush on both banks may prevent any cast from the side. A direct downstream approach is theoretically possible but because you have to stay farther away from a feeding fish when approaching from above, a safe distance might be around the next bend!

One place that looks ideal for a direct upstream approach, the tail of a pool, is actually the most difficult spot to use this approach. In the tail of a pool, water picks up speed as it approaches the lip at the end of the tail. When fishing directly upstream, the water at your feet is moving faster than the water thirty feet upstream. Sometimes, even with a direct upstream approach, the fast water off your rod tip whisks the fly downstream before your fly drifts more than an inch. In this case, a Parachute Cast is the only answer from a downstream position and it might be better to get out of the river, approach the fish from above, and throw a Reach Cast.

Many things conspire to prevent you from making an easy upstream cast. Sometimes it's deep water. In a wide river, the water between you and fish rising on the far bank might be too deep to wade or the water directly behind a trout may also be too deep to wade. A trout rising just upstream of a low bridge or logjam may also be impossible to approach from behind. Sometimes, especially in the evening, lighting conditions may dictate your casting angle and you may not be able to see your fly in the fading light unless you move to one side.

Quartering Up

Moving to one side or the other from directly downstream of a feeding trout can change your presentation dramatically. If your casting is right on target, a trout will see only your fly and a small part of the leader. A sloppy cast that slams into the water is not usually as serious a problem, as the commotion happens off to the side of a fish instead of directly over its head. Remember to stay a little farther from the fish—as you move off to the side, you move out of a trout's blind spot. A quartering upstream approach seems to be the most comfortable angle for most fly fishers as it balances some degree of protection in a trout's blind

spot with an ability to place the fly carefully above a feeding fish.

The quartering upstream approach works best in places with a uniform current, like long riffles or the slow water in the middle of a pool. It's also a great position for a trout working on the near edge of a fast seam (the boundary between fast and slow water). Quartering upstream, however, is a terrible way to present a fly to a fish rising on the far side of a seam or for fish rising in slow water against the opposite bank. When you cast quartering upstream with fast water between you and a fish, the fast water pulls the fly downstream almost immediately, throwing some serious drag into the equation. It's also difficult to throw a Reach Cast when quartering upstream because the upstream hook part of the reach is tough to produce when a fish is already thirty feet or more upstream of your position. You can always throw a lot of slack but when there is fast water between you and a trout, it's better to cast across the river or even get upstream of the fish.

Across Stream

Getting directly across from a feeding trout is one way to cast to a fish in slower current, provided you add a Reach or Upstream Curve Cast to compensate for the fact that fly line will be drawn into a drag-inducing belly fairly quickly. It's also a good approach in tricky currents, especially in fast, boulder-strewn pocket water. In places where swirls and counter-currents are close together and seem to go in all directions at once, sometimes the only way to avoid drag, if only for a few inches, is to hold all the line and much of your leader off the water. This can at least buy you a short float. I find this approach most useful in rocky brook-trout or cutthroat streams where the fish aren't terribly spooky or selective.

Quartering Downstream

With trout rising in slow water along the far bank, the best approach is quartering downstream. Because the line and leader fall upstream of the fly, it buys you some time before the faster current between you and a trout pulls the fly away from the current lane it landed in and causes drag. Even a straight-line cast can work here but most times it's much better to add an upstream hook via a Reach Cast, giving you even more insurance against drag.

The other reason for quartering downstream to a feeding trout is to make sure the fish sees the fly before the leader. In situations where trout see a lot of artificial flies in a season, they may actually get "leader shy" and refuse nearly anything attached to a tippet. By showing them the fly before anything else, you may be able to induce a rise before the fish realizes something is not quite right. The other time to use a quartering-downstream approach is when experimenting with a twitched or skating fly, as discussed earlier.

Although a quartering-downstream approach has these obvious advantages, use it with caution. Because your position is upstream of the trout, it's easier for them to see you. This may not be a problem in very rich rivers where hatches are frequently so heavy that trout lose their caution and let you get within twenty feet before they spook. I once fished a Trico hatch on Colorado's South Platte where the insects were so thick and the fish rose with such abandon that I was able to walk to within a few feet of feeding trout and touch their tails with my rod tip without spooking them. In contrast, on the Vermont river in my backyard, the fish are so spooky that in broad daylight you'd have to be one hundred feet upstream of feeding trout to keep from spooking them so a quartering-downstream approach is not practical for those of us with mortal casting abilities. Just before dark it's a different story, though, so you can often use a quartering-downstream approach as the light gets low and the trout lose their wariness.

Straight Downstream

You'll seldom fish straight downstream by design as it has everything going against it: You are directly above a trout and very visible, you might kick silt down into a trout's face, and drag happens as soon as the fly hits the water.

One place you may cast straight downstream by design is in tight quarters where brush prevents you from approaching a fish from any other angle. Another is where a trout rises immediately in front of a logjam.

The main use for a direct downstream approach is when trout backdoor you and rise right below your position. Sometimes this happens just before dark when trout leave the cover of deeper water and move into shallow water to feed on mayfly spinners or spent caddis.

Another situation is where trout cruise in big, slow pools. In one pool on the Delaware River, no matter how much time I spend watching the water before I begin wading into position, cruising trout invariably move into position right below me. Wading below them is not an option because in the slow water of these mile-long pools, disturbance caused by wading usually puts the fish down.

There are two ways to fish straight downstream. One is to throw a large amount of slack, hoping the fly will drift drag-free until it floats below the fish. The other is to cast well above and to one side of a fish, then slide the fly into the trout's feeding lane with the tip of the rod. Once the fly is in position, follow the line downstream with the rod, reaching out as far as you can to keep the fly floating without drag. If there is enough line on the water, you may even be able to release line from your stripping hand by wiggling the rod tip from side to side and releasing slack as the fly drifts downstream.

Keeping Track of an Unseen Fly

One of the most important aspects of presentation is being able to track your fly on the water. You can't tell if an invisible fly is dragging. You can't tell if it's drifting over your target. And you can't be sure whether it's your fly or a natural that just disappeared in a rise. The problem does not just happen with tiny midges. Under certain water and light conditions it can be tough to spot a No. 12 Royal Wulff with big white wings. And flies that float low in the water—emergers and spent flies in particular—are tough to see under any light conditions.

If you can't see your fly, the first thing to find out is if it's floating at all. Make a short cast

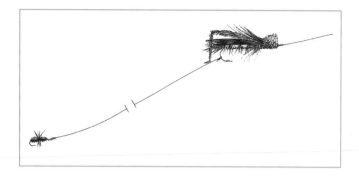

A great combination for summer fishing is a big hopper fly combined with a small ant pattern.

where you can see the surface to check. If not, change flies or apply some desiccant powder. Next, change your angle to the water slightly. Move off to one side or bend down to see if you can spot the fly against surface glare. Because glare actually helps you track a surface fly, especially in low light, I often remove my polarized glasses when I have trouble seeing a fly. The tint in any sunglasses always removes some light, lowering your resolution, so removing sunglasses may help you spot a fly in low light.

Some flies, like midges, emergers, spinners, and spent caddis, are supposed to float low in the water and you have to face the fact that you won't see your fly all the time. False casts are one way of making sure your fly is landing in the right place. As you false cast, try to see where the end of your leader ends up. With some practice, you'll get a pretty good idea of where your fly will land. If you still have trouble, move your cast off to the side and let the fly hit the water lightly at the end of a false cast, or actually deliver the fly with your rod tip pointed at the water instead of parallel to it as you usually do. Then move back to your target and deliver the fly in a normal manner.

Once I was fishing No. 24 olive mayfly imitations on the West Branch of the Delaware in about a twenty-mph wind. I was sure my fly was right and was pretty certain it was not dragging but I couldn't buy a rise. I thought that maybe the wind was blowing my fly off course because of the very long tippet I was using. I put on a No. 16 Adams, a fly I could see, and made the same cast to the rising fish. I quickly realized the wind was blowing the fly at least four feet downstream of where I thought I was casting. I switched back to the tiny olive and cast four feet upstream of where I thought I should have delivered the fly, confident that at least I was putting the fly where the fish could see it!

It's not cheating to use a tiny strike indicator on the leader above an unseen fly. There is a floating putty indicator called Strike Putty that can be used in any size. Some anglers use a blob the size of a BB pellet a few feet ahead of the fly; others just smear some on the tippet above the fly. You can also use a bigger dry fly as a strike indicator, and may be surprised at strikes to the bigger fly as well. Tie on a highly visible fly like a hopper imitation, a parachute fly with white wings, or a small Humpy or Wulff. Tie a two-foot-long piece of tippet to the bend of the hook and tie the less visible fly to the end. Now you have the advantage of a strike indicator—something to tell you where the smaller fly is drifting—and an added chance to fool a trout. The main downside of this arrangement is that it does not cast well in the wind and may tangle.

Effective combinations include the following:

- A No. 16 Parachute Adams ahead of a tiny Trico or olive mayfly
- A No. 10 grasshopper ahead of a No. 18 Fur Ant or Foam Beetle
- A high-floating Elk-Hair Caddis ahead of a Caddis Emerger (the size depends on what you see on the water)
- A Rusty Parachute ahead of a Rusty Spinner (size would depend on what you see on the water)

Finally, assuming you have an idea where your fly is drifting and you see a trout rise anywhere near its supposed vicinity, strike! The strike should not be a vicious yank, especially when fishing tiny midges (it should seldom be when dry-fly fishing anyway). Just a short twitch of the rod tip or a strip of line, enough to tighten the leader all the way to the fly, will be enough to set the hook. If the rise was not to your fly not only will you not spook the fish, you'll also be able to see where your fly is in relation to where you thought it was.

CHAPTER TWENTY

NYMPH FISHING TECHNIQUES

— TOM ROSENBAUER —

Don't ever fool yourself into thinking you'll make your fly look like a naturally drifting nymph for more than a few feet. With the average thirty-foot cast, your fly will behave exactly like a drifting natural for two or three feet, sort of like a natural for fifteen feet, and completely wrong for the other twelve feet. Don't lose any sleep over this. Just as you'll never buy or tie a fly that looks exactly like a mayfly, you'll never get the perfect drift. But trout aren't very bright and pretty close is good enough to fool them.

Fish can be amazingly fussy about the speed and depth of their prey even if the fly pattern is right. Everything you do in nymph presentation should strive to keep your fly at a trout's level as long as possible and at a speed that does not arouse suspicion. With the exception of some caddis pupae, scuds, and swimming mayfly nymphs, most insects drift at the mercy of the current, with an occasional wiggle of their bodies that makes them rise in the current, followed by a period of rest where they sink or stay suspended in the water column. You can't imitate this wiggle—forget about it. The bobbing of a strike indicator in choppy water, however, may cause your fly to rise and fall gently in the water, a benefit of strike indicators that is often overlooked.

Most of the time the trout are within a foot of the bottom where current speed is slow enough to let them maintain their positions without working too hard. They will move for a fly anywhere from a few inches to a few feet,

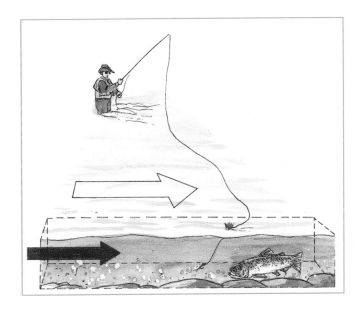

Forces that keep a nymph from drifting naturally.

depending on water temperature, clarity, and the amount of food in the water. Most times they won't move up more than about eight inches (or they may not be able to see a fly farther because of bubbles or turbidity in the water). It's important to get your fly close to the bottom—but obviously not on the bottom. Besides the fact that you'll hang up on the bottom, disturbing the water and losing lots of flies, trout never eat things drifting under them because they can't see them. Almost none of their feeding is done by grubbing on the bottom because they have to tip their

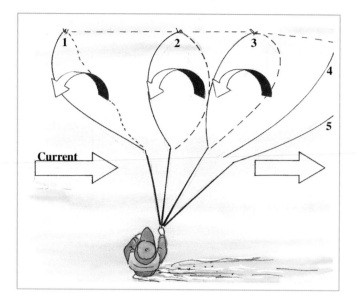

When quartering downstream, make careful mends to keep the fly from skittering across the river.

bodies tail-up, which wastes energy. Plucking food from the drift is far more efficient.

When dry-fly fishing, drag is any pull from the line or leader that makes the fly move contrary to the current, whether it's upstream, downstream, or across-stream. Drag-free drifts are just as critical in nymph fishing but the fly can move slightly upstream or downstream (imitating that rising and falling motion) as long as it does not move across currents. Once you cast your fly, imagine a vertical lane from the surface to the bottom parallel to the direction of the current. As long as your fly drifts along this lane, close enough for trout lying near the bottom to see it, you should be able to tease some of them into eating your nymph.

WET-FLY SWING

Casting a fly across the current and letting it swing below you is the least cumbersome, least scientific—and probably the least productive—way of fishing nymphs. It can be deadly, however, when insects are actively hatching and you see a few scattered rises in a pool. It does not work with a strike indicator and weight on the leader hinders its effectiveness. The fly is cast quartering upstream about

forty-five degrees, followed by a quick upstream mend. As the fly drifts downstream, tension is put on its drift by the line and leader because the currents at the surface are always faster than below. The line and leader begin to belly downstream, pulling the fly out of that vertical lane, sweeping it across the current faster that the natural flow.

There are ways to arrest the cross-current progress of the fly. One is to make frequent small mends in the line. Reach straight out over the water, point the rod tip at the fly, and flip a small loop of line upstream. Try not to move the line lying on the surface, nor the fly or leader, when you mend. It's natural for a drifting nymph to rise and fall slightly in the water column but any movement you make with your clumsy arms is way out of proportion to the distance a natural fly can move. When some species of caddis flies or swimming mayflies are hatching, purposely moving the fly with mends can draw smashing strikes but most times it does more harm than good.

In combination with mends (or instead of mends), try following the suspected position of the fly with the rod tip, keeping as much line as possible off the water by raising the rod tip to slow a fly's sideways skid. And notice I said the suspected position of the fly, not where the line enters the water. This technique works better with short casts; with a fifty-foot cast, it's tough to keep enough line off the water to affect the fly's drift.

The wet-fly swing works best with an unweighted or lightly weighted fly. Of course, it is the method of choice for fishing traditional winged or soft-hackle wet flies. These flies are tied on heavy hooks with soft, water-absorbent materials that sink quickly without added weight and have lifelike mobility in the water. Traditional nymphs can be used as well. I've had better luck with soft, fuzzy nymphs like the Hare's-Ear or hackled nymphs like the Zug Bug than I have with stiffer, harder flies like most stonefly imitations.

The wet-fly swing works better in slow to moderate currents than it does in very fast or broken water. It's a great way to cover the middle or tail of a large pool when you have no

When fishing directly upstream, standing in the same current lane the fly is drifting through will give you a long drag-free presentation.

idea where the trout are; trying to fish a one hundred-foot-wide pool with an indicator and split shot might wear you out before you hook a fish! In smooth water like this, use at least a nine-foot leader or preferably a twelve-footer. Your fly will sink with less hindrance because these leaders have longer tippets (thinner nylon has less resistance in the water) and you'll be keeping the heavy fly line farther from spooky flat-water trout.

UPSTREAM WITH NO INDICATOR

I learned to fish nymphs without the benefit of strike indicators (they have only been widely used since about 1980) and I still love to fish that way if conditions allow. Sight-fishing to spooky fish in shallow water is best done without a bulky indicator because the splash of an indicator often scares trout, but there are other places you can fish effectively without a bobber stuck onto your leader. Generally, the shallower the water and the more aggressively fish feed, the easier it is to catch them without an indicator. It's also better where currents are relatively uniform—tricky pocket water full of swirls really screams for a strike indicator.

Direct Upstream Approach

Let's say there's a caddis hatch on the water, you see a few splashy rises in a fast riffle, but the fish won't touch a dry fly. Here's a perfect opportunity to try a weighted caddis pupa or Bead-Head. Cast straight upstream or slightly across-and-upstream, just as you would with a dry. It helps if your tippet collapses a bit to get the fly below the surface before the leader begins to pull it to the surface. A great trick is

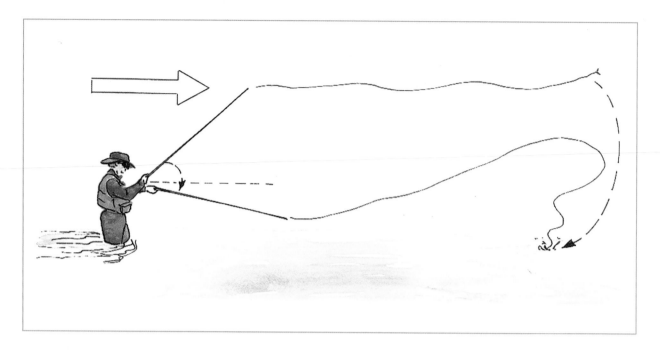

The Tuck Cast gives your nymph the best start to a natural drift.

to employ Joe Humphreys's famous Tuck Cast. This cast drives the fly into the water and piles some of the leader directly over it, giving the fly added margin for sinking. To perform the Tuck Cast, stop your forward cast higher than normal right after the forward power stroke. At the same time, tip your wrist down about thirty degrees below the horizontal. If you're doing it properly, the fly will hit the water with a splat before the line and leader.

If you are fishing directly upstream, keep the rod tip low and strip in line as the current gathers it to you. Strikes will appear to make the line jump upstream, or the leader might tighten, or a curl in the butt section of the leader might straighten. It's not black magic as many anglers would have you believe—set the hook if the line or leader do anything that looks like they are not just drifting with the current. You can hone your technique if you can find some whitefish, chubs, shiners, or bluegills. These fish take nymphs readily and hold onto a fake insect longer than trout.

When fishing directly upstream, try to stand in the same current lane as the water you're fishing and don't mend line. Mending line

without an indicator on the leader makes the fly move unnaturally, no matter how carefully you mend. Everything needs to be done before the fly hits the water with either a Tuck Cast or a sloppy slack-line cast. Casting directly upstream has the disadvantage of putting the line and leader directly over a trout's head, especially if you misjudge a cast. Therefore, it works best in very fast water where the splash of a fly line hitting the water may be ignored over the noise of a riffle.

High-Sticking

The biggest disadvantage of fishing directly upstream with a floating line is that the current is always faster at the surface than down below because friction with the bottom of the river slows the water's velocity. As soon as your cast hits the water, the fly line and leader move downstream faster than the sunken fly. This is why the Tuck Cast is so effective—it both drives your fly down toward the bottom and adds some slack above the fly. The fly has a chance to sink before the line draws it downstream and up through the water column. This effect is accentuated if you're casting to the eddy behind a rock or against the far bank and your line falls on a faster current close to you.

A more typical situation than standing in the same current lane as the fly is when you are standing in the slower, shallower water near shore and you want to fish your nymph in deeper water closer to the center of the river. If the current you're standing in is slower than where you want to drift your nymph, the fly line will bow upstream while the nymph drifts past, quickly forming a whiplash effect, making the fly jerk upstream. If the current you are standing in is faster, the line will tow the fly downstream. You might argue that action like this makes the fly appear to be rising to the surface like a hatching nymph. This might be attractive to a trout under certain conditions but take my word for it—95 percent of the time you'll get more strikes if your fly is drifting just as fast as the current.

One solution is to keep most or all of the fly line off the water by holding the rod tip high, a method developed in Colorado known as "high-sticking." The method works best with short casts, usually under thirty feet, and is ideally suited to fast, swirling pocket water where trout aren't too spooky and you can get very close to them. Stand just opposite to a place where you think a trout might be feeding. Cast upstream and a little beyond this spot to allow the fly to sink to a trout's level. How far above the fish's position you cast depends upon the depth of the water and the amount of weight on your fly and leader. In three feet of water with a moderate current, with a bead-head fly on your leader, cast about ten feet upstream and two feet to the other side of its suspected position. With weight on the leader or a Tuck Cast, you can cut that lead in half.

Two-Fly Rigs

Regardless of whether you try the methods above or the indicator fishing techniques to follow, you may want to fish with two nymphs at once. The advantages are obvious—you get to try two different patterns to see which one the fish prefer and your flies drift at slightly

High-sticking the edge of a deep run. Note the very short cast, helpful in maintaining line control.

different levels. Before you get too excited, though, a word of warning: Where snags are frequent, you'll lose two flies at a time as opposed to one and when it's windy this arrangement is on a par with a root canal. Tangles are frequent, so be patient.

The most common two-fly arrangement is to add the second fly by tying it to the bend or eye of the first fly. For instance, let's say you're fishing a No. 12 Hare's-Ear Nymph on a 4X tippet and want to try something smaller and in a different color. Tie a twelve-inch piece of 5X tippet material to the bend of your Hare's-Ear with a clinch knot and then tie a No. 16

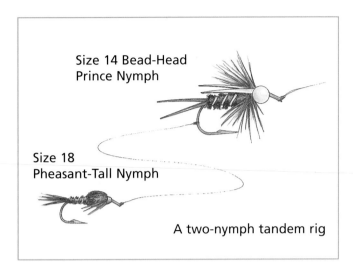

A two-nymph tandem rig

Size 14 Bead-Head Prince Nymph

Size 18 Pheasant-Tall Nymph

Two-fly rig. The smaller fly could also be attached to the eye of the larger fly with a clinch knot.

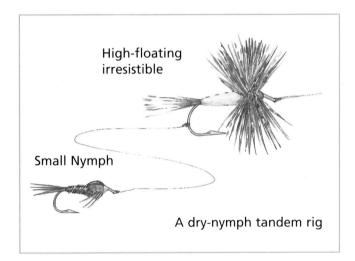

High-floating irresistible

Small Nymph

A dry-nymph tandem rig

Using a dry fly as a strike indicator.

Green Caddis Pupa to the end of the 5X. The lower fly is typically smaller than the upper fly and the tippet used for it is one size smaller than the main tippet.

There is a temptation to try a really large fly for the upper one and a tiny fly for the lower but I've found this doesn't work well for reasons I can't begin to fathom. Perhaps seeing two flies of vastly different proportions does not seem natural. You'll have better luck if you don't vary the size of the two flies by more than two hook sizes. Often you'll see two flies on the water at once; for instance, a No. 14 caddis and a No. 18 mayfly. This makes your choice easy—put on imitations of corresponding size and silhouette. If there aren't any visible hatches, try the nymph most recommended for the stream in question and the same pattern two sizes smaller. If you are mixing and matching, take your best shot with the upper fly and use the lower one for experimentation.

When putting weight on the leader, it's best to put all the weight above the upper fly. You can also experiment by adding weight on the tippet between the two flies, but that arrangement has never worked well for me and it induces tangles. You might also occasionally foul hook trout when fishing two flies. What usually happens is that a trout takes the upper fly but ejects it before you set the hook. By the time you strike, the lower fly ends up in the trout's butt. You can avoid this by making the lower tippet longer (around sixteen inches) and perhaps by changing the upper fly to the same pattern one size smaller.

INDICATOR FISHING

As I stated before, strike indicators have become much more than bite indicators. You'll also find them handy as drift indicators and the bigger ones also function as drift regulators. I urge you to experiment with several styles, especially when you fish different water types. My vest contains at least four different types of indicators and three styles of weight at any given time. New flavors come out every year and I urge you to watch magazine articles and fishing catalogs for the latest varieties. The perfect indicator has yet to appear and it only costs a few bucks to try a new one.

Whatever else you do when fishing a nymph with a strike indicator, the most important part of the game is to keep the fly and indicator drifting in the same current lane and to make sure both continue in the same current lane throughout the drift. Any way you can accomplish this, no matter how unorthodox it may seem, will make nymph fishing more productive.

Using Dry-Fly Indicators

Using a dry fly as an indicator couldn't be easier. Tie a piece of tippet to the bend of the dry-fly hook and tie a nymph to the end of the tippet. This rig will not cast as well as you think—just adding a piece of nylon and even a small nymph can do nasty things to your casting and you'll have to sacrifice tight loops and long casts for a more relaxed style with an open loop. Also, if you're fishing heavy fast water and need weight on the leader, a dry fly won't be up to the task of suspending a pair of large weighted flies and a hunk of soft lead. But for fishing shallow riffles or slow pools, a dry-fly indicator is just right.

In my backyard flows a small trout stream full of wild and very spooky browns and rainbows with a few brookies mixed in. My favorite rig for this shallow, clear river is a No. 18 Black Caddis Pupa fished underneath a No. 14 Foam Beetle. The tippet to the beetle is about three feet of 6X and the nymph is separated from the dry by two feet of 7X. I can't cast more than forty feet with these flies but it seldom spooks trout and I catch fish on both the beetle and the nymph.

Cast upstream with a slight Tuck Cast so the nymph enters the water first. Watch the dry fly's progress as it floats back to you. Avoid drag as you would fishing a single dry and if you see the floater hesitate or bob slightly, set the hook quickly but not viciously. Enough tightening to move the dry fly a few inches will be enough force to set the hook. If a trout splashes at the dry but does not take it, watch the fly carefully as many fish drop back and take the nymph.

Silicate dry-fly desiccant, a white powder sold under names such as Dry Flotant, is invaluable when using a dry-fly indicator. When your dry becomes hard to spot, grind it into a small amount of this miracle powder and blow on the fly until most of the powder is removed. This process removes moisture from the dry and coats it with a layer of hydrophobic silicone powder.

For most riffles, two feet of tippet between the dry and the nymph is about right. If there are insects hatching and you see an occasional rise, the distance between the two can be as short as a foot. But this technique is also deadly in deep, slow water where takes are so subtle that sometimes a standard indicator won't register the strike. In a pool over three feet deep, use about five feet of tippet between the nymph and the dry. Warning: This rig is harder to cast than it seems. Your casting will feel clumsy even if both nymph and dry are quite small. But the rewards are often worth the effort.

Using Foam and Yarn Indicators

Foam and yarn indicators have made nymph fishing a technique that even first-time fly fishers can understand and use effectively. An experienced guide in a drift boat can rig up an angler who has never held a fly rod with a pair of nymphs and some weight on the leader, plus a high-floating indicator, and have the client catch scores of trout in a single day. The guide keeps the boat drifting even with the indicator and can often fish through fifty yards of water without even mending the line; all the angler has to do is set the hook. Some anglers look down on this kind of fishing, calling it bobber fishing. Make your own decision and don't be intimidated by self-righteous "experts." There are times when only a big indicator with weight will interest trout and most of us would rather play a few trout in a day of fishing than not.

I'll assume that most of your fishing will be on your own where you won't have the benefit of a guide's prudent advice and accomplished boat-handling skills. The best advice I can give you about indicator fishing is to pick a flexible arrangement. If you can quickly move the indicator up and down the leader, and add, subtract, or move the weight, you'll spend more time fishing and less time fussing with tackle.

A Typical Scenario

The best rig for fast currents and water over two feet deep is a clip-on yarn indicator and tungsten Sink Putty for weight (if needed).

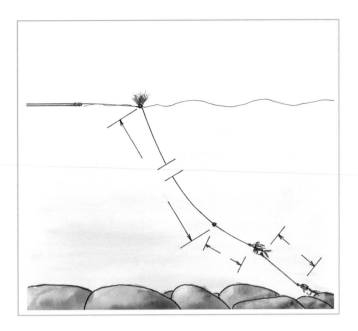

The most common way to fish nymphs with an indicator.

Let's say you're starting out in a moderate riffle in the middle of a pool with current about as fast as a walk and two feet deep. You have a nine-foot, 5X leader and you know the fish in this river like a No. 14 Bead-Head Prince Nymph. Without a lot of weight on the leader, your fly will invariably drift at an angle to the indicator, not directly below it. A rule of thumb is to set the indicator at twice the depth of the water, so tie on the nymph and clip the strike indicator four feet up the leader.

If the fly is weighted and you don't have a strike in two dozen casts and notice the indicator has never hesitated, you are probably fishing nowhere near the bottom. It takes far more weight than you might think to get the fly close to the fish. The fly might also be dragging unnaturally because the indicator at the surface is drifting much faster than the nymph below. To slow down the fly and get it deeper, roll a piece of Sink Putty half the size of a pea to the tippet a foot above the fly. The weight will get the fly deeper and help slow it down as it drifts.

If you still don't get any sign of hesitation in the indicator, add enough Sink Putty to the original clump to increase its size about thirty percent. Now, every half-dozen casts the indicator hesitates slightly, as if the fly were ticking along the bottom. Each time you set the hook but there is no weight at the other end. Another few casts and the indicator hesitates more decisively—set the hook and land and release a nice rainbow.

Since adding some weight increased your success, you decide to add more. Now you double the size of the lump of Sink Putty and on every cast the indicator hesitates. After a few more casts it really stops dead and you are firmly attached to a rock on the streambed. You've learned two important lessons. First, when you find the right combination of weight and indicator setting, don't change a thing. Second, it's possible to be too close to the bottom. Not only will you hang up frequently and lose many flies but the trout may be missing your fly because it's drifting too deep. Remember, they may be close to the bottom but they feed on stuff drifting above the bottom.

You decide to move closer to the head of the pool where the water is deeper—about four feet. You make a dozen casts and suspect the fly is not getting deep enough as it never hesitates. Instead of adding weight, you move the strike indicator four feet closer to the fly line to match the water's depth. You also make a more pronounced Tuck Cast, putting more authority into the downward flick of your wrist. The combination of the increased depth of the indicator and the Tuck Cast is enough to drift your nymph at the right level, and you take another small rainbow and a frisky, butter-colored fourteen-inch brown trout. Equal success might have come from adding more weight to the leader, but casting and fishing are more pleasant if you can get to the same place without additional weight.

Ways to Get the Fly Deeper and Avoid Drag

Avoiding unnatural drag and getting the fly deeper go hand-in-hand. You have a number of arrows in your quiver of techniques:

- **Cast at an angle closer to directly upstream.** Any time you cast off to one side, the current will pull the indicator and line directly downstream faster than the nymph. It will also pull them to one side, toward you and the tip of the rod.
- **Add more weight to the leader.** Adding weight—about 30 percent at a time—seems to be about right. When the indicator hesitates at the end of the drift, bumping bottom every three or four casts just before the line straightens, your nymph should be drifting about right.
- **Move the indicator closer to the fly line.** Make sure it's somewhere around twice the depth of the water (unless you have a very heavy chunk of Sink Putty). If you've pushed the envelope in weight, the indicator can be set to slightly less than the water depth.
- **Use a Tuck Cast.** It's an extremely useful technique that helps the fly drift deeper and free of drag.
- **Use a Post-Cast Tuck.** I have never seen this used or described before but it works for me. After the fly and indicator hit the water, lift your rod tip sharply while pointing it straight at the indicator. This lifts the line and indicator, giving the nymph some slack to sink, and the nymph and weight pivot around the indicator, driving them deeper. It's like a mend but you are not moving the fly line to one side or the other.
- **Make an upstream mend.** Similar to the technique above, throw a loop of fly line upstream of the indicator. Try to do this without moving the indicator so you don't make the nymph jump like a grasshopper caught on a hot sidewalk.
- **Make shorter casts and hold the rod tip high.** The longer you cast, the harder it is to control the fly and indicator. Keep casts short, as in the high-sticking method, while keeping most or all of the line and leader above the indicator off the water. It is a deadly way to fish fast, deep water, if you can wade close enough.
- **Lengthen Your Tippet.** The finer the connection between the leader butt and the nymph, the less resistance the leader offers to the water and the faster the fly can sink—and the more naturally it will drift. Adding more tippet material can give you a deeper, more natural drift; four feet of 5X instead of two feet can dramatically increase your success.

When Deeper Isn't Better

Usually, you'll be fishing too shallow if you don't pay attention to the amount of weight and the setting of your indicator. There are times, however, when you'll want a nymph to drift higher in the water column. Early in the morning and in the evening, it's hard for a trout to see your fly when it's close to the bottom. Try moving the indicator closer to the fly until it's at the water's depth or even half the depth. Setting the indicator so the fly rides higher can also make a difference during a hatch when insects are rising toward the surface.

Extending the Drift

Despite your best efforts, at some point the line between your rod tip will tighten, pulling the nymph and indicator toward you and the surface. This usually happens right after the fly is at its deepest and most drag-free position—most often as it drifts past where you're standing. You will catch most trout just before this spot but there are ways to get a longer drift and cover more water with each cast. Sometimes just lifting the rod will extend the drift. Follow the indicator with the tip of the rod and hold the rod high but horizontally above the indicator. On longer casts, it's difficult to raise the rod without pulling the indicator toward you. In this situation, you can mend a large loop of slack line upstream and beyond the indicator. As the indicator floats downstream, keep the rod tip pointing at the indicator. Feed line into the loop by wiggling the rod tip gently from side to side while letting slack line slip through the guides. The loop absorbs the slight movements of the rod tip so the indicator and the fly

Extending the downstream drift of a nymph. Note the angler feeding line and the rod tip pointed at the indicator.

don't move. Keep feeding slack until the indicator starts to slide sideways. At this point there is nothing else you can do except let the fly and indicator hang below you in preparation for the next cast.

Sometimes trout strike when the line tightens and the fly rises toward the surface. This usually happens when there is an insect hatch and they are chasing emerging flies to the surface. It seems like this would be a natural movement and a prime time for strikes but it happens less often than you might think.

At times, wading conditions or snags along a bank may make it impossible to fish any way but directly downstream. This is a far tougher way to fish and trout are more likely spooked when you are above them. Still, if it's the only way to get your nymph into position, cast downstream with a serious slack-line cast by overpowering the cast and stopping it short, so line, leader, and fly land in a pile. Immediately start feeding slack into the drift (as if you were

extending a normal drift). Strikes will be even more subtle than usual so set the hook at the slightest hesitation of the indicator.

When fishing a rig with lots of weight on the leader, casting is difficult, dangerous, and clumsy. The best way to make another cast and reposition the fly for the next drift is to wait until the line, indicator, and fly hang directly downstream. Extend the rod tip all the way back until it points directly at the indicator, then sling the whole thing back upstream by moving the rod tip in a broad, quick arc. The line hanging in the water will load the rod and there is no need to make a false cast. With no false casts, you are less likely to tangle the leader and less likely to skim your ear with a big chunk of tungsten. Another trick is to move the rod tip to one side or another just at the completion of this upstream lob. This movement creates an upstream loop that will give you a longer, deeper drift.

Other Ways to Rig Indicators

The clip-on yarn and Sink Putty rig described previously is the most flexible arrangement and it allows you to instantly switch to a dry fly if trout begin feeding on the surface. Alternatively, you can use a yarn indicator with a rubber O-ring or slip-knot a piece of yarn to the leader butt. With most cork and foam indicators, fishing techniques are the same but to add or remove them you must remove all flies and weight from the leader because the leader gets threaded up the middle of these.

Big, extremely buoyant plastic or cork indicators come into their own when you want to suspend a heavily weighted rig in deep, fast water. Yarn is not buoyant enough to hold a big stonefly nymph plus two peanut-sized chunks of weight off the bottom. When water is over five feet deep and very fast, especially with strong turbulence that tosses your fly around like a milkweed seed on a fall day, no cast is long enough to sink the fly. Here you must get your nymph down right now and under control. The only way is to attach as much weight to the leader as you can sling, with an indicator that will hold it just above the bottom.

One of the most difficult places to fish nymphs is in swirling currents where your leader and indicator are pulled in many directions and it's difficult to tell if your nymph is drifting at the same speed as the indicator. Strikes are also tough to detect. A double-strike-indicator technique I learned from guides in Colorado makes these conditions much easier to handle. Place one strike indicator where you normally would at about twice the depth of the water from the fly. Then add a second indicator two feet above the first one. Mend line so that both indicators form a straight line, pointing toward the place you think your fly is drifting. Keep mending as the fly drifts toward you. This avoids arcs in the leader that can cause drag.

In fact, this double-indicator method is great for novice nymph fishers in any current; it's easier to follow the progress of the fly than with a single indicator and it teaches them about drag caused by loops in the line.

Right-Angle Nymph Rig.

Strike Putty is wonderful stuff for the double-indicator method because it's not as important that the indicators float as high when you have two of them. I also use Strike Putty with unweighted flies and leaders such as when fishing tiny Pheasant-Tail Nymphs in shallow riffles. When fishing with weight on the leader or where it's tough to keep the fly and indicator in the same current lane, however, Strike Putty is not as effective as a yarn or foam indicator. A round ball of Strike Putty offers little resistance to the pull of the line or leader butt so it gives a drifting nymph little defense against drag.

One final strike indicator setup is the Right-Angle Nymph Rig (or Suspension Rig) developed in California. It places the tippet and fly at right angles to the indicator and helps them drift deeper, suspended under the indicator. Start with a short, heavy leader, about seven and one-half feet long and ending at no lighter than 2X. The end of the leader can be even

Sight-fishing in a rich tailwater—in this case, Colorado's Frying Pan—can be exciting and productive.

heavier for big flies and stiff winds. At the end of the leader, attach a yarn strike indicator with a clinch knot. You can either knot the leader to the rubber O-ring of a pre-made indicator or knot it to the center of a loose bunch of floating yarn.

Use a clinch knot to tie a tippet about equal to the depth of the water either to the O-ring or to the end of the leader. The tippet is usually 4X or 5X material, depending on the size of the fly and clarity of the water. Lighter tippets can be effective but they tangle easily. You'll notice the tippet and the fly at its end come off from the indicator at a right angle so once the rig hits the water the fly is forced toward the bottom quicker than if it were on one continuous length. This arrangement gives great drifts but it's difficult to cast and you must rebuild or replace your entire leader if you want to change to a dry fly.

Other Ways to Fish Weight and Multiple Flies

In the examples above, we've been looking at a single fly and weight on the tippet about a foot from the fly. The nymph can be weighted or unweighted depending upon the depth and speed of the water. I prefer to try a weighted nymph with no lead on the leader first because I feel it's more natural and easier to cast. As I stated earlier, some anglers feel an unweighted fly looks more natural but I don't agree. I'll often change from a lightly weighted nymph (tied with a wire underbody) to one with a brass bead to get deeper. Finally, I'll try a fly with a tungsten bead head before adding weight to the leader.

Instead of putting Sink Putty or split shot directly on the tippet, you can place it on a dropper tied above the fly. Here you leave a two-inch-long tag end of the blood knot used to attach the tippet (the heavier tag is better). Attach the weight to this tag dropper. The advantage here is that if the weight hangs up, you'll lose just the lead but not the tippet and fly. I've also seen rigs where you put the weight on the end of the tippet and put the fly on the dropper. With this rig, the weight should bump along the bottom and the fly should ride just above. This makes perfect sense but I've seen it mostly in magazines. I've tried it and found it to be no better or worse than putting the weight above the fly. None of my friends use it, so maybe that tells you something.

Fishing a second lower fly—typically a smaller one on a lighter tippet—seems to work best with weight only above the upper fly (with no additional weight between the two flies). This keeps the lower fly actually drifting higher in the water column than the upper fly because current welling up from the bottom pulls it up. If the water is cold or very fast, however, and you suspect the trout are glued to the bottom, you might try adding a smaller amount of weight between the two flies. This keeps both of them close to the bottom but it also makes casting tougher and tangles more frequent.

SIGHT-FISHING

Being able to see your quarry makes any kind of fishing more complex—and more exciting. Flats fishing for bonefish, casting to tailing redfish, pursuing breaking stripers in the surf, dry-fly fishing during a hatch—all bring visual stimulation to a level surpassed by few things in life, plus they add to the primordial satisfaction of the stalk. Sight fishing with a nymph is no exception.

These two brown trout feeding in Utah's Green River are perfect opportunities for a carefully presented nymph. Note that their shadows are more distinct than the fish themselves.

Sight-fishing is usually done in shallow water and in streams with lots of food like spring creeks and tailwaters. It's tough to see trout in deep water and more difficult to gauge their reactions. And because the buffet line of food is constricted into a narrow vertical range in shallow water, trout are more likely to feed in the shallows than in relatively sterile deep water. Despite being in water just deep enough to cover their shoulders, sight fishing is best in shallow streams with lots of food because trout get preoccupied with feeding and are less spooky. And the more frequently they feed, the more likely they'll make a mistake and inhale your fraud.

Sight fishing requires careful observation of the water from as far away as possible. Even binoculars can be helpful. The fish themselves are difficult to spot; look instead for their shadows, which are much darker and more distinct. Also watch for the gentle swaying motion of a trout's tail.

The best setup is a trout in very shallow riffles that is actively moving from side to side. In shallow water, trout see very little of the world above and the riffles mask the landing of your leader and fly on the water. Also, a fish that is actively feeding is far easier to fool. You'll often see trout lying motionless, with no flick of the tail and no short forays from their positions. Fish like this are usually napping, spooked, or lethargic from water that's too cold or too warm.

If you've been watching a pool from afar, the longer you look the more trout you'll spot. If you have a choice, look for one or two fish that are plucking food from the drift, with their tails constantly in motion. Start without a strike indicator or weight on the leader. Make sure your leader is at least twelve feet long, preferably fifteen feet, and your tippet is at least four feet long. The best flies are usually small, drab, and lightly weighted. Pheasant-Tail Nymphs, midge pupae, worm imitations, and scuds are favorite flies for this kind of fishing but try to match what you see in the water or hatching.

The best approach is to pitch your fly above the fish far enough so it has time to sink to the trout's level. If you are fishing from directly behind it, try to place only the tippet over the fish. If you are fishing off to one side of the

Pat McCord sight-fishing to a big trout. You can feel the intensity of his gaze even from this angle.

fish, try to cast so that nothing falls on its head and only the fly drifts over its position. Placing the fly line over the trout's head is a sure way to send it bolting for deep water. How far ahead of the fish you cast depends on the size and weight of the fly, the water's depth, and the speed of the current. A typical distance in shallow water is three to four feet.

Since it is usually impossible to see your fly in the water, keep your eyes glued on the trout. Often, if you look away for just a few seconds you'll lose sight of the fish or it might move into a place where it's not as easy to spot. Try to gauge when your fly is passing the trout's position. If the fish moves sideways or lifts off the bottom, gently "pre-strike"—which is a soft but quick movement of either the rod tip or the fly line—to take slack out of the line. Continue to tighten if you feel resistance; if there is no resistance, the trout either refused your fly, moved for something else, or spit it out quickly. At any rate, since you did not rip your line off the water, the fish won't be spooked and occasionally the darting motion will even make the fish chase your fly.

Sometimes you'll see a fish move way off to one side when your fly drifts even with its position. This fish is probably frightened by either your leader or fly—a good sign that you should change position, go to a smaller fly, or add a longer, lighter tippet. Some fish will also get so frightened with your approach that

they'll spook and swim away. Some days most of them will. Chuckle or curse and move on.

Signs that a trout is ready to take your fly are a quickening of its tail beats, dropping back in the current, or moving to one side. If you are fishing across from a trout, you might even see a white flash as it opens its mouth. My friend Pat McCord, a Colorado guide and the best sight-fisherman I know, likes to strike just as he sees a fish move back to its original position. They'll invariably do that after eating something and it avoids a typical problem of striking too soon—when the fish is moving for your fly rather than after it has eaten the fly.

Strike indicators are not very useful when sight fishing; in fact, most times they're a hindrance because they spook the fish and cut down on your casting accuracy. Besides, fish lying in the shallows feeding on nymphs can inhale your fly and spit it out without ever moving the indicator. Many times I've been watching the strike indicator instead of the trout and when I glance back to the fish I wonder why it's moving its head like a puppy with a rag. By the time I realize the fish is trying to get a piece of metal out of its jaws, it's too late. A very tiny piece of yarn, a small dry fly, or a smudge of Strike Putty on the leader, however, can help you gauge the position of the fly. Make sure the indicator is so small that it does not disturb the water when you cast and keep it at least two feet from the fly. Don't watch the indicator. Use it in your peripheral vision to keep track of the fly's progress but never take your eyes off the fish.

There will be times when the water is deeper or faster and you'll need a small piece of shot or sink putty on the leader to get your nymph to a trout's level. You'll seldom need weight if you are directly behind a fish but if you approach them from any sideways angle it's much harder to get the fly down drag free because the current is yanking on the leader. Keep the weight as small as possible and at least eight inches from the fly. Here, adding two small indicators instead of one helps keep the fly from dragging and lets you approximate its position. Mend softly, keeping both indicators in line and pointing at the fly.

CHAPTER TWENTY-ONE

STILLWATER TROUT TECHNIQUES AND STRATEGIES

— JIM LEPAGE —

When approaching a stillwater you will discover that there are really only three fishing situations you will find yourself in: You will be prospecting the pond for fish, fishing a fly or technique that mimics something you have observed while on the water, or you'll be in the middle of a hatch. Other variables including weather, time of year, the size of stillwater, fishing methods used, and more will affect your fishing but you will still find yourself in one of these three situations.

STILLWATER PROSPECTING

More often than not I find myself on a stillwater with no apparent hatches to give away the trouts' location. Fear not, this does not mean the trout are not feeding. In fact, studies estimate that anywhere from 80 to 95 percent of a trout's diet is subsurface. I see this as an opportunity to prospect for trout as opposed to kicking back and waiting for trout to start rising. It's more interesting when fisherman leave or turn around to go home when they see no evidence of rising fish. I can confidently tell you that I have taken many more trout subsurface than on top with drys. I can also tell you that windy, churned-up water has the potential to produce more fish than a pond that is lying still, although either situation offers a good prospecting opportunity when fishing stillwater.

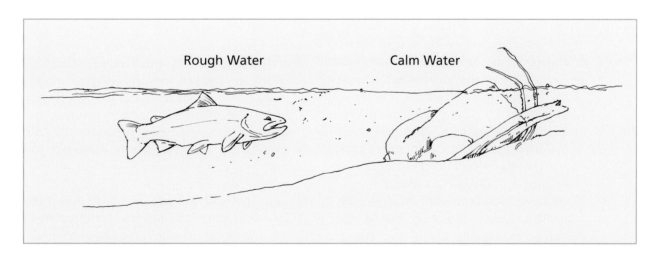

Rough Water   Calm Water

On windy days, rough water can stir up food and trout will often feed in the lee of a point or rock. Feeding can happen both at and below the surface.

Windy conditions do not hamper trout feeding, in fact they may prompt it. Choose your fishing location carefully.

Conditions

On windy days, ponds become easier to read yet harder to fish because casting can be a challenge and seeing rising fish may be next to impossible. But if you think fish are not feeding, think again. The wind creates many areas for trout to feed, similar to streams and rivers. A back eddy may form in a cove where the wind is blowing off a point of land, creating a calm area in the lee behind the point. You will often find a scum line forming in this lee as the wind blows debris and insects into the water and deposits them in a well-defined line just behind and out of the wind-blown water. Fish will often congregate under the debris and feed opportunistically on insects or wounded baitfish being deposited in this area.

Although you can see the debris floating on the surface, just as much and maybe more is often below. Feeding activity can take place throughout the water column in these situations and fishermen should observe the area for rising trout before prospecting below the surface. The fact that many of these debris lines form in the lee of a cove makes spotting rising fish a little easier in windy conditions. Because fish are less spooky in windy, churned-up water you can often get fairly close to a debris line without disturbing feeding fish, which allows you to spot rising fish more effectively and cast shorter distances.

The fish instinctively know that the insects are helpless so feeding activity is very slow and deliberate. A fisherman concentrating his efforts on a debris line will often see only a subtle, slow rise, or a fin and tail of a feeding trout. Eddies like these can be tricky to cast dry flies into as the wind may create some current, making this similar to stream fishing. If you find your cast is crossing windswept water as you try to present your fly to a rising fish in a calm spot and you just can't seem to get the long drift you're looking for, reposition yourself downwind closer to shore and cast into the wind. This not only takes you out of the wind but also allows you to present your fly with a long drift that eventually works back to your position. As long as your presentation is subtle, accurate, and without drag you may be able to work the fish until you find the right fly and presentation to entice a strike. This is important, as a fly dragged across a rising fish could put the fish down for awhile. The downwind position allows you to work the fly over and over again until you find the right combination to take the fish. If you see no evidence of rising fish, then prospecting the debris line with streamers, nymphs, Woolly Buggers, or leeches can prove deadly.

There is one other important debris line phenomenon. As the wind picks up and waves start to grow, the action of the waves hitting the shoreline and bouncing back into the pond or lake against the wind forms another line of debris that is visible from the lake. These debris lines will often run the entire length of a shoreline. I usually don't bother looking for risers in this situation as they are generally impossible to see unless a fish decides to really thrash the surface looking for a meal. Stick to subsurface flies in this situation, casting beyond the debris and retrieving your fly through or along the edge. This will eventually result in a fish.

I recently had occasion to learn how deadly streamer fishing can be in these situations when fishing Lago Tromen in Argentina's northern Patagonia. Host Ronnie Olsen guided my friend Mike and me to this beautiful lake in the Andes that forms the headwaters of the famed Malleo River. Crystal clear water and a calm day made for tough fishing conditions but Ronnie knew something we didn't. The wind would blow, as it always does here, and the fishing would get good as soon as it did. As we settled into an early lunch we could feel the wind start to pick up. Ronnie smiled and said "Let's go." Instead of finding a lee shoreline, Ronnie went to the most windy area of the lake. Waves made standing in the boat to cast a challenge but as we cast toward shore and started to retrieve we could see the distinct line of debris form as the waves hit shore and rebounded back into the lake. Rainbows in the eighteen-to twenty-four-inch range came readily to our olive Woolly

This angler makes a short cast toward the shoreline where the wind has formed a shady debris line . . .

. . . and takes a nice rainbow as a result!

Buggers and fishing was fantastic the rest of the day. As we drifted our last shoreline and I snapped the last few pictures of another of Mike's many rainbows, I realized how important it was to have someone like Ronnie who so graciously allowed us to have this great experience. Without his knowledge of this fishery, we probably would have headed home when the wind picked up.

I have had some twenty- and thirty-fish days fly fishing on stillwaters that were churned up from the wind. Popular fisheries in your area that are normally crowded with anglers are often empty on windy days. Windy conditions can result in some of the year's best

This angler is casting straight into the wind. This is challenging but most windswept debris will be here on the windward side, as will the trout.

Sometimes casting into the wind can pay off handsomely.

fishing if you are able to venture out. You must fish either from shore or in a stable boat to make this successful but it's worth it.

Not all prospecting occurs in windy conditions. There are many days when calm waters can be productive, especially in early spring when fish are well dispersed, and again in midsummer when warm surface water temperatures send fish looking for cooler depths, sometimes forty or fifty feet below the surface. Paul Bruun and I share a passion for stillwater lake trout called togue in Canada. They tend to be deepwater fish, hugging bottom most of the year. One of Paul's stillwater techniques involves a deep, slow retrieve of small streamer flies. The trick is feeling the take, often only a very subtle hesitation in your line. You need to be quick to react in setting the hook. It's easy to overlook the take and not hook the fish, or not even know it was there. Using a Depth Charge line, nine- to twelve-foot leader, and small streamers, Paul lets his line settle to his retrieve depth, usually measured by counting after his line and fly land on the water. It takes some

experimentation to know just how deep your fly is. Anchor off shore in twenty-five feet of water (measured with your anchor line) and count as your fly sinks; your fly will eventually hit bottom. Back off on your count and you will be fishing just off bottom.

Another important requirement for this deep-water technique is to feed slack into the water as the line is sinking. If you hold onto the line as it sinks, you act as a pivot or hinge point for your flyline and fly. This causes the fly to swing in an arc back toward you. If you feed slack line into the water as the line and fly is sinking it will allow the line to settle parallel with the bottom and your retrieve to cover more of the water's bottom than if it had hinged back toward your position when sinking. Add to this a slow retrieve and your fly will stay just off the bottom longer than if you were to retrieve quickly. Many times fish will take as the fly is swinging up toward the boat so keep your retrieve steady and be ready for the take all the way back to the boat. This technique works well for trout all year in most deep stillwaters.

Retrieves

When prospecting for trout in any weather condition, one becomes proficient at casting and retrieving the fly, over and over again. Change your retrieve and pattern often until you find the right combination for the fish you are seeking. When fishing streamers or nymphs, I may start with a floating line and weighted fly so that I am fishing just below the water's surface but may change to a full-sinking Depth Charge line that allows me to get deeper more quickly. In these conditions I like to have two rods rigged, one with a floating line and the other with a fast-sinking line.

When fishing nymphs use a longer twelve- to fifteen-foot leader on either a floating or sinking line. The nymphs I fish are always smaller than any streamer I would cast and so will turn over with the longer leaders. The retrieve is slower and more deliberate than the retrieves used for streamers or leeches, therefore I believe stealth is much more important when fishing nymphs, as the fish has more time to inspect what he is eating.

The retrieve I find most successful is small six- to twelve-inch strips, varying them from slow to fast. The takes can be very subtle and it is therefore super important to pay attention. There are many fish that eat a nymph and spit it out before the angler even knows that he has had a take.

Rule number one, when fishing nymphs with a floating line: Always look at where you think your fly is in the water and at the same time keep an eye on the end of your fly line. Many times a fish coming for the fly, even though it is subsurface, will make some sort of swirl that you can see from your vantage point. If you don't see the swirl, you should watch for any hesitation, stop, or pull at the end of your fly line that may indicate a fish taking your nymph. Making a long strip or lifting the rod to set the hook when you see any indication of a strike will often result in a hookup. If you think you are missing a lot of fish, increase the speed and length of your retrieve slightly. This will help you feel the strikes as it keeps a tighter line between you and your fly.

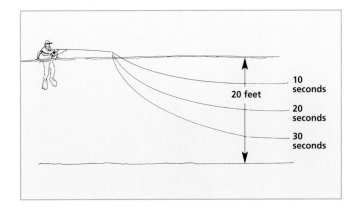

When fishing a sinking line, counting after your fly hits the water will give you an idea how deep it is when you get a strike. Keep fishing to the same count!

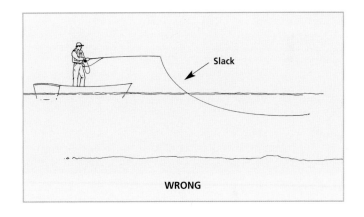

WRONG: Holding the rod tip high on the retrieve will cause slack and make strikes difficult to detect.

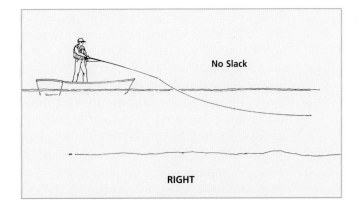

RIGHT: Holding the rod tip low keeps a straight line between you and the fly, making strike detection easier.

Tom Rosenbauer took this monster landlocked salmon while fishing a New York stillwater in October. The fish chased the streamer several times before hitting hard.

and releases the same amount when you stop. The combination of looking for a change and feeling a hesitation or pull results in a much more harmonious approach to detecting a strike. Any change in this rhythm should be met with a long strip or a lift of the tip to set the hook. If there is nothing there, go back to your retrieve but never think that what you felt and saw was not a fish. Always react as if a fish has just eaten your fly. More often than not you will be right. Don't second-guess yourself because it's too late if you do.

Two Nymphs Are Better Than One

As a variation on the above techniques, two nymphs can be better than one. I have a few good friends in Colorado who, many years ago, taught me never to tie only one nymph on my rig. Monroe Coleman, Mike Clough, and Kevin Gregory are the best nymph fishermen I have ever seen. Each of them has his own unique deadly technique but they all tie on at least two nymphs when fishing.

The key to fishing two nymphs is in how you set up your rig before you cast. The larger or heavier nymph should be at the top closer to your fly line, followed by the smaller nymph trailing sixteen to twenty-four inches behind the first. Tie the dropper directly to the bend of the hook on the heavier fly. This prevents the rig from twisting and spinning as you retrieve it. You will hear fishermen tell you that hooking fish on the top fly is harder because there is a piece of tippet attached to it and the fish may feel it as they try to take the fly. I think they are right but I have taken a good number of fish on the upper fly that I would not have caught had it not been there. I also feel that a fish will often see the larger nymph and approach for a look; when confronted with the smaller nymph trailing behind, they quickly eat it. This method simply gives the fish two choices of food, which they would not have had otherwise. It works very well when searching for a pattern the fish will eat. Have I ever taken two fish at once while fishing two nymphs? Rarely, but yes. If they are big, your chances of landing both are slim.

Rule number two: When fishing a full-sinking line you must concentrate on your senses of sight and touch. Your rod should be positioned low to the water so the tip is actually touching the surface as you retrieve. This removes any slack line that would form if you had your rod a foot or two above the surface of the water. Any slack will prevent you from feeling those subtle takes during the retrieve. When fishing nymphs on a full-sinking line it is much harder to feel the takes than with a floating line, so your concentration is key to knowing that a fish has just eaten your nymph. As you are retrieving your fly, watch the tip of your rod closely. You will see it fall into a rhythm with your retrieve: It dips the same amount as you pull

Using Streamers

Never have I witnessed a more dedicated streamer fisherman than my good friend Wayne MacDougall. His vest holds several fly boxes crammed with flies of every color, pattern, shape, and size you could imagine. When most fishermen give it up, Wayne is just getting started, and he produces. His methods include covering all water depths so he is ready with a Depth Charge as well as a floating fly line. His flies are gaudy creations that include lots of marabou and Krystal Flash in all imaginable colors, although his most successful colors are yellow and black. He varies his retrieves along with the depth until he hits on a combination that works. I have seen few occasions when Wayne is not catching fish using his deadly techniques.

I recall a memorable occasion where several of us, including Wayne, had a tremendous hatch of blue-winged olives (BWO) coming off a stillwater on a calm evening. Trout were readily sipping duns that sat on the water's surface, but trying to catch a trout seemed an impossible challenge. I had covered rises for an hour with nary a bite while Wayne was reeling in his fourth fish. Last I knew he was fishing a No. 20 BWO trying to trick these fish into eating so as he brought in his fourth fish I thought he had found the right combination to take these finicky trout. But as I gathered the courage to ask, I found his deadly fly was a No. 2 black marabou creation he had whipped up.

When fishing streamers, Woolly Buggers, and leeches, use slightly shorter leaders. I recommend a longer twelve-foot leader on a floating line and a shorter nine-foot (seven-and-a-half-foot if you are trying to stay tight to bottom) leader on full-sinking lines. Unlike the nymph fishing we discussed above, the takes are aggressive and quick, so 2X or 3X leaders should be used, especially when fishing in windy conditions. In lakes and ponds with large eight-pounds-plus fish, a 0X or 1X leader is not too big. Be ready for the yank of a lifetime when you least expect it. When retrieving flies on either floating or sinking lines use long, full strips with varying rates of speed. I often find trout turn on to very fast, long

Wayne with a nice rainbow taken on one of his many streamer patterns. Note the fly patch on his vest.

strips of a Woolly Bugger or leech and here the strikes are the most vicious of all. This is one of the most successful prospecting techniques going as you can cover a lot of water quickly and efficiently.

Baitfish can get disoriented or separated from their schools in windy situations, so trout are on the lookout for an imitation that looks like a lost soldier. When fishing streamers that are imitating baitfish, use lighter 3X to 4X leaders to start. To make the fly act like a wounded baitfish, make a few quick strips, stop, then two or three longer strips, then stop. Change it up so your retrieve is not monotonous. Takes will range from the subtle to the explosive so you need to be ready for either. In the fall when fishing for Northeast landlocked salmon on lakes and ponds, where fish are more likely to take small attractor streamers slowly stripped, the takes are more similar to those you get when fishing nymphs. Watch for swirling fish. Fish that make a pass at the fly but do not eat it will often take a different pattern presented to them. I have found that if a fish comes up and looks a couple times at a pattern and then disappears it will often come back and eat a different pattern presented as a follow-up. Fish will invariably come back and investigate until they see something that triggers the take. So quickly change your fly and recast to the same area, and keep doing this until he takes.

A big mayfly and its dry-fly imitation. On calm days, prospecting near shore with a dry fly is often an effective strategy. (Tom Rosenbauer photo)

Using Dry Flies

As deadly and persistent as Wayne is with streamers, my father (Chuck) is the same with his dry-fly fishing. Dad has been a relentless dry-fly fisherman for years. He just really hates to take off a dry fly and would rather prospect with drys than go to a nymph or streamer even if someone is catching a bunch of fish on them. He likes the challenge of fishing drys and will figure it out. In the end he catches fish, a lot of fish. He is patient and works to put together the same combination of pattern, size, color, and presentation that Wayne has worked out with his streamers. His relentless pursuit of trout on dry flies has given me insight into successful techniques that take trout.

Of all the fishing experiences I have been able to share with my dad, the one involving dry-fly fishing that sticks most in my mind took place on Pierce Pond in Maine in the early 1980s. We had, for a number of years, tented in a remote cove (called the Scott Paper site) for a week in early July in anticipation of the giant

Hexagenia limbata mayfly hatch that was prolific on this pond. I always fished floating nymphs early in the hatch before the fish started to rise. I could occasionally get fish to take a nymph stripped slowly just under the surface but never fished drys this early on. There were no flies on the surface so logically why would I want to prospect with one? Dad tied on a large Black Wulff pattern we had tied during the day and started prospecting. Patiently casting and letting his fly sit on the water, he soon had an aggressive take from a big brook trout. Bringing the fish to the canoe, I could see that it was one of the bigger trout I had ever seen on Pierce Pond. We landed the fish, measured it at twenty-one inches, and released it. It didn't stop there and Dad proceeded to have the best single night of prospecting for trout that I have ever seen. One trout measured twenty-five inches in length and must have weighed all of eight pounds. He still glows when we talk about that evening. It has been a valuable reminder of the success you can have prospecting with drys.

On really calm days I will often prospect with dry flies close to shore or in areas where deepwater shoals rise to within a couple of feet of the surface. You'll be surprised how many fish will come to a dry fly dropped within a few feet of their position. In these situations it is important to read the water around you. Fish looking for food along these shorelines are feeding opportunistically subsurface, close to shore, and on the surface. They spot a fly in their path and rise to eat it as they continue on their way looking for more.

Work the shorelines in these situations, making a few casts in one area, then move on. Once you catch a fish, concentrate some time and effort in the area before moving on. You will often find a shoal, point, or section of shoreline where fish are feeding more readily than in other areas. Spend some time in such spots, as different fish will come in and out in search of food.

On stillwater, a dry fly should be cast and left for some time before picking it up to recast. I have seen too many anglers who do not have the patience to leave a fly in one spot long enough. They seem to think they need to keep the fly in the air or strip it back to get fish to strike. Remember that the fish are moving and may not instantly take your offering. There are several tricks to the cast-and-wait method that you should be aware of. Most important is the relationship of your fly line to the fly on the water. You will find that after you cast a dry fly on stillwater things don't stay exactly the same until you pick up your line for a recast. You must constantly tend your line to keep slack from forming between you and your fly. If you are in a moving canoe or float tube, you will find that a belly or arc forms between you and the fly, making it hard to set the hook. It's pretty exciting to see a fish you didn't anticipate come up and gulp your offering, so be ready.

ANTICIPATING A HATCH

While prospecting on stillwater, something you observe while fishing will usually be a key to some later activity that will increase your

An early Hexagenia limbata mayfly, a sure sign of what's to come in the evening.

fishing opportunities. Careful observation of the areas you are prospecting will often reveal a subsurface swirl, the remains of nymph cases floating in the water or gathered along shorelines, or flies in the trees.

In any stillwater the majority of hatching or emerging activity will take place in the shallows. Because sunlight and water temperatures are important to insect life, areas with rocky points, shallow silty coves, overhanging trees, undercut banks, weedy shorelines, and areas with subsurface structure like sunken logs or half-submerged fallen trees may create the conditions for a hatch you will see later today or tomorrow. A sure sign that a specific cove or section of a stillwater is experiencing a hatch is nymph cases floating in the water or washed up on shore. These cases are left as nymphs emerge to become flying adults. By either swimming or floating to the surface they shed their outer skins and emerge like a butterfly from a cocoon, leaving an empty hull floating in the surface layer. The insects are most vulnerable during this emerging phase, drawing fish to feed during the transformation. If you are there right after a hatch you may find these cases still floating in the area where they emerged. If you find cases later in the day, they have usually been carried closer to shorelines with the wind and are bunched together in a debris field.

These nymph cases can unlock a door to some intense fishing activity during the right time of day. If you are just arriving at a stillwater for the first time or the trip is just getting started, make it a point to search windward shorelines or coves for these remains during your day on the water. If you have done your entomology homework you will be able to determine whether the cases are from caddis, mayflies, stoneflies, midges, or other insects that have hatched.

The length and width of the case also gives you an idea of the fly size you should start with. If there is no apparent emerging activity, start with a nymph resembling the remains you have found. Fish it below the water's surface at varying depths. Chances are the nymph cases you have discovered along the shore represent an increase in the activity of a particular species.

I love to fish the *Hexagenia* hatch in the Northeast. I know from years of fishing this hatch that it occurs at night from the last week of June into the first week of July. I also know that certain coves are better than others. If I have only a day to fish this hatch (I would rather stay a week), I will arrive early and survey coves that have silt bottoms, looking for last night's cases bunched up along the shore. Once I have found an area with cases, chances are I can count on the hatch to take place again tonight in this same area. I will anchor or stake out an area close to where I think the highest activity will take place and will immediately start to prospect with large *Hex* nymphs. I know these nymphs are in the area and if they are emerging they must be in a state of increased activity, drawing the fish. As evening approaches I will switch from fishing nymphs deep to fishing nymphs just under the surface as I expect the real ones will be making their way up to emerge. And just at dark, and hopefully just before the major hatch, I fish a dry-fly in hopes of taking a trophy.

Keeping an eye skyward will often show flies that may be coming off intermittently. An occasional rise on stillwater should be enough to make you look in the air to see what may be emerging. This early indicator to a potential hatch can result in an opportunity for you to get an early start on some great fishing action.

Observation is key to anticipating what is going to happen and I believe that anytime you fish stillwater you should be trying to predict what might happen next.

FISHING THE HATCH

When a hatch starts, I have seen even the best fishermen fumble, bumble, and grumble their way through wind knots, tangles, and misguided casts. Keen observation is very important both before the hatch occurs and again after it starts. Fish are often seen swirling subsurface at emerging nymphs. Often this is your clue of a hatch about to come.

You should fish floating lines during a hatch. Pick a color that is bright enough to see during the day but that also can be seen easily in dimming light. Yellow is a good color for both situations. Bright colors like orange are great during the day but become a challenge to see in dimming light.

Leader length and tippet size depends on the flies you will be using during the hatch. Large wind-resistant drys in No. 6 to No. 8 call for seven-and-a-half- to nine-foot leaders in with 2X to 3X tippets. Any longer or finer and the leader will twist during casting. If this happens at dark just as the hatch is reaching its peak you may find yourself in quite a mess. Worse yet, you usually do not see it happen until it gets so bad you have to start over again. Flies in the normal No.10 to No.16 range can be cast with a nine- to twelve-foot leader and tippets in the 4X to 5X category. Flies smaller than No.16 need a leader of twelve-feet or longer and tippets of 6X or 7X. Dress your dry flies with a floatant before casting them; this keeps your fly on top for awhile before you have to pick up and recast. If fishing extremely

Shaking the trees along the shoreline produced a cloud of caddis flies. A couple of hours later, trout were rising to the egg-laying adults.

calm water, I like to use fluorocarbon tippet as it breaks the surface tension of water and sinks slightly. A commercial preparation called Mud can be applied to nylon tippets so they also break the surface tension. In very calm water, your tippet and leader close to the fly will be just below the surface thereby avoiding any shadows made by dimples as your leader sits in the film. The shadows make your fly, and the area around it, look suspicious to cruising trout. They will often turn away from your fly if this happens. This is one reason I like to locate spots that have a slight riffle when fishing drys. The small waves or riffles help hide the leader and tippet, so fish are less likely to spook.

Stillwater trout do not rise in the same place over and over again. They cruise, and you may find one particular fish working an area back and forth but covering large sections of stillwater looking for insects. When a hatch reaches its peak, you will find the fish with the insects. If only one cove has emerging mayflies, there will be more fish here than anywhere else on the pond. This is another good reason to do your pre-hatch homework.

Large western brown and rainbow trout, and eastern brook trout, are normally lone cruisers. As a hatch gets started they can be seen rising and a few seconds later they rise again some distance away. This usually gives you an indication of which way the fish is moving. A cast aimed to intercept the fish will often result in a rise to your fly. Eastern brookies seem to move consistently in a straight line and are more predictable than western browns and rainbows. Nonetheless it is possible to get the fly in the area of a brown's or rainbow's next rise if you spend some time watching them.

In the Northeast, landlocked salmon will often move together in schools to feed during a hatch. Activity is much more erratic as the school moves through the area and picking a single fish is next to impossible. A cast in the middle of the area where activity is highest will often be met with an aggressive rise due to competition from neighboring fish. In

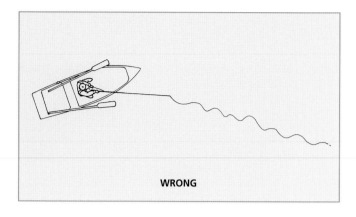

WRONG

WRONG: Slack in the line will prevent you from having a direct connection with the dry fly in the event of a strike.

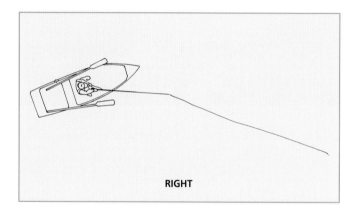

RIGHT

RIGHT: Take in enough line to keep slack from forming but do not strip in so much that you actually move the fly, which should remain still on the surface.

addition, I have seen trout in a given size class school together on stillwater both in the East and West, exhibiting this same behavior.

If the hatch is sporadic yet consistent, fishing will often be much better than if the hatch is a full-blown whiteout. When fish rise close to you, casting your fly to cover the rise will sometimes bring the fish back up in the same spot to take your fly. Get your fly quickly to the rise ring before the fish moves away. If fish are consistently rising all around you, disregard them, be patient, and wait for a fish to move to your fly. Trying to cover all the rings in the middle of a good hatch will have your fly in the air more than on the water. Remember also that when fishing from a boat or float tube,

chasing rising fish will only result in chasing more rising fish. Stay put, let the area around you settle down, and trust that the fish will move in to feed. They will come to you if you have the patience.

When presenting your dry fly on stillwater, unlike with nymphs and streamers, you seldom strip your fly back. With drys, leave your fly on the water and wait. Don't be impatient. Many anglers cast, let their fly land on the water, and if not met with an immediate take they pick up and cast again. Two things happen when an angler does this: The action of lifting the line off the water over and over will eventually spook most of the fish around you and they'll stay outside of the circle of your longest cast. Be patient, cast your dry fly, leave it, and watch it.

You *will* have to do some line management when fishing drys. As you watch your fly on the water it appears to be staying in one place but it isn't. If the wind is moving directly away from you, the fly line will usually stay fairly tight, requiring little management. Usually in this situation I find that the fly sinking is more of a problem than managing slack line. If the fly sinks, bring it in, dry it off, and recast.

More often than not you will see slack forming in your fly line that needs to be taken in so that you have a direct connection to your fly in the event of a strike. Take in only enough line to keep the slack from forming; do not strip in so much that you start moving your fly. When the fly gets fairly close to you, pick it up and recast to another area. Fan your casts around to cover the water. If you do this, you will not be spooking fish by constantly picking up line off the water and you will have more fish cruise in close to you. I have had fish take the fly within a couple of feet of the boat so don't think you have to have the fly sixty feet away. Remember, the trout are cruising, so less wriggling and more patience will pay off.

In the midst of a heavy hatch when it appears to be raining flies or the water's surface looks as if it has a blanket of insects covering every square inch, you will probably need to change your tactics. During these times I have had fish spend way too much time examining my fly, then pass on it with a swirl just to let me know they were looking. Going to a different size fly, either bigger or smaller, or maybe a caddis instead of a mayfly, is the ticket to breaking the ice. Something a little different will often make them rise without hesitation, while mimicking the hatch would have gotten you nothing.

SIGHT-FISHING FOR TROPHY TROUT

When conditions are just right, sight-fishing for cruising trout is like hunting for big bone-fish in the Bahamas. It will take some patience and practice but the thrill of watching a trout cruise the shore, see your fly, and then take it brings a new level of excitement for the stillwater angler. I love sight-fishing for trout but weather, light conditions, shorelines, fish movement, and more need to be in your favor before you go prowling the shorelines in search of a trout.

There are three methods of stillwater trout fishing that could be called sight-fishing: Shoreline wading in search of cruising trout, sight-fishing for weed bed trout that are either sipping insects or looking for scuds and midges, and shallow cove sight-fishing from a boat. For the most part, these three situations cover the majority of your stillwater sight-fishing opportunities. In all of these situations you should fish a floating line. Leaders of nine-feet minimum and preferably twelve-feet or longer should be used in all sight-fishing situations. The diameter of your tippet will range from 4X for larger nymphs to 7X for midges in weed beds.

Lee Wulff once told me that if a fish had refused his fly, before he changed it he always dropped down one tippet size first. I have never forgotten that bit of advice and now pass it on to you. Usually if you are getting refusals the fish is attracted by your fly but is turning off because of something else he sees just before he eats it. A heavy tippet sometimes gives the fly a stiff look or the fish can see it in really clear water. So try a finer tippet before changing your fly.

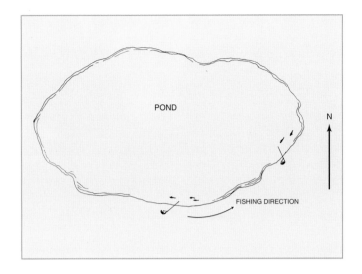

When sight-fishing at high noon, the best strategy is often to move east along the south shoreline. But keep the wind in mind as well.

Before we start talking about the various opportunities for sight-fishing, I need to mention that in sight-fishing more than anywhere else, a good pair of polarized sunglasses is a must-have item. Amber or copper lenses are my choice for sight-fishing. Amber is best in all conditions but I have found that copper out-performs amber in low-light situations. I like carrying both but if you have to choose one color I would recommend a good pair of amber polarized sunglasses.

Cruisin' for a Bruisin'

Clear days with low winds offer the best sight-fishing opportunities. Do a little homework before jumping into the pond, though. The sun will be your best friend when sight-fishing but it can turn into your enemy if you are not paying attention to its relation to you and your quarry. The best hours for sight-fishing are from midmorning through late afternoon. Depending on the season, these hours range from long in midsummer to only a few hours in late fall or winter. It is an advantage to have the sun somewhere behind you so locate a shoreline where the sun will be at your back. It does not have to be directly behind you but it should be in a position that allows you to see into the water for the greatest distance. If the

Sight-fishing can produce some great catches, like this trophy rainbow trout.

sun quarters off one shoulder or another it should be fine.

Generally speaking, in the United States, where the sun rises in the east and sets in the west, here is a good rule of thumb that you can use to find good shorelines for sight-fishing at various times of the day:

- In early morning, when light just starts to get strong enough so you can see into the water, south shorelines moving west, north shorelines moving west, and east shorelines moving north will be your best bets.

- At high noon, look for south shorelines moving either east or west, or east and west shorelines moving north.

- As the sun sets, fish north or south shorelines moving east, or west shorelines moving north.

After sun position, wind direction is the second order of business when looking for a shoreline to wade. Keep in mind that you have several options of shorelines to fish depending on the time of day. If it is high noon and you have a strong wind coming from the northeast, the east shoreline moving north would be a good bet. It will be slightly out of the wind and will keep your line away from you if you're a right-handed caster. Consider this before hiking to a fishing spot.

Obviously, the shoreline of the pond you are fishing must have other important attributes in order to sight-fish. You must be able to see bottom along the shoreline you are fishing. The shoreline needs to be wadable, with firm footing for a long distance. A shoreline that does not drop-off quickly, yet allows you to see into waist-deep water easily, is prime. The bottom should be fairly light colored and rocky with stretches of hard sandy areas to make spotting fish a little easier. The water must be relatively clear as sight-fishing in churned-up water just does not work.

Normally, when you are sight-fishing a long rocky shoreline, like that on Duck Lake in Glacier National Park, fish cruise and feed on anything that strays into their path. On occasion they may come up for dry flies but more often than not they are feeding on nymphs when cruising shorelines. I like to tie on a No. 12 or 14 nymph to start my sight-fishing. If I am fishing deeper water (twenty-four to thirty-six inches) a beadhead mayfly or weighted scud pattern that will sink fairly quickly and get to the fish's cruising level, would be my choice. In shallower water, use the same patterns without beads, epoxy-back mayfly nymphs, soft-hackle caddis, or other nymphs that simulate insects found in the pond you are fishing.

Walk the shoreline slowly in search of your first fish. Trout are not always easy to spot. I have spent many days with anglers who are not familiar with spotting fish even when wearing the best sunglasses. Some people pick it up very quickly while others don't see the fish until they are too close for a decent cast or presentation. Keep practicing! The key is to look for a shadow or a movement that is not attached to the bottom. Don't worry about casting to what you thought was a trout but turned out to be a rock. The situation will soon improve. When it all comes together you will be spotting fish at thirty or forty yards with plenty of time to get your knees to stop shaking and make your cast.

On lakes like Duck Lake, where you can spend a morning working a single shoreline, fish over ten pounds are not uncommon. Your

Clear days with light winds offer the best sight-fishing opportunities. This can be like stalking tailing bonefish on a tropical flat.

Sight-fishing can produce some great catches like this trophy rainbow.

sented fly. Don't cast over their backs or let the fly land on top of their heads, that much I can tell you for sure!

When you make the right cast, the fish will react to your offering, and now comes the next critical step in catching it. When fishing nymphs I have found that free-falling nymphs work better than nymphs stripped back. Trout see the nymph falling, move toward it, and almost always turn slightly to eat. You need to meet this with either a lift of the rod or a strip strike, as more often than not you will not feel the take but will only see it. Although I utilize strip strikes for bonefishing or tarpon fishing, I find it more difficult when fishing stillwater. Stillwater anglers like Tom Rosenbauer and Marty Cecil utilize a strip strike once the fish takes the fly. To make a strip strike, keep your rod pointing at the fish with the tip low, almost touching the water. As the fish takes the fly, a long strip will often be met with the resistance of the fish on the other end. If not, your fly, still in front of the fish, will often be pursued and eaten. In either case, if you wait to feel the fish on the end of your line it is too late as it has had time to spit out the fly and move off.

As you move slowly and look for cruising trout you will find some areas with little or no activity and others where every few feet you have another trout come along. If you go through a hot spot, reel in, go back to where you started, and work this area again, or look for the next area along the shoreline that has the same attributes as the one just fished. Usually a point of land will mark an area of increased activity as trout tend to bounce off points. Also food is deposited more readily in these areas. Be on the alert for patterns and areas of increased activity.

Sometimes you find trout cruising high up in the water looking for dry flies on the surface, sipping in whatever happens to be in their path. Changing to a dry in these situations is recommended if you have seen fish hover close to the surface or have spotted a good bit of rising activity down the shoreline. Once you have seen the fish and marked his rising activity, cast your fly to intercept him. Watch the fish closely as he approaches your fly and

cast should land far enough in front of the fish so the fly will be at his level when he gets to it. If you lead him too much, the fish can easily change direction and you will have to cast again to get back in front of the fish. Many factors must be considered: How fast is the fish moving? How deep is it? Is it swimming erratically or does it seem to be cruising in a straight line? Make your own calculations; each situation will be different. I have seen shallow cruisers in a foot of water with their noses in the rocks looking for nymphs so I had to put a fly a couple of inches from their snouts, while deepwater trout may move twenty feet out of their way for a poorly predon't get overly excited and pull the fly away from him. It's hard to do but if all goes well the fish will inhale your fly and turn away with fly in mouth. Lift your rod to set the hook. You will have a higher success rate hooking stillwater trout if you can wait until the fish turns and starts back down with your fly. It's just a split second but makes a huge difference in hookup rate.

Midge Cruisers and Weed Bed Sippers

In this section I'll focus on trout that are found cruising and feeding selectively on smaller nymphs. These trout are not the free-ranging cruisers discussed above but rather are found in shallow, weedy, stillwater areas. They often stay in one small area, circling or moving back and forth along a shoreline in a repetitive feeding pattern. I consider these trout to be the most difficult fish to take on a fly for several reasons: They are usually really focused on a specific nymph, in many cases swimming with their mouths open taking in clusters of midges that have been blown in large groups onto the water's surface. They are the most erratic of feeders and the hardest to figure out in terms of where they are going next. And they are usually found in areas of dense weed growth so once you hook them the challenge begins all over again as they put their heads down and bury themselves in the weeds.

Use tippets or leaders in the 5X to 7X range for this fishing. If using scuds you may be able to get away with 5X, but for midge larvae or nymphs in the No. 18 to 24 range use tippets in sizes 6X or 7X.

I highly recommend fluorocarbon leader or tippet material for this fishing. You can often get away with one tippet size larger when using it, and thus gain an advantage when the fight begins but also this fishing is usually in shallow, calm water where a material that blends in or disappears in the water becomes a great stealth advantage. I prefer twelve-foot knotless tapered leaders here as a minimum length.

This fishing is found in smaller stillwaters or in small areas of big stillwaters. Wading may or

Fishing the weeds can be very effective, especially when you do it from a float tube.

may not be an option, as weed beds may be so heavy near shore that you will need to be in a boat or float tube fishing the outside edges of the weeds. In others you will see areas between the weeds and shore where cruising fish can be found. I have found that on smaller stillwaters fishing from shore is usually a good bet, whereas small areas on large stillwaters where weed beds are found are often better fished from a tube or boat.

Remember that the sun position and wind direction are factors to consider in deciding where you will start fishing. Once you have done that, standing back from shore and observing the area you are fishing will often reveal fish that are within a couple of feet of shore, moving slowly down the shoreline looking for their next meal. Take some time to watch these fish. When do they eat? Are they rooting around the bottom? Are they sipping off the top? If you spend time watching the trout before casting, your success rate will increase.

These trout may be taking small flies, often not even apparent to you. If the trout are cruising and rooting the bottom, try a Brassy, small glass beadhead midge pupa, or another slow-sinking nymph in a No. 18 or 20. You will need to use at least a 6X to start, but before changing flies, if you have no interest from the trout, try going to 7X first. If they are sipping off the top and seem to be feeding just subsurface, tying on two nymphs can often be a good bet. A small midge dry at the top followed by an emerger or nymph about sixteen to twenty inches back can be a deadly presentation in these situations. You may have to cast more line on shore than in the water. There is a small spring creek in my yard that flows into a small stillwater area the size of large bathtub. Anyone walking within thirty feet of this pool sees nothing but riffles as small brook trout take cover under a large rock that sits at the head of the pool. I occasionally try my luck casting to these wary trout, and in order to catch one I need to position myself about forty feet from the pool and thirty-seven feet of line lands on the grass.

Some stillwater situations demand this same technique. When presenting a fly this way you cannot strip line back in or you will get caught on everything between you and the water. You must lift the line straight up and out of the grass and rocks. If all goes as planned you can cast back into the area for another try at the trout you have your eye on. If all does not go as planned you will get your hook caught on a blade of grass or the only stick between you and your fish. It's decision time: Break it off or go and get it? If the trout is still in casting range and I expect it will be cruising a small area for a while, I'll break it off and tie a new fly on. I hate to leave fish to look for other fish I may or may not find. A hookup on the other hand, carries a whole different set of rules.

If the cast is rewarded by a trout on the end of your line, the work has just begun. I said earlier that trout found in weedy areas require special care. You will lose fish. Don't be disappointed, the best anglers in the world lose them too. But you can improve your odds. Keep your rod high, I mean really high. Reach up as far as you can over your head and leave your rod there. The fish will head for the weeds and the high rod angle makes the fish work hard to get there. If he makes it and appears to be caught up don't panic but keep steady pressure on. Often the fish will back very slowly out of the weeds and you can begin the battle again. In the event the fish seems to be stuck and not moving, release all pressure on the fish and let him think he has gotten off. The fish will often back out of the weeds on his own, allowing you to bring the line tight on a surprised trout and resume the battle. It is a real thrill when the trout finally comes to net, covered in the debris of the weedy bottom.

Sight-fishing from a boat for cruising trout along weed beds that lie in deeper water is a slightly different game. Float tube or canoe sight-fishing is not easy and all conditions must be perfect for this to be successful, as your low angle to the water is poor for spotting fish. I would recommend a boat that you can stand in for sight-fishing. You will be higher off the water at a much better angle for spotting fish.

Stillwaters that have coves or shorelines lined with weed beds will bring trout from deepwater sections in to feed. They move into weedy areas and cruise for dislodged or swimming nymphs or scuds, and may opportunistically rise to a fly during this activity. Watch the fish as it feeds along its cruise path. Is the fish cruising high or low in the water column? If the fish is high up in the water, just under the surface, I will often fish a small dry and a dropper. A midge dry-fly with a small midge dropper eighteen to twenty-four inches behind or a caddis with a scud dropper are two combinations to try. Giving the trout a choice helps you to narrow down what they are feeding on and gives you twice the chance to catch them. If fishing clearwater ponds try not to cast too close as this often spooks the fish. A cast ten feet away on the same line that the trout is cruising will not spook the fish and I have seen trout go well out of their way to take a fly presented some distance from their actual location. If the fish swims in the vicinity of the fly and refuses it, wait for him to cruise well past your fly before picking it up to recast. He may not have seen your first presentation and a second or even a third cast may be needed to catch him.

Western stillwaters offer abundant opportunities for sight-fishing in shallow coves.

Shallow Cove Sight-Fishing

There are times when you will find fish just cruising in shallow bays and coves looking for a meal. I have found few eastern stillwaters that have good sight-fishing for fish cruising in the shallows but western stillwater opportunities abound. I have learned a lot by fishing with western anglers who have made fly fishing stillwaters their favorite pastime.

On Trapper's Lake outside of Meeker, Colorado, I have had the opportunity to fish for cruisers that could be seen easily a hundred feet away coming into shallow coves looking for a meal. My son Brian, a well-seasoned Colorado fishing guide and stillwater angler, turned me on to the Trapper's Lake fishery a couple of years ago. On this special trip we encountered a great *Callibaetis* mayfly hatch in a shallow silty cove across the lake from our access site. From a distance we

could see an occasional rise and when we got closer we found trout cruising the bay eating both nymphs and emerging mayflies. There was a constant stream of cutthroats and rainbows moving in and out of the cove, and we found the fish were happy taking either the nymph or a low-riding emerger. We sat anchored up in this cove for a few hours of nonstop dry-fly fishing, all the while seeing each fish we cast to.

In these situations I have found that fish tend to move into a cove mainly from one specific direction. Whether it is the contour of the bottom or unseen currents that cause the fish to cruise in a set pattern and rhythm, I don't know. But you will find after awhile that there is a pattern to their approach and you will start looking toward the same area for cruising trout to enter your field of vision. I like to cast well in front of these cruisers so as not to spook them but into their path so that they will swim by my fly. Long,

Streamers and Muddlers are effective patterns for fishing a fry bash.

twelve- to fifteen-foot leaders are an advantage in this situation and will help keep fish from spooking as the fly lands on the water. Takes are subtle, slow, and deliberate, so don't get overly excited as the fish approaches your fly. Wait until he eats it before yelling and screaming.

FISHING FRY BASHES

"Oh yeah, we fish fry bashes in late summer or early fall. You wouldn't believe the brook trout we catch," Jeff said with excitement as evening approached on King and Bartlett Pond. Jeff Charles, head guide and manager of King and Bartlett Sporting Camps in Maine, has discovered a connection between schooled-up bait along the shorelines and a trouting opportunity I had often overlooked. Although I had

observed and fished to schooled-up bait pods in late summer and early fall, Jeff had observed that these baitfish schools were the result of several trout corralling bait toward shore and then bashing the schooled bait, thus Jeff's term "fry bash." (This term may have its origins in England, according to well-known author Tom Rosenbauer.) The result of this bashing is often dozens of stunned, half-alive baitfish that become easy targets for feeding trout.

The first sign of this activity will often be the slight dimpling of baitfish along shore as they are being schooled up. Occasionally you will see an aggressive splash along the shoreline. Investigating this activity is worth it. In these situations, fishing a baitfish imitation that exactly imitates the schooled-up bait is key. A Black-Nosed Dace, Muddler Minnow, or Grey Ghost streamer would be my first choice.

If fishing to the dimpling of bait along the shore, cast your streamer to one side of the pod, not directly into it. Trout often cruise the edges of the pod and may not take a streamer cast into the middle. A baitfish that strays outside the pod will often be hit as trout prepare to bash the school. If trout are actually crashing bait, cast your streamer directly into the fray. Let it settle, twitch it once, and let it sit still again. Try to make it look like a stunned bait. Trout sweeping back through will often take your streamer as it settles toward bottom, so be ready.

BEAVER POND TROUT

Some of my most memorable stillwater experiences have been on small beaver ponds scattered throughout the western and eastern United States. Often overlooked by many fishermen, these little gems can be both a challenging and rewarding experience. I met my wife Deb while fishing a small beaver pond flowage in Rocky Mountain National Park, so my fond memories encompass more than the trout I caught but also the catch of my life. Even before I met my wife I was hooked on beaver ponds, as my father took my brother and me to the far reaches of the headwaters of Bemis Stream in the Rangeley Lakes region of

Maine. I can remember days when trout came to net one after another, some as large as twelve inches, a good trout on any beaver pond. In more recent years Tom Rosenbauer, who shares a love for beaver pond fly fishing, has been both a partner and a teacher. Tom observes beaver ponds in New England through the winter months in search of the springs that feed them. The springs, often unfrozen in winter, will be key in the summer as trout congregate there in search of cooler water temperatures.

Beaver pond trout are often easy prey for a well-presented dry fly. They do not see many fishermen so they are often voracious feeders, eating almost anything presented. I have been to many small, remote beaver dams that offer fishing for small trout in the six- to nine-inch class, where every cast will be rewarded by a trout hitting your fly. Whether fishing a dry, nymph, or streamer, it appears you can do no wrong. In still others, one good six-inch fish will be the fish of the day.

A more humbling experience is fishing to the large trout that inhabit some beaver dams in the West. Bob Auger, for many years the riverkeeper on DePuy Spring Creek in Paradise Valley, Montana, was one of the best technical fishermen I ever fished with. Before the floods of the Yellowstone wiped out most of DePuy Creek in the mid 1990s, there was a large beaver dam in the lower reaches of the creek that everyone went around in order to fish the lower creek before it emptied into the Yellowstone River. Bob brought Tom and me to this beaver dam in the early 1990s and proceeded to show us the trout that everyone was passing up. Fishing an Orvis One-Weight rod and light tippet, Bob cast and landed a five-pound brown that looked as though it had never been caught. It looked easy, as trout slowly sipped midges off the pond's surface. Tom and I soon found that imitation and presentation were key to getting one of these finicky trout to take our offerings. Once a fish was hooked, the beaver pond offered its challenges in the downed timber that had been flooded in the making of the pond. It took us a while to land a trout but the fishing was spectacular, with no pressure from other fishermen. This is not an uncommon experience when fishing spring-fed beaver ponds of the West.

PART III

STEELHEAD

CHAPTER TWENTY-TWO

GREAT LAKES SALMON AND STEELHEAD: PRESENTATION AND THE FLY

— MATTHEW SUPINSKI —

By combining the fundamental techniques of presentation with learning how to read the rivers where Great Lakes salmon and steelhead are found, as well as understanding the behavior of the fish under all conditions, total mastery is attained.

The proper presentation is a function of the best method for the conditions, time of year, fish species pursued and its behavior, along with personal preferred fishing style. As with all art forms, there is not one absolute method a person must use. The successful salmon/steelheader has an open mind for creativity and experimentation. Redundancy of technique and fly patterns often leads to condi-tioned behavioral responses by the salmonids, and they avoid being hooked and almost become bored to tears by the angler's habitual lack of creativity. How often do we get stuck using the same drift and flies when along comes someone who, either out of sheer dumb luck or purposeful intention, pulls some odd looking fly out of the box and casts it in an unconventional way and—voilà!—catches a large fish. These humbling encounters show the enigmatic aspects of salmon/steelheading and illustrate how one must learn the basics and then improvise for success.

BOTTOM DRIFT NYMPHING— CHUCK-AND-DUCK

This has become the classic presentation for the cold water Great Lakes salmonid angler. With the rig described in the tackle chapter, the cast uses lead weight to propel the thin running/shooting line and penetrate the swift, cold waters immediately. The cast is usually executed by swinging the weight and flies behind the angler. On the "water load," the weight touches the water for a fraction of a second to load the rod tip. With a snap of the wrist, the line is propelled to the desired point of entry into the water as the rod tip follows through in the same direction. With one or two slack-line upstream mends of the rod, the lead and flies are allowed to sink to the bottom and the egg and nymph patterns bounce along the bottom drag free. When fishing deep pools

The bottom-drift (chuck-and-duck) technique is easy for novice salmon and steelhead anglers to learn. Here, it allowed Jared Adler to take this beautiful steelhead in front of the Gray Drake Lodge on Michigan's Muskegon River.

Casting and presentation are art forms that develop through practice.

and runs with this method, all of the angler's focus should be on the rod tip. A steady bouncing of the tip indicates contact with the bottom, which is the goal of this method. If the tip droops very slowly, a snag on the bottom has occurred. By lifting the rod slowly upstream and pulling very gently on the line, 90 percent of all snags can be eliminated and the terminal tackle saved. If the angler sets the hook on a snag, it is certain he will lose the whole rig. So when does the angler set the hook? By watching the rod tip very closely; the sudden throbbing of the tip will signal the fly being struck and the salmonid shaking its head to dislodge the fly. The fly usually hooks the fish with the force of the water's current. A quick strip set and a sharp hook will ensure contact.

In order for the line to penetrate the water at the desired ninety-degree angle, hold the rod handle straight out at nine-thirty or two-thirty (clock positions). This keeps as much line off the water as possible, which reduces unwanted drag. Holding the rod too high will create more slack. The goal is to lift line and create tightness of feel to detect strikes.

To penetrate deep lies, a more upstream cast is needed. In shallower runs and lies, use a down-and-across approach. If your rod tip is not bouncing, you are not on the bottom and must feed out more line. This method is very effective for fishing egg patterns, nymphs, small wets, and streamers for fall salmon, steelhead, and lake-run browns, and for winter and spring steelheading. It can also be used to swing flies through pools for early holding chinook salmon. When fishing the pools and runs for holding fall and winter steelhead, a "slip-sinker" weight system that slides up and down the leader is desired. This is best for deeper and slower waters that lack the current of the faster runs and gravel areas. Also, this method allows steelhead to inhale the fly and not feel the weight, giving the angler more time to set the hook.

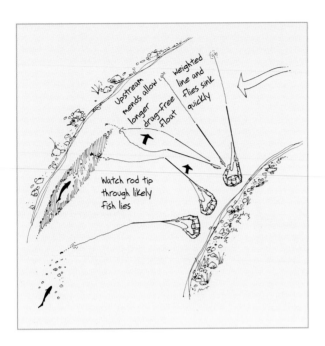

Upstream mends allow longer drag-free float

Weighted line and flies sink quickly

Watch rod tip through likely fish lies

Bottom Nymph Drifting

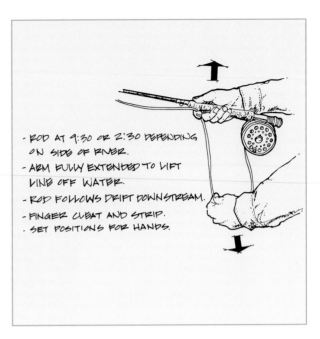

- ROD AT 9:30 OR 2:30 DEPENDING ON SIDE OF RIVER.
- ARM FULLY EXTENDED TO LIFT LINE OFF WATER.
- ROD FOLLOWS DRIFT DOWNSTREAM.
- FINGER CLEAT AND STRIP.
- SET POSITIONS FOR HANDS.

Bottom Drift Technique

A twenty-pound St. Mary's summer Atlantic salmon taken by strike-indicator nymphing a scud pattern.

In shallow spawning gravel and runs, quick strike detection is required. A three-way swivel is used where the leader is attached to one eye, a dropper weight off the second, and the fly or flies off the third eye. When fishing gravel spawning runs, the angler's eye turns away from the rod tip and now focuses on the line. A sudden stopping of the line usually signals a mouth grab by a salmon or steelhead—a quick hook-set is usually required. This technique is effective for fall chinooks, lake-run browns, and spring steelhead on or near gravel.

STRIKE-INDICATOR NYMPHING

Strike-indicator nymphing is becoming ever more popular with anglers wanting to use floating fly lines without massive amounts of lead and running lines. The technique is best used in moderate to shallower rivers and streams, or on or near gravel spawning areas. A single- or double-handed Spey rod may be used. A weight-forward floating or salmon/steelhead taper line is used. By using the leader described earlier in the tackle section, the sliding strike indicator is placed first on the leader, followed by the fly or flies (in states that allow two-fly rigs). The split shot can be applied in two areas. Many anglers prefer it six to twelve inches above the fly. In the "panfish" style rig, the split shot is applied at the very bottom—below the flies. To be legal, however, the flies must have a three-inch tag off the main leader—dropper style. I personally prefer this rig because it is easier to accurately set the strike indicator to ensure that the flies are in the proper strike zone. As a general rule, the indicator is usually set one and a half to two times the depth you are fishing.

The "Indy" or indicator rig uses a floating line, strike indicator, nymphs/egg patterns, and split shot to provide a near-bottom, drag-free presentation. The strikes are detected by the indicator bobbing down. In addition, the indicator provides a ninety-degree angle presentation that induces less drag.

Executing the "Indy" rig method is best achieved by using longer rods or Spey rods that get additional lifting of the line off the water for drag-free floats. The effect is similar to cane-pole bobber fishing. Setting the weight or split shot is determined by the depth and speed of the current. During the drift, you want to eliminate any belly in the line that might create drag. A proper float of the rig should be slower than the current and the strike indicator should be ticking ever so slightly to show that the flies and shot are drifting close to the bottom. If you hang up on snags, you are in the ballpark—a slight shortening up of the strike indicator will fine-tune the presentation. Your rod should be high-sticked over the strike indicator as it moves downstream with continuous drag-free mends. Set the hook each time the bobber dips below the water. The most common strikes are a steady underwater pull in a sideward direction from the indicator or a quick take as the indicator takes off fast.

Indicator rigs are very effective for fishing to salmon and steelhead in shallow-water gravel runs. They are also preferred for pool and pocket-water fishing on moderate to smaller rivers containing lots of wooded debris where bottom drift nymphing creates a snag-filled proposition. Michigan's Pere Marquette River is an excellent river for this technique.

High Stick Nymphing

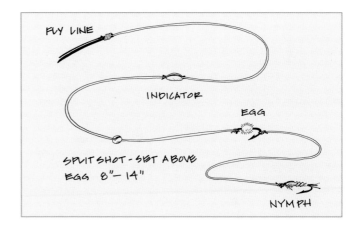

Basic Indicator Rig

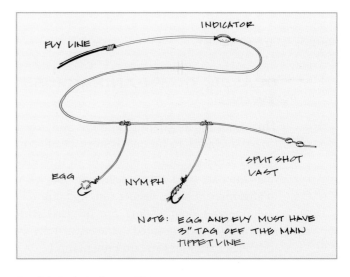

Panfish-Style Indicator Rig

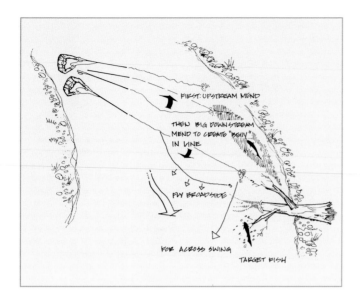

Down-and-Across Swing Method

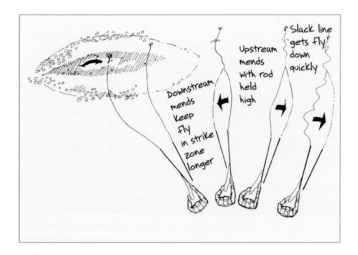

Deep Sink Tip Presentation

CLASSIC DOWN-AND-ACROSS SWING

This traditional Atlantic salmon and West Coast steelhead technique is very deadly on Great Lakes salmonids. Sinking-tip or intermediate lines are used when presenting Spey wets or streamers in faster, deeper runs and tail-outs and pools. A floating line can be used with some weight incorporated in the head of the fly for smaller river and stream presentations.

The basic objective is to present a wet fly swinging crosscurrent to pique the interest of a fresh-run salmon or steelhead. The technique is best executed by a parachute or puddle cast. The check cast is stopped similarly to the puddle cast and by zigzagging the tip to produce snake-like coils. Proper depth penetration is achieved with constant up- and downstream mending.

The key is to envision the holding lies that you believe the fish are occupying. The downstream, broadside drift should be executing its swing slightly upstream of the taking lies, and then swing through them. To start, position yourself upstream of the holding lies. Mend the cast several times upstream for depth penetration; follow with a long downstream mend to create a belly of line that is tight to the reel and allows for the swing. Strikes are often violent, with the fish hooking itself—keep drags set lightly. With the clockwork method, which breaks the pool run down from nine to three o'clock, each quadrant of the pool can be fished as the angler progressively moves down the run and casts to the envisioned clock position.

Keep in mind that this technique is most effective under ideal water with a clear to slight strain, and river temperatures between forty and sixty degrees Fahrenheit.

DEEP-DRIFT SINKING-LINE TECHNIQUES

This is a very effective method, especially when our Great Lakes rivers are running cold, high, and off-color. Pioneered by Trey Combs and Lani Waller on the fast-flowing British Columbia rivers, it will get a large Spey wet fly or streamer down and deep in the strike zone for a long time. Use a sinking-tip or full-sinking line at the various weights two hundred to six hundred grains or Class II to VII combined with a short three- to five-foot-long leader to the fly. These custom-made depth–charge lines either have long bellies in either floating, intermediate, or running varieties. By executing a series of up, down, and stack mends, the angler can control the sink rate, depth penetration, and hang time of the drift.

To execute the presentation, one must first focus on the holding and taking lies of the salmonids, whether it be the pocket waters, pool/gut/flats, or tail-out. The goal is to envision where the fish will be and to focus on slowing down the fly's swing and keep it in the prime strike zones as long as possible. Position yourself above the lies you are about to fish. Start upstream and throw roll casts or slack line at the point of entry where the line meets the water to allow the fly to sink. The amount of slack line to add to your presentation is dictated by how fast and deep the water is flowing. As you make mend adjustments, keep the line tight enough to feel a strike which is often slow and sluggish in the cold, high-water conditions. Keep the rod high and upstream to create tension and maximum depth penetration. As you use heavier sinking tips, you'll lose strike detection. Set the hook on any quirky movement of the line. Practicing this technique makes for perfection. This technique is most effective for late-fall and winter steelheading when the fish are hunkered down in the guts of the pools and runs. Ten-foot, 8-weight rods, or Spey rods, work best to handle the long mends and deal with heavy lines.

SPEY AND DRY-FLY TECHNIQUES

The Spey-rod revolution has taken a strong hold in the Great Lakes and is a very practical technique for swinging flies or strike-indicator nymphing. One can utilize the single or double Spey cast, the overhead cast, which is nothing more than a double-handed style single-handed fly cast, or the various specialty casts like the snap-T, snake roll, and underhand cast. I suggest you study the various Spey instructional videos on the market or taking a Spey-casting school with a reputable instructor. The most practical presentation with a floating or sinking-tip Spey line is the classic double Spey.

With the fly anchored below you, the rod and line are swept upstream in a back-handed roll cast as the right hand leads the rod (in an over-the-right-shoulder double Spey) and the left hand is held firmly to the right side of the chest. As the fly and line lay in the water

This female Atlantic salmon was taken from a large pool using deep-sinking-line techniques. She was fooled by a chartreuse Candy Cane Leech.

downstream with an upstream triangle of rod and line formed, a quick sideways sweeping D-shaped cast is made to the downstream, right side of the angler. This allows the direction change to take place for the final step. With a fluid push/pull of the forward cast, the right hand is held high above the head, keeping the rod tip high and stopping it to execute delivery. The tight loop Spey then sails up and across the river. The beauty of two-handed Spey rod presentations lies in the fact that you can cover vast amounts of water, have long-distance line control by mending, cast through a steep canyon or where a bank does not allow for a back cast, and have a tremendous amount of hang time on the tail of your drifts where the fly can be manipulated to swim by pumping and swaying the rod.

A dry-fly presentation is becoming more popular in the Great Lakes, especially for steelhead, lake-run browns and Atlantic salmon. To date, it has had its greatest success on the shallower Lake Erie tributaries like the Cattaraugus of New York and Ontario's Grand and Maitland Rivers. Tom Kurowski, of Buffalo Outfitters, authors Rick and Jerry Kustich, Ontario guide John Valk, and biologist Larry Halyk have been pioneering dry-fly techniques with good success. As with all dry presentations to salmonids, however, timing, water

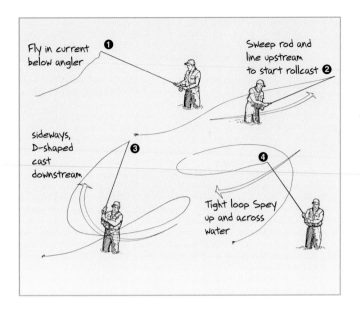

Double Spey Cast

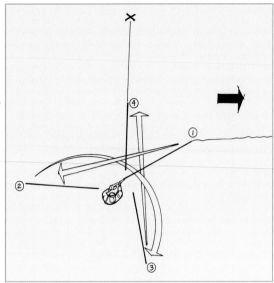

Top View of Double Spey Cast

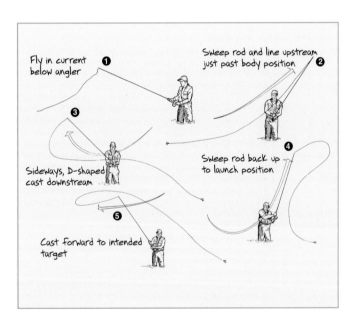

Snap-T Cast

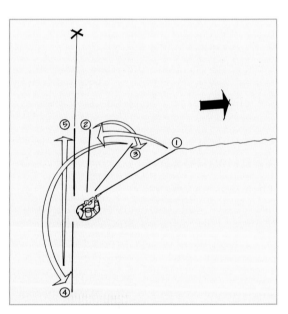

Top View of Snap-T Cast

conditions, and persistence (and a lot of luck) play a major role. It is far from a consistent proposition.

Due to the sheer numbers of steelhead present in these tributaries from heavy stockings, the chrome and aggressive autumn fish will stack into pools and runs, and display territorial holding behavior that is conducive to striking a dry. Most strikes occur by waking a dry on a Riffle Hitch, West Coast style, or by twitching a dead-drift presentation.

Other dry-fly scenarios exist during late spring when drop-back steelhead encounter massive aquatic insect emergers such as gray and brown drakes and Isonychia. This occurs in late May on large insect-rich rivers.

John Miller executes a snap-T Spey cast on Michigan's lower Muskegon River. Wide Great Lakes rivers are ideal for Spey casting.

Michigan's Muskegon, Pere Marquette, and Big Manistee and Ontario's Grand and Maitland Rivers are prime examples. In these cases the steelhead are feeding—chasing and ingesting the flies on their way back down to Lake Michigan. I have personally experienced these feeding fish. As for Atlantic salmon in the Salmon River of New York and Michigan/Ontario's St. Mary's, waking and dead drifting drys at first light can often bring about explosive strikes or boiling refusals. When the *Hexagenia* hatch is in full swing on the St. Mary's, the Atlantics will target and feed on the adults and emergers. Finally, on several Lake Superior tributaries like the Bois Brule of Wisconsin, which attract August runs of lake-run browns, many anglers successfully pursue them at dusk using deer-hair mice and other large dry flies.

TECHNIQUES FOR POOLED-UP PACIFIC SALMON

Unique, early Pacific salmon runs exist on the cold, spring-fed waters of Michigan's Little Manistee and Pere Marquette, along with the Lake Superior-fed St. Mary's rapids. Chrome-silver chinook salmon enter these rivers as early as July and August after a good cold front brings ample rains and cools the waters further. Usually, by late August and early September, the large, deep pools of large chinook rivers like New York's Salmon and Michigan's Big Manistee and Muskegon will be loaded with schools of tail-slapping, surface-boiling fish. It is quite a spectacle to see hundreds of fish, pent up in pools and swimming around in pods. They tend to favor the deepest pools; on the Muskegon and Big

A dime-bright chinook salmon taken in August.

LAKE TROUT AND COASTER BROOK TROUT

One of the only true indigenous salmonids of the char family in the Great Lakes, the lake trout still prospers quite well due to the help of the U.S. Fish & Wildlife Service and many of the Great Lakes states and province of Ontario's stringent management regulations. The lake trout is found in all the Great Lakes in substantial numbers, except for perhaps Lake Erie. The coaster brook trout, on the other hand, is now strictly limited in its native range to the northern shore of Lake Superior (Nipigon District) with a slow but steady resurgence in micro populations on Lake Superior's south shore. This fish is being studied and managed carefully in an effort to restore populations throughout its historic range.

The lake trout is a strong baitfish predator and favors deeper waters and low-light conditions. It will also spawn along rocky reefs and shorelines, often foregoing river migration during fall spawning cycles. Good numbers of spawning fish ascend Michigan's Grand River and New York/Ontario's Niagara to create a visible trophy fishery. Any given river during the fall on Lakes Superior, Huron, Michigan, and Ontario could see a sporadic school of these fish. As with all of the char family, they are extremely non-selective eaters and are very gullible to fly presentations. White and chartreuse Zuddlers, baitfish streamers, and chartreuse Glo-bugs will hook many fish. Their fight is very dogged and deep-throbbing like a giant brown. They can be a lot of fun on the fly rod.

The coaster brook trout of Ontario's Nipigon/Thunder Bay district are very large, thick-girthed creatures with the magnificent color display of a resident stream brookie. They run the Cypress River as early as late July and usually peak around late August. Good rains always bring in a fresh batch of fish, averaging three to five pounds. They are extremely aggressive when they take the fly. They are very strong fighters and equally important is their radiant spawning-color beauty. Rabbit strip Zonker-style streamers in chartreuse, white,

Manistee that could mean water twelve to twenty feet deep.

These fish, "not ready and ripe enough" to spawn, have perplexed salmon anglers for decades. They often come in on rising water levels and pool up when waters recede. Still, at times, fall water temperatures heat up during a warm spell and drive the salmon down deep and off the spawn. Understanding their behavior is the key to catching these fish on a fly rod. Since they are not eating, aggression and territorial dominance is their main cue. First light and dusk show the most porpoising, jumping, tail-slapping, and boiling at the surface by the fish. The key is that these fish are hovering in the pool, suspended from the bottom to the surface. Bottom drifting a fly is futile. One must swing or drift to these fish at various suspended depths. At first light or dusk, fish bright chartreuse, orange, black, and gold Comet/Boss imitations. As light approaches, switch to dull-colored nymphs and small baitfish streamers. The Bead-Chain Boss and Comet, West Coast patterns, show an uncanny ability to agitate pooled-up Pacifics. The action could be fast and furious—or dead. Swinging flies on sinking-tips (clear intermediates preferred) or chuck-and-duck style will be effective. Inclement weather with rain seems to be the best producer.

olive, and beige tones produce the best results. Scott Smith, the regional coaster brook trout expert and guide, ties a Green-Butt Monkey streamer that is deadly; I can personally attest to twenty-hook-up days for these magnificent fish when the run is on.

A GREAT LAKES SALMON/ STEELHEAD FLY BOX

From the hallowed Atlantic salmon rivers of Scotland to the wild majesty of British Columbia's steelhead Valhalla, a colorful, intriguing and artistic fly-tying tradition has evolved. Though the Great Lakes salmonid fishery is fairly new in comparison, it has made great innovations in a short period of time.

To beguile a salmon or steelhead to strike the fly takes confidence in one's pattern, persistence in presentation, patience, and an effervescent state of mental optimism. The age-old enigma of why a migratory salmonid strikes the fly will amuse the ocean-run fish advocate and fill the angler's perplexing diaries and hard-fought riverside experience for a lifetime. Natal imprinting to food forms, aggression, territorial dominance, and a programmed genetic urge to strike when provoked, based on an evolutionary predator/prey response behavior, sum up the experiences with our quarry.

If there is any variance from the anadromous (ocean to fresh water) behavioral disposition of Pacific and Atlantic salmonids, it must lie in the simplicity of the complete freshwater lifecycle found in the Great Lakes. Living a potamadromous (fresh water to fresh water) life may alleviate some of the physiological complications of adjusting to salinity when migrating, and may indeed enhance the ability of these fish to eat food—and flies—on a longer and more sustained basis. Special regard must be given to the biological richness and complexity of food in the Great Lakes and its river ecosystems. Baitfish such as alewives, herring, chubs, emerald shiners, gobies, and shad are evolving in density and being enhanced with new exotic species entering the system, having both positive and negative impacts. Aquatic and terrestrial insects, along with Mysis

A coaster brook trout is always a special catch. This one was taken on Scott Smith's Green-Butt Monkey in Lake Superior's Cypress River.

and *Diporeia* shrimp, round out the food chain. Where significant natural reproduction of salmon and steelhead populations exists, particularly in Lakes Superior, Michigan, Huron, and Ontario, one can walk the riverbanks and see the baby salmonid fry feverishly feeding on the emerging midges, mayflies, and stoneflies, a conditioned learned response at this early developmental stage. Compared to the significantly more food-sterile environments on some of the Western rivers, the Great Lakes are a food factory for salmonids.

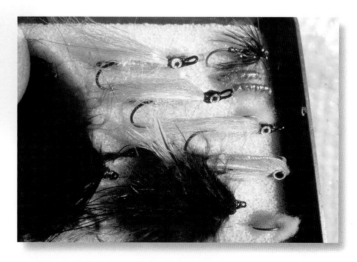

Nymphs, egg patterns, Speys, and baitfish streamers are all effective at times for Great Lakes salmonids.

Curt Collins with a chrome St. Mary's Atlantic salmon that took an emerging caddis pupae. Sometimes it pays to try different patterns, particularly on hard-fished rivers.

If anything novel exists about Great Lakes salmonid fly patterns, it is in the tremendous diversity and complexity of offerings that the angler must be well versed in.

NYMPH AND EGG PATTERNS

These form the "meat and potatoes" of the salmon and steelhead fisheries fly box. Based on the massive density of aquatic insects, along with salmonid and sucker eggs in the river's biological drift, patterns are selected and modified with both naturalistic and impressionistic motifs. The first nymphal patterns, like Michigan's Spring Wiggler, were developed off the Brindle/Woolly Worm concept. These shell-back flies imitate the *Hexagenia limbata.* With a tremendous diversity of mayflies, stoneflies, caddis, and shrimp in the river sys-

tems, nymph imitations should be based on these food forms.

Suggested Nymphs

- Green caddis larvae—No. 8–16
- *Hexagenia* (Hex)—No. 4–8
- Oliver Edwards's black stone and other black and golden stonefly—No. 8–12
- Black & purple Disco Stone and Prince—No. 8–14
- Hare's Ear—No. 6–14
- Gartside Sparrow—No. 6–12
- *Mysis* shrimp and scuds—No. 8–16
- Alevin sac-fry—No. 6–8
- Steelhead Hammer—No. 10–12
- Polish Woven—No. 10–12
- Czech-mate—No. 10–12
- Quill/peacock soft hackle—No. 8–14
- Bead-head Pheasant Tail—No. 8–16

The egg pattern has evolved from the simple Glo-bug pioneered by Anderson, of California's Bug Shop, to highly specialized patterns using yarn with flashy synthetic materials like Estaz. The sheer volume of eggs being extruded by spawning salmon, steelhead, suckers, walleye, etc., make them the number-one choice of all Great Lakes fly anglers. It is important to know the metamorphosis and colors of the natural egg, chinook, coho, pink, and Atlantic salmon, along with steelhead, have a more orange/yellow tint. Sucker spawn is caviar, small and bright yellow. The metamorphosis of an egg, once it is free flowing in the river, goes from the orange/yellow to a paler cream to almost a purplish/blue color in its final stages of decay—thus the appeal lately of blue egg patterns.

Suggested Egg Patterns

- Glo-bugs—all sizes and colors—No. 6–18
- Nuke eggs—No. 8–16
- Sucker spawn or cluster weaves—No. 8–16

Note: Eggs can be enhanced by adding Krystal Flash, Flashabou, Mylar Motion, and other glitter.

WETS, SPEYS, TUBES, STREAMERS, AND DRY FLIES

This group incorporates the traditional Atlantic salmon and West Coast steelhead patterns with baitfish motifs, which allows for ultimate creative expression. The first Great Lakes wets, as tried by the Richey brothers of Michigan and early trout guides on the Pere Marquette like Zimmy Nolph, incorporated West Coast brightly colored motifs. These flies, which are meant to be swung on the down-and-across drift, trigger aggression, playfulness, curiosity, as well as the desire to eat baitfish. Drys are meant to be waked on a Riffle Hitch down-and-across pools and tail-outs or dead drifted and twitched in faster pocket water.

Suggested Wets

- Winter Hope—No. 4–10
- Burlap—No. 6–10
- Micro Signal Light and Freight Train—No. 6–12
- Golden Demon—No. 4–6
- Macks Canyon—No. 4–8
- Purple Peril—No. 2–8
- Purple polar bear Matuka—No. 2–6
- Christmas Trinity—No. 4–6
- Washougal Olive—No. 4–6

Spey Flies

- Sol Duc series—No. 2/0–6
- Picasse—No. 2–8
- Marabou Paintbrush—No. 2–6
- Bronze Brad's Brat—No. 2–8
- Marabou Popsicle series—No. 2/0–6
- Thugmeister—No. 2/0–8
- September Spey—No. 2–6
- Tequilla Sunrise—No. 2–6
- Steelhead Stinger—No. 2/0–4
- Steelhead Ackroyd—No. 2/0–4

Tube Flies

- Willie Gunn—1–2 inches
- Temple Dog—1–2 inches
- Tippet Shrimp—1–2 inches
- Maygog Smelt—1–2 inches

The late great Ohio steelhead guide Dr. Mike Bennet searches for the perfect egg pattern from his well-stocked sucker spawn box.

The wide variety of fly-tying materials now available makes it easy for salmon and steelhead anglers to experiment with new patterns.

The surf and open waters of the Great Lakes are fast becoming an important fishery for fly anglers.

An angler probes a run for salmon and steelhead on a crisp autumn day while a black Lab checks out dying chinook salmon near shore.

Streamers/Matukas/Bucktails

- Egg-Sucking Leech—No. 2–10
- Halo Harlot—No. 2–4
- Steelhead Woolly Bugger—No. 4–10
- Bunny Bugger—No. 2/0–4
- Leechsicle—No. 2/0–4
- Comet/Boss—No. 4–6
- Opossum Sculpin—No. 2–6
- Tasmanian Sculpin—No. 2/0–4
- White Cone-head Zuddler—No. 2–4
- C-4 See Me Alewife and Smelt—No. 2/0–4
- Electric Candy Cane—No. 2/0–4
- Muddler Minnow—No. 2–8
- Stickleback Sculpin—No. 2–6

Dry Flies

- White & Red Wulff—No. 4–8
- Steelhead Bee—No. 4–6
- Waller Wakers—No. 4–8
- Steelhead Caddis—No. 6–8

SEASONAL FLY PATTERN GUIDE BY SPECIES

Autumn

Salmon in pools: Comets and Boss, Speys and larger nymphs.
Salmon on gravel: Nymphs, eggs, and Woolly Bugger/Muddler/Matukas; Egg-Sucking Leeches.
Lake-run browns and coaster brook trout: Light egg patterns; white Zuddlers; olive and black Matukas; bushy nymphs.
Steelhead: Baitfish and sculpin style streamers; fluorescent Speys and wets; egg patterns; Woolly Buggers; white Zuddlers; Hex nymphs.

Winter

Steelhead: Micro Nuke Eggs; stonefly, Hare's Ear, *Hex,* and green caddis nymphs; olive and gray sculpins; baitfish patterns in river estuaries; purple and blue Disco Stone and Prince Nymphs; *Mysis* shrimp; Steelhead Hammer.

Spring

Steelhead in pools and on gravel: Alevin sac-fry nymphs; various egg fly imitations; Sparrow, Hex, green caddis, Hare's Ear, stonefly, Disco Prince and *Mysis* shrimp nymph; Steelhead Woolly Buggers and fluorescent Speys.
Drop-back steelhead: Various baitfish imitations, salmon fry patterns, and mayfly emergers.

Summer

Atlantic salmon: Smelt/shiner baitfish patterns; natural and yellow Muddlers; caddis, shrimp, and Hex nymphs; Wulff, Adams Irresistible, and Bomber drys; Stickly Sculpins; small classic salmon wets.
Summer steelhead: Alewife baitfish and white Zuddlers; fluorescent Leechsicles; Tasmanian Sculpins; Thugmeister; black/blue/purple Speys and leeches; Electric Candy-Cane Bunny Buggers.
Early King Salmon in pools: Comets and Boss, Egg-Sucking Leeches, chartreuse and orange Speys.
Late-summer lake-run browns and coaster brook trout: Olive leeches and sculpins; smelt/herring baitfish patterns; white Zuddlers; mottled yellow, gold, and red Muddlers; deer-hair mice and yellow Wulff drys.

HOW TO HOOK, FIGHT, AND LAND SALMON AND STEELHEAD

Perhaps the most exciting aspect of salmon and steelhead on the fly is the spectacular fighting performance of these fish. Their spectacular aerial leaps, hard thrashing runs, and bearish refusal to submit will keep the angler addicted to the ocean-run fish for life.

The strike and hook-set vary with each encounter, time of year, species, fly presentation, and fly pattern. Strikes can be rod-throbbing smashes, subtle head-shakes, or pauses in the drift. Newly migrated fish that haven't seen a lot of pressure usually crush the fly due to their lack of caution. This often occurs on the down-and-across swing method, and

Face to face with a chrome fall steelhead.

when bottom-drifting egg patterns, when the current hooks the fish as it takes the fly on a broadside presentation. In winter bottom-drift (chuck-and-duck) or strike-indicator nymphing, strikes can be subtle, especially in cold-water conditions and when using small nymphs or eggs. When casting to fish on gravel, the line stopping in the drift often signals that the fly has been intercepted. Regardless, a firm strip-set downstream of the fish will drive the hook home. On the bony mouth of a kyped male salmon or steelhead, the firmer the hook-set, the better but don't overdo it or your fish will break off.

Peter and Matt Supinski with a late-summer chrome chinook salmon from Lake Michigan.

A fat chrome male chinook from Lake Michigan's surf.

Once you're ready to land the fish, be aware that it will make one last run when it sees the net or your tailing hand. Some fish play possum and then—wham!—a quick break-off occurs. Bottom line: Stay focused throughout the fight—it ain't over till it's over! Lighting of cigars, flashing cameras, and nips from the flask come after the fish is landed—not during the battle. Photograph your fish quickly, revive it carefully by using a tailing glove, and enjoy the experience.

SURF-FISHING GREAT LAKES SALMONID

This is a new and exciting frontier for the Great Lakes fly fisher. As river conditions become more crowded and water levels unpredictable, and with the sheer predator aggression that big lake salmonids possess, the lure to target these fish "in the surf" is compelling. And with the pioneering work done by innovative saltwater anglers, fly casting in the surf is now a very productive option.

Pacific and Atlantic salmon, steelhead, lake trout, and brown and coaster brook trout can be pursued on a seasonal basis. During the late winter and spring, coho, chinook, Atlantics, lake trout, and browns will be found off the pierheads of tributary rivers and off warmwater electrical and nuclear discharge. The amount of baitfish schooling near these areas will be significant. Alewives, smelt, shiners, and shad will use these areas due to the warmer water flows and also as a pre-spawning gathering place. Surf anglers should look for onshore winds which bring in the warmer offshore waters in the forty-degree Fahrenheit range. A gentle chop and overcast days are ideal. Look for porpoising salmonids along with seagulls herding baitfish. Fish the rocks and drop-off ledges where the river channels empty into the big lake. Also concentrate on the line marking the boundary between the clear lake water and the cloudier river water. Double-haul sinking lines on one- or two-handed rods with very large baitfish streamer patterns. Target moving schools of salmonids by casting in front of the prowling

Once the fish is on, carefully reel the loose line onto the reel as you pinch the line with your other hand to keep tension. Not enough tension in the line at the onset of the fight will allow a fish to shake the fly free. Often, a hooked fish will charge and you'll be stripping or reel scrambling to maintain tension. The best way to ensure proper tension is to drop your rod tip a foot or so below the water. This will allow the water to provide resistance on the line to the running fish. Once contact is made, let the fish run on the reel's drag system. On direct-drive reels, don't touch the handle or allow it or the spool rim to hit your clothing, vest, etc. Keep a bow in the rod, pointing it in the direction of the fish. If the fish jumps, bow to it with the rod to release the drag system quickly. By constantly changing rod direction to the nine o'clock and three o'clock horizontal positions, you'll tire a fish and confuse its equilibrium orientation quicker. If the fish drives left, your rod should sweep laterally to the right and vice versa.

Thanks to new equipment and techniques, more fly fishers are now targeting the Great Lakes surf.

The tremendous leaping ability of summer Skamania steelhead will test an angler's fighting skills.

This lake-run brown trout was fooled by a streamer.

fish. Be prepared for a jolting strike and aerial battle like you've never seen!

Summer brings on the greatest surf opportunities with summer Skamania steelhead. Since the fish's natal rivers often run hot and dry, these July/August river-run fish will often stack up along the pier-head river estuaries. The key to this occurrence are offshore winds which will push the warm beach temperatures, often averaging seventy-five to eighty degrees Fahrenheit, out into the big lake and bring in a cold undertow of cold interior lake water. Beach temperatures can drop to the upper forties and lower fifties with sustainable offshore winds, creating a summer steelhead and alewife baitfish "surfs-up" magic carpet ride. If river temperatures

remain hot, the river-sick Skamanias will stage for days or weeks, foraging on alewives. Surf and pier casting with a Spey rod or trolling can be extremely productive. Early dawn and dusk periods are recommended. Target schools of seagulls and watch for surface-boiling alewives and seagulls on the hunt. Bright chartreuse, orange, and pink bunny Leechsicles are hot producers at the low-light levels of dusk and dawn.

Late summer will find chinook, coho and pink salmon in the surf. Once again, the key is a brisk offshore wind, and low and warm rivers that will keep the fish beach-bound. These fish are noted for incredible circle-schooling behavior. Target the stragglers and you'll often find curious fish that want to take a baitfish imitation.

Finally, autumn brings in lake trout and browns along with roaming fall steelhead looking for food. Though baitfish patterns work well, dead drifting cluster egg patterns is the choice since the rivers will be emanating the sexual scent of spawning Pacific salmon and their smorgasbord of dislodged unfertilized eggs.

GETTING TO THE FISH

Whether you wade, or use a drift boat, jet sled, or pontoon/belly boat is a matter of personal choice. If you wade, make sure you know the water, its level, and crossing-point areas well. Drift boats are ideal for covering large distances of river and can put you onto holes and runs too deep to wade. Jet sleds can further increase your advantage, allowing you to go up- and downstream, draft in six inches of water, and open up your game plan for the river on a daily basis. Pontoon boats are great for smaller boulder-strewn rivers and shallow tight-water streams. Belly boats are becoming popular; however, they can be dangerous on fast-flowing, ice-cold waters.

Do your homework, get advice on the waters you fish, and use common safety sense in all of your endeavors. Be courteous to both boat and wading anglers, and give them space. The waters are becoming much too crowded and etiquette can go a long way.

CHAPTER TWENTY-THREE

THE WET FLY SWING

— JOHN SHEWEY —

"The main idea is to let the fly race across current, across that particular slick or riffle where after a long, long while you somehow know Old Dynamite is waiting."

—SYL MACDOWELL, 1948

The wet fly swing, the basic steelheading technique, derives from a centuries-old method of fly angling for Atlantic salmon. The basic idea is to cast downstream and across, mend upstream to straighten the line and leader (not always necessary), and then allow the fly—under tension from the current—to swing back to your side of the flow.

In short, you make the fly drag. We spend most of our trout-fishing days learning to eliminate that evil thing called drag. No wonder steelheading is so easy: We want the fly to drag. Throw the fly down and across, mend once, and allow the fly to drag back to your side of the river. Take two steps downstream and repeat. Pretty simple.

It's a matter of covering as much water as possible during the course of a day, hence the cast-swing-step approach that gives every available fish at least one chance to see the fly. Most of the time, if a steelhead wants to chase it, she'll do so at the first opportunity. That's why—unless perhaps you are covering visible fish—you want to keep moving.

The learned British author John Ashley-Cooper, in his book *The Salmon Rivers of Scotland*, could as easily have been discussing western steelheading when he wrote: "In big pools, and in these rivers the majority of them

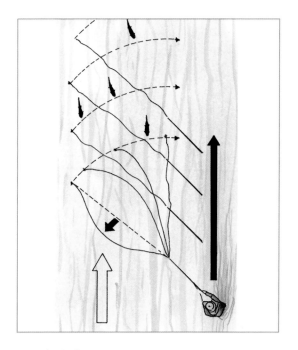

Wet Fly Swing
LEFT: Move downstream one or two steps between casts. **RIGHT:** Begin the wet fly swing by casting at approximately a forty-five-degree angle across the current (far left). An immediate upstream mend (second from left) allows the fly to sink and dead drift for a few feet before the line comes taut. As the current tightens the line and sweeps it down and across, the fly follows, swinging across the stream (third from left). You may need to make additional mends to control the speed and depth of the fly. At the end of the swing, the line hangs downstream (far right). Take one or two steps downstream, make another cast, and repeat the process.

The wet fly swing: The angler casts down and across stream (above) and allows the fly to swing back to his side of the river (page 165).

are big, you should normally fish quickly, especially when fish are scarce. On no account pause to do two or three casts in the same place (this is almost an endemic fault in nervous waders). This leads to a deplorable waste of time. Keep moving on steadily at a rate of two or three yards between each cast and so get the water covered. Only if you locate a spot where likely takers are lying, or if you rise fish that do not take hold, should you slow up. It is much better to fish a big pool twice, fairly fast, in a given period of time than once, slowly."

Specific current structures dictate the angle of the downstream cast but generally speaking, the steeper the angle, the easier it becomes to control the fly's speed as it swings across the flow. In fact, the speed of the fly and its depth in the water column comprise the two critical elements in steelhead presentation. When fishing floating lines and wet flies during the summer, fly depth more or less takes care of itself, especially when you control the more important element of fly speed. Steep angles of presentation and some timely mending control the speed of the fly. In short, a slow, controlled swing accounts for more hookups than a fly zipping rapidly back across the river.

Controlling depth and speed becomes a more critical issue with winter steelhead, which won't chase down a fly as aggressively as will summer-run fish. Thus, you must present the fly closer to the steelhead's level. You needn't dredge the bottom but you must swing the fly deeper in the water column, often just a foot or two above the streambed.

A couple tricks help with fly control during winter: First, you can hold a large loop of line in your hand during the swing and steadily release this slack line to slow the fly's speed and thus increase its depth. Second, try stepping downstream after the cast rather than before. In summer, the typical pattern is to fish out one swing, take a step or two downstream, and then cast again. During the winter, however, try fishing out one swing and then making the next cast from the same position. After making the cast, take those two steps downstream, allowing the line a few more feet of drag-free drift to gain depth.

Another trick is to cast down and across but at the end of the cast leave the rod tip elevated in preparation for a quick stack mend. In other words, as soon as the fly touches down, make a quick roll cast, shooting a loop of line that rolls the floating portion of the fly line partway out. This stack mend gives you a few feet of slack line—and thus dead drift—that helps the sinking portion of the line gain depth before the fly begins to swing.

Your choice of casting stations often dictates the methods used to control fly speed and the degree to which these methods prove effective. An often overlooked pool on one of our local rivers exemplifies the importance of the angler's position: Located at the lip current, deep in the tail-out of a much larger pool, a narrow pocket in the bedrock allows migrating steelhead a respite after negotiating the falls immediately below.

We can fish this slot from either side of the river but only if we position ourselves above and within a rod's length laterally of the pool. In other words, we stand almost directly upstream from the holding area. Try to fish the slot from a steeper angle, and the fly and line either latch onto ledge rock or dash across the pocket so quickly as to render the presentation ineffective.

I could cite countless similar examples. In short, the steeper your angle of presentation, the easier it becomes to control the speed of the fly without mending. The importance of fishing at steep angles may be the best justification for casting a long line on large western rivers. Basically, it's a matter of geometry. When thrown at identical down-and-across angles from the same position, the longer cast covers a wider swath of water at the appropriate speed than does a shorter cast.

Initial positioning in the pool allows you to fish the best possible angle of presentation but rod position and rod movement also play critical roles in fly control. You can either follow the fly or lead the fly with the rod, depending again on particular current structures in relation to the path of the line and fly. Following the fly means that once the line straightens, you keep the rod tip pointed out over the river.

The fly is now directly downstream of the angler.

Using a steep angle of presentation, this angler swings the fly through the seam between the bank and the rapids.

Doing so allows you direct contact throughout the presentation and gives you the opportunity to hang the fly in particular places, at least toward the end of the crosscurrent swing.

One of my favorite local pools perfectly illustrates the principle of following the fly. The pool features a major current seam well out in the flow, formed by a huge submerged slab of rock. Steelhead often hold on the far side of the seam in the slower water thirty feet below the rock. To present the fly effectively to these fish, you must cast well across the flow and then make a big upstream mend. Then you must hold the rod tip as far out toward the middle of the river as possible so the fly can come around and begin its swing in or near the seam. If you fail to do this, the fly darts through the seam as the current pulls it quickly to your side of the river. (See diagrams.)

Leading the fly, meanwhile, is a technique that can help slow the fly in swift currents or help speed it through slow currents. A slow-moving fly is good; an unmoving fly is not so desirable. So in some cases you may need to lead the fly with rod tip—in effect using the rod and line in conjunction with the currents to pull the fly through slow water. Or in some cases you might lead the fly to slow its speed by allowing the rod tip to drift downstream slightly faster than the fly. Doing so causes the fly to swing across stream in a more angled arc—a valuable ploy when you can't get a steep enough angle on a narrow slot well out in the flow.

Regardless of the particulars of your presentation, success ultimately hinges on your ability to fish the fly in the proper place. In other words, reading a river and identifying the likely holding water rank as the most significant factors in determining your ability to hook fish consistently. In some rivers, the good pools are so well known that you need only watch for other anglers. Still, learning such pools yourself allows you to find the sweet spots in any given stretch of water.

Meanwhile, each day spent fishing adds to your arsenal of skills. As I have said, the basic technique for steelhead fly angling is decidedly easy to learn and execute. Yet there remains ample room for skill to prevail over a common

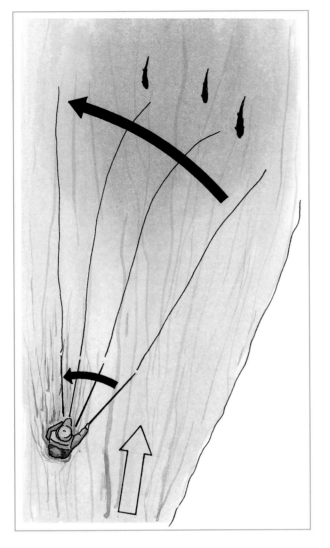

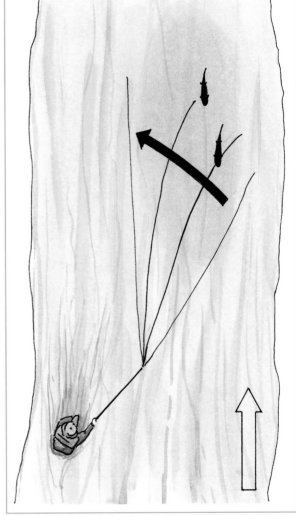

"Leading" the fly across a broad, slow pool.

"Following" the fly in a fast, narrow run.

flogging of the water and fly control lies in that realm of skills in which we should tirelessly aim to improve.

EXECUTING THE SWING

Begin fishing at the upstream extent of the pool or run (this is called the head of the pool) where the riffle or rapids above feeds into slower, softer, deeper currents. Strip from the reel a few yards of line and begin with a short cast aimed down and across stream. Allow the current to pull the line taut, swinging the fly back to your side of the river until it hangs in the current directly downstream. Now strip two more yards of line from the reel and repeat the same cast. We call this "fishing out the short casts." These first few casts cover the water closest to you and cannot be neglected.

Lengthen the line by about two yards on each successive cast until you have arrived at the maximum amount of line you need or want to cover the water. Then, instead of lengthening the line, take two steps between casts, fishing out each cast and stepping downstream before making the next presentation. Continue in this manner until you

The author swings a fly through a typical steelhead run.

have fished down through the length of the pool or run.

On some rivers—Oregon's North Umpqua offers the perfect example—many pools must be fished from a single casting station or from a few such stations. (This is called "station-to-station" fishing.) Some pools are essentially impossible to wade from top to bottom, the water typically being too deep or otherwise inaccessible. So anglers choose a particular rock, ledge, gravel bar, or position on shore from which to cover as much of the pool as possible.

In these cases, you simply lengthen the line by two yards or so with each successive cast until you have either covered all the water or covered all you can reach. In the station-to-station pools, start at the uppermost casting station, cover all the water you can reach, then

reel in, move downstream to the next station, and begin the process anew.

Whether you're wading through the pool or casting from stations, learn to minimize false casts. The fewer false casts, the more quickly you deliver each successive presentation, thereby covering the pool as efficiently as possible. Each false cast you eliminate adds one more fishing cast that day, and the more casts you make the more chances you have of presenting the fly to a biter.

Properly executed, the swing technique develops a beautiful, efficient rhythm: You cast, fish out the swing, strip in a little line, pick up the line, turn the cast back out over the river with the first false cast, and deliver the next fishing cast immediately. Practiced steelheaders make the wet fly swing seem like a well-ordered dance routine.

THE IMPORTANCE OF LINE CONTROL

When you chase steelhead—especially summer-run fish—on the big western rivers, you need to cover water and cover it effectively. Reading and covering water are the two most important aspects of fly angling for these wonderful game-fish. Much of the available literature talks about different kinds of casts and mends, often ascribing them fancy names like "stack mend." Yet even myriad, carefully categorized casting and mending techniques cannot begin to address the immense variety of real-life, on-the-river fishing situations. After all, every steelhead pool offers its unique nature, its particular structure and flow. Such characteristics affect the location and behavior of steelhead in that pool and thereby determine our tactical approach.

Because of the unique characteristics of each steelhead run or pool, I find it rather limiting to teach particular line-control skills in context with specific water types. Instead, I like to teach instinctive steelheading: Learn to cast, mend, and control line; learn to read a steelhead river. Then use whatever combination of learned and off-the-cuff skills you need to swing or swim your fly as slowly as possible across the pool. Most anglers, once they understand the virtue of controlling fly speed, easily learn to instinctively manipulate the line and the presentation.

Occasionally we find pools called "self-menders." Such pools require nothing in terms of line control beyond the cast itself. Self-menders are arranged so perfectly that they do everything for you: They straighten the line and they swim the fly at the perfect speed. Mending the line is wasted effort and might even cost a hookup.

At the other extreme are the complex pools where the initial cast must be delivered specifically to set up a subsequent series of mends. One of my favorite pools, in fact, offers a productive slot that requires an across-stream cast delivered with an upstream reach so that the fly lands slightly downstream of the line. At the same time, I must complete the cast with a high stop so the rod and line are positioned for an immediate, underpowered roll cast that positions a loop of slack line upstream from the fly. All this

Casting down and across to present the fly on the swing.

During the swing, the rod usually points downstream.

is done just to set up the fly for a nice, controlled swing through the bottom of the slot.

A few years ago I had the chance to introduce some Midwesterners to a big western steelhead river replete with complex pools. Standing on a rock beside one such pool, I pointed out the sweet spot where the fish was likely to take if indeed a steelhead occupied the run. One of the fellows, Dave, accepted the challenge. The cast alone covered eighty feet but Dave was equal to the task. He wasn't mending the line quite right, however, so the fly, even when it landed in the right place, darted away too quickly. I yelled instructions from atop my perch: "Put it in the same place again, Dave. Perfect, okay, now

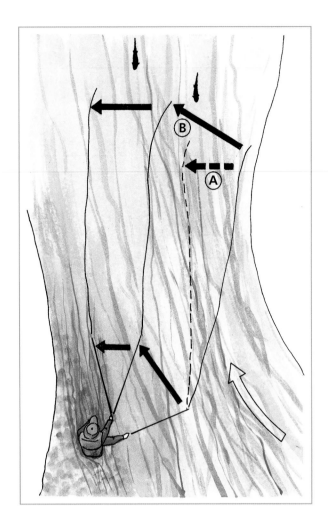

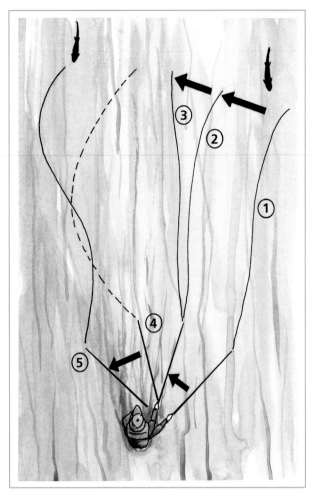

Here the angler leads the fly to slow its progress through the flow. In this fast, narrow seam, the angler cannot gain a steep enough angle of presentation to "follow" the fly, so the second-best option is to allow the rod tip to swing downstream slightly faster than the drift of the fly. This causes the fly to swing in a wide downstream arc (B) rather than a narrow arc straight across the flow (A).

"Backmending" is another method of mending line to the downstream (or inside) side of the fly but in this case the mend is used to extend the swing into good holding water located between the angler and the near bank. (Normally the angler would wade inside of all the good water but in this example the angler wades aggressively to cover the good water, knowing that at the lower end of the pool the current pushes toward the left-hand bank and the water deepens on that side.) The angler casts down and across (1) and allows the rod and fly to swing down and across (2). Soon the fly hangs directly below the angler (3) and stops swinging. To fish the potentially productive water to the inside, the angler can either flip a mend to the inside (4) or switch hands with the rod and point the tip down toward the near bank (5), causing the fly to swing in that direction.

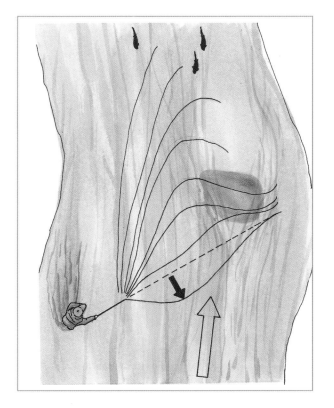 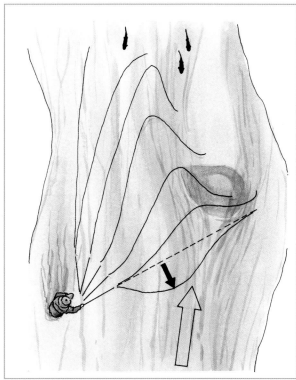

These diagrams show one of the author's favorite pools, where the angler must hold the rod out over the river throughout most of the presentation to get the proper swing. LEFT DRAWING—CORRECT: If the angler reaches the rod across stream and holds it there, the fly comes around and begins to swing effectively while still within the current seam created by the submerged boulder.

RIGHT DRAWING—INCORRECT: If the angler allows the rod to drift downstream, the fly gets held up in the slow water while the line bellies badly in the fast water. Consequently the fly darts straight downstream, pulled along by the fly line, and doesn't begin a controlled swing until it drifts beyond the current seam at midriver.

mend upstream, quick, and hold your rod tip out toward the slot."

Soon the light went on. Dave saw how an incorrect presentation caused the fly to dart out of the soft water that offered the only haven for a steelhead. No steelhead would chase a fly into the rushing white water immediately adjacent to the little slot so the angler had to hang the fly in the slow water long enough to draw a reaction. Quite suddenly my friend, who had honed his skills on streams of a different nature, understood why I had admonished him all day to swing the fly slowly through the pools.

Dave finally got one just right: Perfect cast, perfect mend, and perfect rod position. Just as the fly straightened into the slot, I yelled, "Now that cast deserves a fish."

Wham! Fish on. Dave landed a beautiful native buck, and I was worshiped as some kind of divining fish god. My partners failed to realize, of course, that I mutter that same phrase, at least to myself, every time I make a decent cast. Save some knowledge of the pool on my part, it was Dave's ability to depart from his normal thought processes and make the perfect cast and presentation that earned him that fish.

Later, as we ate dinner, Dave and I talked about the nature of that presentation. The configuration of the river dictated his choice in line control: A fast current ran a path straight through the middle of the river, which here was bounded on both sides by ledge rock. The far bank offered a narrow slot where a seam in the current offered ideal holding water against a rock ledge. This slot—just a bathtub-sized, miniature pool—was unfishable unless an angler stood on a narrow gravel berm way up at the head of the fast water.

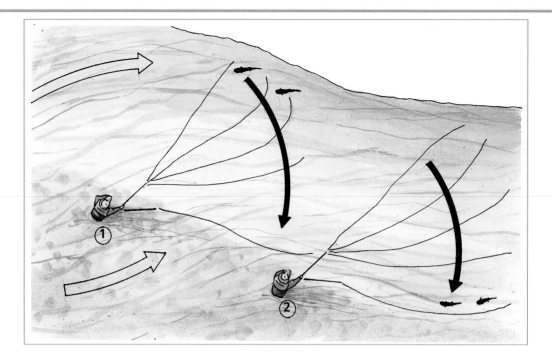

This diagram shows one of the author's favorite pools that requires the angler to first "follow" the fly (1) and then "lead" the fly (2) with the rod tip on each presentation. A cobblestone bar extends to mid-river and then drops off, creating ideal steelhead water. But owing to the curvature of the current structure, the angler must swing the rod to the downstream side at the end of each presentation to make the fly swing in toward the drop-off, where fish often hold.

The long cast dropped the fly atop the slot. An upstream flip and loft positioned all of the fly line above the fly and well to the left of the current. The angler's position left him at the steepest possible angle to the pool, and he held his rod out to the left and kept it there as the line came taut. Combined with his initial positioning, Dave's cast, mend, and rod position allowed him to dance the fly slowly through the narrow slot. No written labels describe the presentation that earned Dave his fish—it was an instinctive reaction to the structure of the pool. Once Dave understood why the fly had to swing slowly through the little pool, he simply flew by the seat of his pants and did what needed doing. I was yelling instructions, sure, but Dave's fishing instincts translated my simple instructions ("Okay, now mend!") into the perfect presentation.

CONFIDENCE COUNTS

Steelhead fly anglers constitute a decidedly twisted lot. We have little choice in the matter because our chosen pastime assures that we spend far more time fishing than actually catching. We operate on faith, on the assumption that if we just keep fishing we will, sooner or later, hook a steelhead.

Here in the Northwest, most of us fish big water—the Deschutes, Skykomish, Thompson, North Umpqua, Clearwater, Skagit, and many more. For some of these rivers you can watch the fish counts at the dams and garner at least some rough guess as to how many steelhead have migrated up to your favorite reaches. Even so, you simply assume that each pool holds fish, because only rarely on these rivers can one actually spot fish in the water.

Your faith must never falter. You must always believe that fish are in the river, in your favorite pools, and in a mood to chase your flies. In fact, confidence may well constitute the single most important attribute of the successful steelhead angler.

Confidence transcends technique and strategy. More than that, confidence elevates your angling skills because it instills in you a belief that there exists no doubt about the fact that you will hook a steelhead. Not burdened by doubt, you come to decide that casting, wading, and reading water are skills at which you will tirelessly try to better yourself.

Any doubts about hooking steelhead are pushed far out of your mind. As you deliver a cast, there exists not a shred of doubt that a steelhead will grab the fly on that presentation. When this fails to happen, you are at the very least mildly surprised. Your confidence doubles on the ensuing cast—after all, if the last cast failed to tempt a fish, there is simply no question that the next one is sure to score. When this next presentation goes fishless, you find yourself quite flabbergasted, and when you fish out the pool without touching a fish you are entirely astounded.

Your astonishment only redoubles your confidence. No question about it: You will certainly hook a fish in the next pool. Should the day pass without a hookup, you find yourself brimming with confidence about your chances the following day. Should a week pass without a hookup, your confidence has reached epic proportions: It builds in direct proportion with your astonishment over not catching fish.

Never does your confidence wane; rather it follows this inverse relationship, mounting appreciably with the passage of fishless casts, pools, and days. Your reasoning is simple, fundamental. How can there exist any doubt that the next cast will hook a steelhead since the last five hundred have failed to do so?

Indeed, doubt never enters the confident steelheader's mind. In this way you become a better angler, concentrating fully on your efforts. When your fly hangs in the current directly downstream at the end of the swing, you stand there entirely befuddled that a steelhead did not give chase. Then you can't wait to deliver the next presentation because you are more certain than ever that the forthcoming cast will hook a fish.

The confident steelheader, unencumbered by doubt, appreciates that reading water and effectively covering water rank as the two most significant factors in hooking fish. The confident angler never worries over pattern choice. He chooses a favorite, ties it on, and forgets about the fly. The confident angler believes in

A beautiful wild summer steelhead caught with a well-executed wet fly swing.

every pool and fishes each one from top to bottom, knowing full well that giving up even one cast short of the lip current might spell the difference between success and failure.

Unburdened by worries, the steelhead angler now begins to appreciate the fact that few angling pursuits place him in more intimate quarters with a favorite river. As the seasons mount and the wading and casting miles add up; as those cherished hookups become many; as lifelong angling friendships are forged; as new rivers become old stomping grounds, the steelhead angler learns that he persists in this game simply because he loves to fish and because these noble gamefish and the rivers in which they live deserve a special reverence.

CHAPTER TWENTY-FOUR

BASS ON TOP

— WILLIAM G. TAPPLY —

We'll look first at floating flies—bass bugs—because there's nothing in all of fly fishing that matches that heart-stopping implosion a big bass makes when he swirls at the surface to suck in bug. When conditions are at all favorable, I always fish with bugs.

Every bass-bug aficionado I know has his favorite bug. He ties it on because . . . well, because he's had good luck with it in the past, because he likes the way it acts on the water, because he enjoys casting it, and sometimes because he made it himself. None gives much thought to imitating anything particular, although they all believe that the way they manipulate their bug makes it more or less imitate bass prey in general.

I happen to do most of my bass bugging with the deer-hair popper my father invented about fifty years ago. Tap's Bug resembles no natural bass food. Dad designed his bug to meet the needs of the fisherman, not the imagined appetites of bass. It's easy to tie, floats well, casts easily on midweight fly rods, and can be made to burble, gurgle, plop, glug, and slither in ways that smallmouths and largemouths in all types of water consistently find irresistible.

Usually when I go bass fishing, I just tie on a Tap's Bug and fish with it all day, unless a pickerel or a pike tears it up or I break it off in the bushes or in the mouth of a big bass. When that happens, I tie on another one.

When the bass show little interest in a Tap's Bug, and I'm not yet ready to concede that a streamer or a jig is the answer, I experiment with different bug designs. This makes me feel as if I'm doing something constructive and I usually do it with a purpose in mind. When I do try different bugs, I have logical reasons, although not much science, for doing so.

CONDITIONS TO CONSIDER

My choice of bugs depends on the conditions I encounter on the water, not on the particular food I imagine bass are looking for.

- *In shallow, flat-calm water,* I worry that my bug might spook fish when it hits the water. So I cast smallish, soft-bodied bugs that land with a natural-sounding, quiet *splat* rather than an attention-getting *splash,* and I prefer bugs with rounded faces that gurgle and burble seductively rather than those with flat faces that pop loudly.

- When I'm casting to *small pockets and tight holes* such as openings in a bed of lily pads or under overhanging bushes or among the limbs of waterlogged trees, where the bug must do its work without being moved away from the hotspot, I like a design that vibrates and wiggles when I give it just the slightest twitch. Rubber arms and legs and hairy or splayed hackle-feather or marabou tails impart subtle, lifelike movements to a bug while it rests on the water.

- When *a breeze riffles the surface,* I tie on something big and loud to command a bass's attention, such as a flat-nosed deer-hair bug or a hard-bodied lure with a cupped face that will move water and send out strong vibrations.

- When I'm casting over *dropoffs, shoals, sunken weedbeds, and other cover in deeper water,* I like big, low-riding bugs with tails made from marabou or rabbit strips and Krystal Flash or Flashabou to flutter, pulsate, and glitter under the surface while the cork or deer-hair body chugs along on top.

- When I'm casting to *water that's blanketed with lily pads,* I tie on a large, lightweight foam bug with a weedguard. I want it to slither over the weeds without getting fouled but I want it to draw the attention of any bass lurking in the shadow of the pads.

- When all else is equal, I prefer smaller (No. 2) bugs in natural colors (gray, white, or tan) for smallmouths, and bigger (No. 2/0) in combinations of white, yellow, green, and red for largemouths. On dark days and at twilight I go with darker colors. For nighttime bugging, I like all-black, which presents a sharp silhouette to a bass looking up at it, with a white face for my own eyes. I doubt if *size and color* actually make much of a difference for either species but when the fishing is slow, this is how I think.

When we analyze the qualities of a good bass bug, we must look beyond the baseline question, "Will it catch bass?" We already know the answer to that one.

BASS BUG CHARACTERISTICS

Here, in their order of importance, are what most bass-bug fishermen consider to be the characteristics of an effective bug:

- *Aerodynamics.* A good bass bug is lightweight and streamlined. It offers little air resistance when you cast it. It does not

Tap's Bug—an old favorite.

River-dwelling smallmouths love large attractor dry flies such as these.

twist the leader or plane or flutter off target. You should be able to cast it fifty feet with a tight loop, pinpoint accuracy, and minimal false casting on a medium-weight fly rod, and you should be able to do it all day without tearing your rotator cuff. Most commercial bugs come with more legs and arms and tails and other air-resistant materials than they need. Cut off some of that stuff and you'll have a bug that bass like just as much but which casts far more easily.

- *Noise.* Burbles and gurgles are more lifelike and, under most conditions, attract bass better than either sharp pops or no noise at all. The angler should be able to impart a variety of noises, from soft and subtle to loud and attention grabbing, to a good bug.

- *Behavior.* The best bass bugs are never absolutely motionless. When they're twitched and retrieved, they vibrate with life. Between twitches, they quiver and shiver, shudder and flutter. A bug with rubber legs, hackle, hair, or feathers—just enough to give the bug the illusion of life when it's sitting quietly on the water but not enough to make it hard to cast—will entice reluctant bass to gulp it in.

- *Touchdown.* The way a bug falls upon the water will either attract or frighten any bass in the area, particularly if you've read the water accurately, executed a pinpoint cast, and dropped your bug onto his nose. Most natural bass prey hit the water with a muffled *plop* or *splat*, not a startling *splash*. Bass bugs should, too.

- *Feel.* All fish feel with their mouths but the bass's mouth is especially sensitive. If a bass takes something into his mouth that doesn't feel right, he'll eject it so fast that you'd swear he struck short and missed it completely. Bass hit anything that looks edible. Only if it *feels* edible, however, will they hold it in their mouth long enough for the fisherman to react and set the hook.

- *Buoyancy.* Bass bugs are supposed to float. If they absorb water and begin sinking after a few casts, they are inefficient regardless of their other qualities. A bug that rides low in the water with its belly submerged, however, offers the bass a more natural profile, emits more lifelike, fish-attracting noises, and creates more enticing wiggles and twitches than a high-rider that floats entirely atop the surface.

- *Hook.* The gape, or "bite," of the hook should be wide relative to the size of the

bug for consistent hookups. The point should be sharp and the barb should be mashed down. Barbless hooks not only penetrate better than those with barbs but they also enable you to unhook and release your fish—not to mention yourself or your partner, should you have a casting accident—quickly and harmlessly.

- *Size.* In general, the ancient wisdom that largemouths prefer bigger bugs than smallmouths seems to hold true. But when the fish are uncooperative and the water is flat calm, I have often found that small, even panfish-sized, bugs entice more strikes from both species. On riffled water and at night an outsized bug usually draws more attention.

- *Shape and color.* These are the features generally touted in catalogs, and in much bass-bugging literature, to distinguish one bug from another. Catalogs assume their readers have a trout-fishing, hatch-matching mentality, so they emphasize imitation, and they imply that you need the "right" bug, meaning the one that imitates the prey species the bass are supposed to be looking for at that moment, to catch them. That's why so many commercial bugs are shaped, colored, and named for the prey they theoretically represent—diving frog, wounded minnow, fluttering moth, etc. On the water where it counts, however, color or shape or even both of these factors taken together are less significant than any one of those other qualities. The shape of a bug needn't imitate anything. Overall shape matters because it affects how well the bug casts and how it behaves on the water.

Some fishermen theorize that a long, thin bug resembles baitfish and should be fished around boulders, along the edges of weedbeds, and over points and dropoffs, and a short, fat bug resembles the various pudgy terrestrial species that fall onto the water near shore. Thinking this way gives these anglers confidence in their choice of bug, which encourages them to fish it thoroughly and carefully. This will produce the kind of results that reinforces their thinking.

My strategy on color is to use a bug I can see on the water because I haven't noticed that the bass give a hoot. They see only the belly of a floating bug. Everything above the water's surface is a blurry silhouette from the bass's perspective.

- *Durability.* Bass are toothless creatures so a good bug should survive dozens of chomps. If your bug frays, comes unraveled, or falls apart after a few fish have glommed onto it, it was poorly made. If you encounter toothy fish such as pike and pickerel (which smash bass bugs with heart-stopping enthusiasm), all bets are off.

- *Weedlessness.* A bug that slithers around, over, and through weeds and snags allows the fisherman to cast closer to the places where bass lurk. A properly constructed weedguard will not significantly reduce your chances of hooking any bass that takes your bug in his mouth. The most effective weedguard is made from one or two strands of monofilament attached to the rear of the hook, looped around the bend, and fastened behind the eye.

- *Imitativeness.* Underwater flies and lures that resemble specific prey—common species of baitfish and crayfish in particular—arguably work better than generic, suggestive lures. In my experience, at least, the opposite is actually true of topwater bass bugs. Sometimes, in fact, I like to show the fish something that looks dramatically different from their prevalent species of prey, on the theory that it will get their attention quicker than a bug that looks like just one more of everything else in the water.

On the other hand, bass rarely pass up any hapless frog, kicking grasshopper, or half-dead shiner they find twitching on the sur-

This hefty smallmouth took a big deer-hair popper, proving the theory that big bugs take big fish. (Will Ryan photograph)

face. If you get a special kick out of "fooling" fish into thinking they're eating the real thing, by all means tie on an imitative bug. The bass won't object.

BASS BUG VARIETIES

Bass bugs are constructed from any lightweight material that floats: Cork, balsa, soft and hard foam, and spun deer hair are the most common. For all practical purposes, there are just two types: Hard-bodied (cork, balsa, hard foam, plastic) and soft-bodied (deer hair and soft foam). Each type has some advantages and disadvantages.

Frogs can be imitated in many ways. Both hard- and soft-bodied bugs can be deadly.

A soft bug probably feels more natural and lifelike to a bass when he clomps down on it so he's less likely to spit it out instantly. It can be manipulated to gurgle and chug, or it can be twitched and slithered, flirted and fluttered in a variety of ways. Soft-bodied bugs can be dropped softly or splatted onto the water.

Hard bugs, of course, never get waterlogged, and, if they're well made, they'll last forever.

You don't need a steamer trunk full of bass bugs to be prepared for every occasion. If you carry just half a dozen bugs with you, you can usually stimulate a hungry bass's conditioned predatory response.

- *Popper.* The most versatile bug has a flat face, a tapered body, and a streamlined tail. It imitates nothing in particular and everything in general. All irrelevant decorations have been eliminated. It casts like a bullet and produces a variety of seductive noises when retrieved, which is everything you want.

Give it a slow tug to make it burble irresistibly. A harder, quicker pull makes it pop. Cast it against a fallen tree, along the edge of a weedbed, or against a rock, make it go *ploop*, and let it sit until the rings disappear. Give it a couple of little tugs. Rest it again. Keep it right there in the strike zone. Imagine the big bass that has come over for a look-see. Give it a twitch.

A popper with a wide, flat face that makes a big ruckus is your best choice for riffled or discolored water and at night, when bass hunt by sound rather than sight. Cup-faced bugs make an even louder pop than those with flat faces but they tend to dig into the water when you pick them up to recast.

- *Slider.* On clear, flat, shallow water, a noisy popper might frighten bass. Here your best choice is a bug that slithers and undulates quietly. A slider such as a

Feathered Minnow or a Sneaky Pete is one of the oldest floating bass lures and it's still deadly. It has a small, bullet-shaped head and a long, wiggly tail. The slider rides low on the surface and gets its action from the creative manipulation of the angler.

Whether bass take the slider for a wounded baitfish is arguable but it's certain that the same instinct that impels them to eat crippled minnows, worms, lizards, and any other unfortunate long, skinny creature that finds itself struggling on or near the water's surface prompts them to strike sliders.

A slider is a good choice when you want to cover a lot of water. Cast it among the reeds or over a sunken weedbed or a rocky point. Keep it moving at a steady but irregular pace and vary the speed until the bass tell you that you've got it right.

- *Deerhair Mouse.* I call it a mouse because to me it looks like a mouse. I'm not sure bass see it that way. Bass rarely pass up the chance to grab the unfortunate mouse or mole that finds itself on the water. Such opportunities, however, are rare. I don't show them a mouse to imitate what they're eating but simply to tempt them with an easy-to-catch and nourishing bellyful.

When bass see a mouse "bug," they see a lure that splits the difference between a popper and a slider. It won't pop but it will burble and gurgle when you twitch it, and it will slither and slide and leave a wake of bubbles if you retrieve it slowly. The wiggly little whiskers and the long, sinuous tail are irresistible.

Try a mouse toward nightfall. Throw it right against the bank. Make it plop onto the water the way an unfortunate terrestrial creature accidentally falls in. Let it sit. It's momentarily stunned. Now bring it to life. It's disoriented. It's panicky. It twitches, swims, pauses—the bass that swallows it in an implosion of

The Feathered Minnow slider is one of the oldest types of bass bugs.

Mouse imitations featuring long slithery tails are extremely effective.

water may not know it's supposed to be a mouse but he's absolutely convinced it's good to eat.

- *Diver.* Larry Dahlberg designed this unique deerhair bug that works both on and under the surface. The flat bottom, pointed nose, and high collar cause the diver to dart underwater when you give it a tug, while the long, sinuous tail gives it plenty of seductive action. The faster you retrieve it, the deeper it goes. Pause, and it bobs back to the surface. This up-and-down swimming motion mimics

The Dahlberg Diver darts under the surface on the retrieve.

An assortment of panfish-sized bugs featuring wiggly rubber legs.

that of frogs and several other species of bass prey.

Use a Dahlberg Diver when sunlight or riffled water seems to discourage bass from coming to the surface. The diver also brings up bass when they're lying in deeper water. On a sinking line, the diver can be fished deep and made to hop along near the bottom, a happy option for those times when bass simply refuse to come to the top to eat.

- *Big Bug.* The theory is, "For big fish, use big lures." The theory seems to work, especially for largemouths. Nick Lyons introduced me to the specialized fun of hunting for the biggest bass in the pond with outsized deer-hair bugs tied on 4/0 and larger hooks. Any design will work, provided it offers a big silhouette, has legs and a tail to exaggerate the illusion of size, and makes plenty of noise when you give it a tug. Small bass might flee in terror but every potbellied old lunker in the neighborhood will come over for a look.

  Tie on a big bug at dusk and after dark, when the water goes flat and the cautious old big boys begin marauding in the shallow water. Cast it near likely cover, let it sit, make it go *glug* and *ker-ploop*, rest it again—and hold on.

  If your big bug doesn't have terrible aerodynamics, it's not big and bulky enough. It takes a 10- or even a 12-weight rod to throw a big bug and a sturdy (six-foot, twenty-pound) leader to turn it over. Of course, you'll need a sturdy outfit to subdue the bass that might inhale it.

- *Bluegill Bug.* Many anglers believe that no hungry bass will pass up an easy meal, regardless of how small it is. I'm convinced that there are times when bass of all sizes, particularly smallmouths, actually prefer something dainty and inoffensive.

  I don't hesitate to try a little generic foam- or cork-bodied bluegill bug with wiggly rubber legs whenever my full-sized bugs aren't doing the job. Sometimes the minibug turns the trick, and even if it doesn't, it casts like a dream on a trout-weight outfit. Bluegill bugs on No. 8 or 10 hooks are just right for the panfish that you always find in bass ponds, without being too small for bass. I tie one on whenever I just want a relaxing afternoon of no-pressure fishing, and I'm content to catch whatever wants to eat.

CHAPTER TWENTY-FIVE

BASS UNDER THE SURFACE

— WILLIAM G. TAPPLY —

Although bass are usually eager to slurp deer-hair and cork-bodied bugs off the top of the water, they're conditioned to find most of their food under the surface. So when conditions for bass-bug fishing are poor or if you want to give yourself a slightly better chance of catching bass regardless of the conditions, a subsurface fly is your best choice.

Most commercial subsurface bass flies, like commercial bass bugs, are designed to imitate some form of natural prey—baitfish, leeches, crayfish, salamanders, or nymphs. Some flies are remarkably imitative and others are vaguely suggestive. It's no more important for the angler to imitate a particular species of bass prey with subsurface flies than it is with bugs. Bass are opportunists. The creatures they encounter in the water make a bass buffet and they eat whatever they can catch. Most of the time you can tie on a time-tested Woolly Bugger and be confident that you've got a fish-catcher on the end of your leader.

There are exceptions to this rule, especially with smallmouths. I have on occasion found them so keyed in on crayfish that only a fly that resembled and acted like a crayfish would catch them. When mayflies are hatching on a smallmouth river, the fish can be as selective as trout. In some Northeastern rivers, small-mouths feed almost exclusively on hellgram-mites, a nymph the size of a grown man's thumb, and only a fly that resembles a hell-grammite will catch them.

Experience—and reliable local sources—will tell you when to expect any of these exceptions. Otherwise, frankly, your choice of which fly to tie on is far less important than where you cast it and how you manipulate it in the water.

SUBSURFACE BASS FLY CHARACTERISTICS

Here are the characteristics to consider when selecting a subsurface fly:

- *Color.* In clear, shallow water under bright sun, go with a light-colored fly. Combinations of white, cream, tan, and yellow are good choices. Minimize the amount of flashy material in the fly. In bright sunlight, anything more than a hint of glitter is more likely to spook bass than to attract them.

    In clear water under cloud cover, use the same light colors but go with a bit more flash.

    In murky water, darker colors such as black, purple, and dark olive work better. A hint of flash helps.

    Under almost any conditions, you can't go wrong with combinations of yellow and red, red and white, and green and white.

- *Size.* The old adage, "Big flies for big fish," generally holds true. For most conditions, a streamer four or five inches

Old-fashioned bucktails in attention-getting colors still fool bass. Big eyes are added attractants.

Variations on the old favorite, a yellow-and-red Mickey Finn bucktail. A touch of red at the throat helps imitate the flare of a baitfish's gills.

long on a 1/0 hook is a good choice for largemouths, and something two or three inches long on a No. 2 hook works best for smallmouths.

When the fishing is slow and you wouldn't mind catching a few perch, crappies, or bluegills while still having a chance for a bass, tie on a one- or two-inch streamer tied on a size 6 or 8 hook. Bass eat a lot of small baitfish. At the other end of the spectrum, if you want to go big-game hunting for lunker bass and maybe a big northern pike or pickerel, and you're willing to get snubbed by small bass, tie on a big saltwater streamer. What you add in bulk, of course, you subtract in casting pleasure.

- *Decorations.* Baitfish, the number one bass forage in most waters, have prominent eyes, and many experts believe that predatory fish focus on the eyes of their victims. Glued or painted eyes on streamers help trigger strikes.

  Panicky baitfish flare their gills, which excites the predatory instinct of bass. A touch of red at the throat or behind the eyes of a streamer always helps.

- *Action.* The action of a fly—that is, how it moves in the water—should be lifelike to trigger the strike of a bass. Flies made from soft materials such as marabou, hackle feathers, wound hackles, and bucktail breathe and flare in the water. Rabbit strips wiggle and undulate. One of the great advantages fly fishermen enjoy over those who throw hardware with spinning rods is the ability to present soft lures that appear lifelike and appetizing to hungry bass.

- *Weight.* Even small beadhead or dumbbell eyes on a sinking fly make casting difficult and tiring but a little weight gets a subsurface fly down a foot or two where bass won't have to expose themselves near the surface to eat it. Weight near the front of the fly enhances its action in the water, too. It's a tradeoff.

  When you're not finding bass in the shallows—that is, in water less than five feet deep—your best bet, if you stick with a floating line, is a fly with enough weight to sink it down to where the fish are. If you decide your only alternative is to go deep, switch to a sinking or sink-tip line. For me, a heavily weighted fly or a sinking line is always a reluctant last resort because casting them on a fly rod is simply no fun, and fishing blindly in deep water is, frankly, boring. Sometimes, however, it's the only chance to catch fish, and when the choice is fishing or quitting, I vote for fishing.

Coneheads, dumbbell eyes, lead-wrapped bodies, and beadheads make any fly plummet toward the bottom. When they're retrieved with a series of tugs and pauses, they jig up and down in the water in an enticing manner. Let your weighted fly sink close to the bottom before beginning your retrieve, and then twitch it over the rocks and rubble where bass look for food. Over deep-water structure such as sunken weedbeds or brush piles, count down before you begin your retrieve, and keep experimenting until the fish tell you you've found their depth. If you can put weighted flies near bass, they are deadly.

- *Weedguards.* A monofilament loop around the bend of the hook prevents snagging in weedy water and allows flies to crawl over stumps, tree branches, and rocks without hooking up. There's no reason not to arm all your bass flies with weedguards.

IMITATING BASS PREY

Bass are rarely finicky about what they eat. Drop an appetizing fly near them, make it move seductively, and they'll usually devour it, whether or not it happens to resemble the particular critter they ate most recently. Time-proven bass attractors such as Mickey Finn bucktails, red-and-white streamers, Woolly Buggers, Clouser Minnows, and bunny flies continue to work most of the time. Maybe these flies look like something the fish recognize but it's more likely that their action and color are what seduce bass into striking.

Nevertheless, it does no harm, and sometimes it does a lot of good, to tie on subsurface flies that at least suggest a species of prey that is commonly found in the water you are fish-

Sometimes bass ignore everything except crawfish imitations. Bead eyes help attract fish.

ing. The movement you give your fly should likewise imitate that of the natural prey.

- *Baitfish.* All bass feed on other fish, including shiners, minnows, sculpins, sunfish, and baby bass. Baitfish imitations with eyes and gills, therefore, are always productive, and the well-equipped bass angler will carry an assortment of bucktails and other streamers in a variety of colors and sizes. Experiment with the speed and cadence of your retrieve until you hit upon the one that catches fish. Sometimes bass want a series of fast, hard strips; other times you'll need to slow it down to a slow twitch . . . pause . . . twitch.

- *Leeches.* We called leeches "bloodsuckers" when I was a kid. These wormlike critters ranging from about two to four inches long are abundant in most lakes, ponds, and rivers. Bunny flies, Woolly Buggers, and marabou streamers in olive, tan, black, purple, and orange imitate leeches. Extra-long leech flies up to seven inches long may not imitate the

Bucktails in combinations of red and white are always deadly.

Woolly Buggers work anywhere, anytime.

general, a very slow retrieve works best for crayfish flies.

- *Nymphs.* In cold-running smallmouth rivers, hellgrammites, caddis pupae, and mayfly and stonefly nymphs are important bass foods. These nymphs range in size from one-half to nearly two inches long. Turn over a few rocks to see what's crawling underneath. That will help you decide what to tie on. Precise imitation is unimportant but when you fish a river, carry an assortment of dark-colored (black, olive, and brown) buggy nymphs in sizes ranging from 12 to 4. Woolly Worms—or Woolly Buggers with the tails cut short—make excellent generic nymphs. Nymphs for moving water should be weighted and fished with a dead drift right along the bottom.

  In ponds and lakes in the early summer, bass gluttonize on the inch-long nymphs of damselflies and dragonflies as they swim toward the shore where they will hatch into adults. Again, Woolly Buggers and Woolly Worms do an acceptable job of suggesting these creatures, although closer imitations sometimes catch more fish. Still-water nymphs should be unweighted. Retrieve them like streamers with irregular twitches and tugs.

A FEW GOOD FLIES

You don't need hundreds of subsurface flies to be prepared for all situations. Here are seven designs that you can tie on with confidence any time. They're all a bass fisherman will ever need:

- *Woolly Bugger.* The Bugger, in a reasonable assortment of sizes and colors, may be the only underwater bass fly you'll ever need. It is a suggestive imitation of virtually all bass prey, although I suspect its flaring hackle and wiggly marabou tail simply seduce bass regardless of what it might imitate. Supply tan, olive, and black Woolly Buggers in Nos. 6, 2,

actual leeches that live in bass water but they often bring strikes from otherwise lock-jawed bass. Leeches swim slowly in an undulating motion so a steady tug-pause-tug retrieve works best.

- *Crayfish.* In waters where crayfish are found, primarily cool, rocky smallmouth lakes and rivers, bass eat them voraciously. Woolly Buggers usually do the job but closer imitations in tan and pale olive sometimes do it better. Crayfish crawl around on the bottom except when they're frightened. Then they move in a series of quick darts. In and 2/0, some with a beadhead, some unweighted.

- *Mickey Finn bucktail.* The combination of yellow and red and the lifelike look of bucktail in the water have been catching bass for decades. A six-inch Mickey Finn is the best pike and pickerel fly I know.

- *Bunny fly.* This is simply a strip of rabbit fur and skin lashed to a hook. In olive, black, and brown, it makes a deadly leech imitation although its wiggly movement in the water unquestionably seduces bass regardless of what they take it for.

- *Muddler Minnow.* This old favorite resembles all manner of stubby bass prey such as sculpins and tadpoles.

- *Woolly Worm.* Woolly Worms are as versatile as buggers. Worms can be twitched through the water to imitate baitfish, leeches, and damselfly nymphs, or they can be dead-drifted in moving water to imitate buggy stonefly nymphs and hellgrammites. Carry a few olive, brown, and black worms in Nos. 4 and 8, some with a little beadhead up front, and you'll be well armed.

- *Clouser Minnow.* The slim Clouser bucktail with its dumbbell eyes plummets to the bottom and rides upside down to minimize its chance of snagging. It's especially deadly in smallmouth rivers but it works anytime you need to get deep.

In the final analysis, regardless of what you choose to tie to your leader, it's your ability to pick likely targets, cast the fly accurately, and manipulate it convincingly that will draw strikes.

Bass find long, slithery bunny flies irresistible.

Slender Clouser Minnows with lead eyes work best when bumped along the bottom of a smallmouth river.

CHAPTER TWENTY-SIX

CASTING AND RETRIEVING FOR BASS

— WILLIAM G. TAPPLY —

Shallow-water bass fishing is target-shooting—that is, identifying those pockets, alleys, and edges that look "bassy," dropping your streamer or bug right where you want to, and doing it again and again as you move slowly along a brush-strewn shoreline, a weedy cove, or a jumble of boulders. Picking your targets and hitting them consistently offers a continual series of challenges for the fly caster. It's lots of fun. It's also the key to catching bass on flies.

I was about twelve years old the first time my father invited me to go bass fishing with him. A year of trout fishing had taught me the rudiments of fly casting, and it didn't take me too long to get a feel for the heavier rod with the deer-hair popper Dad had tied to the end of my leader. I managed to plop the bug along the edges of the lily pads and near the pilings of the occasional boat dock we encountered along that shoreline and I caught a few small bass.

When we came to an oak tree that grew at a low angle out over the water, Dad held the canoe. He didn't have to tell me that this was a particularly bassy spot.

I dropped the bug along the edge of the shadow cast by the overhanging boughs three or four times, with no strikes.

"Cast it way under those branches," Dad said. "There's a big old bass hiding in that dark hole right against the bank."

"That's impossible," I said. "I'll snag the tree."

He shrugged.

I handed the rod to him.

"Show me," I said, quite confident that he couldn't.

Of course, he did. He made two false casts, and with a sidearm cast and a loop about a foot wide, he drove the bug way under the low branches and dropped it against the bank. One twitch and a four-pound largemouth engulfed it.

He fought the fish quickly, lip-landed it, unhooked the bug from the corner of its mouth, held it up for me to admire, and released it. Then he handed the rod back to me.

"Like that," he said.

It was a powerful lesson—four lessons, really—that still guide me fifty years later: Not all bass targets are easy to hit but they're all worth hitting; the most difficult targets are often the ones that produce the biggest fish; bass won't move far to take a fly so you've got to get it close to them; and, the angler who can cast accurately will have the best luck.

In other words, luck has very little to do with it.

The other key to catching bass on flies, which I absorbed from watching my father do it, is moving the fly on or through the water in an enticing manner once you hit the bull's-eye with it.

CASTING

Fishermen who are used to casting tiny trout flies on lightweight rods often find casting bass-sized flies awkward and laborious, at least

With a strong sidearm cast you can drive a bass fly under overhanging bushes.

at first. Even the smallest, lightest, and most streamlined bass flies are heavier and more air-resistant than most trout flies. Casting them efficiently and accurately requires the right equipment, sound technique, and practice.

- *Equipment.* Nobody can cast a bass fly efficiently if his fly line is too light to overcome the bulk of the fly and if his rod doesn't match his line. No outfit is too heavy to handle a bass fly but it can certainly be too light. The line-and-rod combination you need to move a big, bulky bug or soggy streamer through the air will also cast a small fly easily.

  On the other hand, bass fishing is a continuous process of casting, retrieving, lifting line off the water, and casting again, interrupted now and then, we hope, by fighting a fish. Repeatedly moving a 9- or 10-weight line, with a big,

bulky bass fly tied to the end of it, through the air will cause even a well-conditioned athlete's shoulder to ache. That's why I recommend using stream-lined, medium-sized flies for most situations and reserving the oversized bugs for an hour or so at dusk, and the weighted flies and sink-tip lines for times when nothing else works.

- *Technique.* A 7- or 8-weight line with a bass bug or bass-sized streamer tied to the tippet, even on a well-matched rod, moves through the air more slowly than a thin trout-weight line. The tip-action rod and the quick, wristy casting stroke that combine to work well for false-cast-ing and air-drying tiny dry flies spell dis-aster for bass bugging.

  A medium-action rod and a slow, smooth casting stroke work together to

For backyard practice, use the kind of fly you'll actually fish with but cut off the bend. (Vicki Stiefel photograph)

give the heavy line with the bass fly on the end of it time to straighten out on the back- and forward cast. Keep your wrist stiff and use your entire arm and shoulder to move the rod. Resist the impulse to compensate by trying to overpower the weight of the line and the air-resistance of the fly or by speeding up your stroke. The best way to find the right timing is to watch your backcast unfurl over your shoulder. Don't begin your forward stroke until you see that the line has straightened out behind you. Soon you'll learn to feel the line loading the rod and you won't need to look.

An efficient, powerful casting stroke produces a minimal of false casting, tight casting loops, and pinpoint accuracy. It's all about line speed, and line speed comes from accelerating the rod on both the forward and the backcast and from stopping the rod abruptly when it reaches about one o'clock on the backcast and ten o'clock on the forward cast. Do this properly and you'll see how the rod, not the caster, does all the work.

You can achieve even greater line speed by mastering the single or double haul.

With the right outfit, a strong but smooth stroke, and the proper timing,

you'll have no trouble casting a bass fly as far as you'll ever need to. Smooth, easy casting is just a matter of rhythm and letting the rod and line do their job. If you find yourself straining to reach bassy targets, move a little closer. There's rarely any reason to cast more than fifty feet.

Recognizing likely bass targets and hitting them consistently with a well-cast fly, more than any other factor, including the streamer or bug with which you choose to fish, are what separate successful bass anglers from everyone else. Accuracy, which comes from line speed and tight loops, is more important than delicacy in bass fishing so don't worry if your fly splats down on the water. One of the advantages of flies over hardware is that even big, bulky flies hit the water with a natural-sounding, fish-attracting *plop*. Unless you drop it directly atop a basking bass, that *splat* is more likely to attract a nearby fish than spook him.

Fly casting is inherently more accurate than other methods of delivering a lure. A reasonably competent fly caster controls the distance and direction of his line throughout the cast. He can hit the bull's-eye more consistently than all but the elite bait- or spin-casters, which is one big advantage you as a fly caster have over those high-tech folks. False casting allows for fine-tuning distance and aim before dropping the fly onto the water, and you can pull back a cast before it hits the water if you realize it's destined to be off-target. Don't false cast excessively, however; the flash and shadow of a line in the air can spook a bass.

Bass usually hold tight to bankside logs, rocks, and weedbeds and under overhanging limbs, bushes, and docks. They do not normally like to move far from their cover to eat. If you want to entice them to devour your fly, you've got to put it close to them so cast aggressively. If you don't occasionally overshoot your target, you're probably being too cautious.

If you intend to fish from a boat or canoe, practice casting from a low sitting position. (Vicki Stiefel photograph)

Work on casting those hard, tight loops. By dropping your rod to a horizontal position, you can make a forceful sidearm cast that will cause a deer-hair bug to ricochet off the water's surface and skip under overhanging cover.

Another advantage you as a fly caster enjoy over your spinning and bait-casting counterparts is the ability to make another cast as soon as you've fished the productive water. There's rarely any need to retrieve a fly all the way to the boat. Work it through the good-looking water, usually no more than halfway back to you, then pick up your line and begin your next cast.

To start your next cast, don't try to get the fly airborne until most of your line is off the water. First, be sure that your rod is pointing at the fly and your line is straight. Then raise your rod smoothly and simultaneously pull back on the line with your line hand. This will load your rod, lift your line off the water before the fly, and start it moving into a smooth, strong backcast.

• *Practice.* To get the feel of your bassing outfit and to become a consistently accurate caster, you've got to practice. If you don't mind not catching many fish, of course, you can practice only when you're actually out fishing; but if you want to take advantage of your precious time on the water, get out in the yard or drive to the nearest playground with your bass outfit.

It's wise to use last year's fly line for practicing on grass or asphalt. The abrasion from casting on anything but water will quickly ruin the coating of a line. Cut the bend of the hook off a bug or streamer similar to one you might use on the water, tie it on, and practice casting.

First, work on your technique. Don't go for distance. Bass fishing never demands long-distance casting. Measure out fifty feet on the lawn. That's as far as you'll ever need to cast a bass fly. Practice lifting your line smoothly. Work on your stroke and your timing. Go for consistently tight casting loops. Your goal should be to drive the fly fifty feet with no more than two false casts.

Then focus on your accuracy. The best way to do this is to replicate the actual bass-fishing challenges you're likely to encounter on the water. If you expect to be casting from the bow seat of a canoe or rowboat, for example, bring a stool or milk crate with you, sit on it so that you're at a right angle to your target as you would be when your watercraft is moving parallel to the shoreline, and practice casting across your body from a low sitting position. If you like to wade in knee-deep water, kneel when you practice casting. If you expect to be prowling a shoreline afoot, practice casting sidearm while squatting or hunching over.

With a little imagination, you can create a virtual shoreline in your backyard. Place a dozen aluminum pie plates in imaginary bass holes—alongside the trunk of your apple tree, beside your bird bath, under the branches of your rhododendron, against your stone wall, or perhaps on the edge of your flower garden. Move from target to target and see how many casts it takes to hit each pie plate.

Keep score, if that appeals to you. Make a game of it, like golf. Give yourself out-of-bounds penalties for snagging branches. You can even compete with your fishing partner. When you master your "course," place your pie plates closer to the bushes or in narrower alleys and move back five feet from your targets to the "expert tees."

PUTTING THE FLY TO WORK

- *The Retrieve.* Old-time bass-bug fishermen were almost unanimous in their insistence that you couldn't retrieve a bug slowly enough. The common rule of thumb in those politically incorrect days was: After your bug hits the water, lay your rod across your lap, light a cigarette, and smoke the entire thing before giving the bug its first twitch. Nonsmokers ate sandwiches.

The theory behind this approach depended on a conception of bass behavior that experience bears out only occasionally. Bass, according to the old-timers, needed to be teased into striking. They'd swim over to investigate whatever plopped onto the water, and then they'd lie there looking at it, waiting for it to make the first move, trying to decide if it was good to eat. If it just fell to the water and swam away, Mr. Bass would shrug and return to his lair.

There is no question that the patient waiting game sometimes works. It's a lot easier to execute when your bug has landed beside a shady deadfall or in a pothole surrounded by lily pads where you just *know* a big bass is lurking. When you're working your way down a shoreline that features one likely target after the other, however, and a particularly bassy cove lies just around the next point, spending several minutes to fish out each cast requires superhuman willpower; in the back of your mind, you suspect you might be wasting precious fishing time that could be better invested in that next hotspot.

Fifty years of bass fishing has given me no convincing evidence that leaving a bug motionless on the water for more than half a minute catches bass that wouldn't take it if it moved more quickly.

To hone your accuracy in the backyard, cast to small targets such as pie plates. Include sidearm casts from a crouching position to replicate actual fishing situations. (Vicki Stiefel photograph)

Say what you want about tournament bass fishermen; they know how to catch fish. Rarely do the pros use the super-slow retrieve with their floating lures. In fact, they generally just chuck it out and chug it back. They vary the speed and rhythm of their retrieve depending on the lure and, I'm sure, a vast array of other variables known only to them but they do tend to keep the thing moving.

If eating a sandwich before giving their lure its first twitch would catch more bass, you can be sure that when prize money is on the line, the professional bass catchers would do it that way.

We tend to impute human characteristics to the fish we hunt. We believe "angered" into striking, that they are susceptible to "teasing" or "tormenting," or that they can be "stubborn" or "cautious." Maybe, maybe not. The fact is that most of the time, bass simply do what their instincts drive them to do to survive: They spawn when the urge is upon them, they seek shelter and comfortable water, they flee from danger—and they eat.

Natural bass foods don't all behave the same way and there's no reason to think that the fish prefer one behavior over another. A grasshopper begins kicking desperately the instant it hits the water. A mouse begins swimming as soon as it splashes down. A moth flutters its wings for a moment before lying still. A frog swims, pauses to look around, then swims some more. An injured or disoriented baitfish churns around the surface. Nearby bass will devour any one of these bits of nourishment with equal enthusiasm.

The message for the bass fisherman is this: By all means, vary the speed and cadence of your retrieve, whether you're casting a floater or a subsurface fly but don't waste a lot of time fishing over water that might be barren. If they don't strike on the first couple of casts, they're either not there or they're not hungry.

I have caught a lot of bass, especially, for some reason, smallmouths, by beginning my retrieve as soon as my fly hits the water and keeping it coming steadily back in a series of forceful twitches and jerks, which Dave Whitlock calls the "panic strip." It works especially well over deep-water bass cover such as reefs, sunken weedbeds, and drowned timber, where you need to grab and hold the attention of fish that have to swim up from the bottom to strike. I have also found the panic strip effective when casting to bass during their spawning season.

One of the advantages of bass bugs is the variety of noises and movements you can impart to them, all the way from subtle vibrations to loud, attention-grabbing pops. Leave it motionless, vibrate it, and let it lie. Make it go *glug* and *ker-ploop*. Try a twitch-pause-twitch retrieve, or vary it by alternating a hard panic strip with a pause. Mix and match. Try them all.

The same principle applies to subsurface flies. Vary the speed and the cadence of the retrieve until the bass tell you what they like best.

Some days one method seems to work better than others but I suspect that most of the time, it makes less difference than many experts claim. A hungry bass will eat. If he's not hungry, it may take more than a tantalizing fly to change his mind. Yes, you might be able to anger or otherwise persuade him into striking, and if you're convinced he's there and he's a big one, it's worth trying. In that case, the fast, steady retrieve is just as likely to induce him to inhale your fly as that agonizingly slow twitch-pause-twitch.

• *The straight line.* Regardless of the kind of movement you give your fly or the speed of your retrieve, always keep your rod tip low and pointing directly at the fly. Manipulate the fly by tugging on the line, not by twitching or jerking the rod itself. Maintaining a straight line down the rod, line and leader all the way to your fly, keeps you in control. A one-inch tug on the line moves the fly one inch. Tug hard and it darts forward. Tug gently and it twitches, wiggles, and vibrates.

Moving the fly by lifting your rod or yanking it sideways creates slack in your line that leaves you out of control and could cost you a hookup. By keeping your rod tip low and the line straight, you are ready for a strike at all times. Should you get a hit but fail to hook up, the strip-strike leaves your fly right there where Mr. Bass can find it and, perhaps, try to eat it a second time.

- *Line management.* Be sure the bottom of the boat between your feet is clear of stray tackle, protruding nuts and bolts, your shoelaces, and all the other odds and ends that lie in wait to snag and tangle your stripped-in line and short-circuit your casts, always at the worst possible time. Float tubes generally come equipped with an apron that spreads across your lap to hold your line. When you're casting from the shore, wading in weedy or brushy water, and even casting from a boat, a stripping basket will prevent foulups and give you control of your loose line.

When retrieving, keep your rod tip low and pointed at the fly. This lets you stay in complete control. (Will Ryan photograph)

Use a stripping basket to prevent line tangles in a boat or when wading. (Will Ryan photograph)

PART V
SALT

CHAPTER TWENTY-SEVEN

SALTWATER LEADERS

— TOM ROSENBAUER —

A saltwater leader can be as simple as a single strand of twenty-pound-test monofilament tied to the fly line with a Nail Knot. The best striped bass fisherman I know uses this method about 90 percent of the time, and he has probably caught more striped bass on a fly, and more big bass, than anyone I know. But he fishes in the surf, where the splash of a heavy leader will never spook fish. In most cases you'll want some taper in your leader to slow down the delivery of your fly and make it land without too much commotion.

Saltwater leaders should range from about six feet long for stripers in the surf or redfish in dirty water to fifteen feet for spooky fish in shallow water. Bonefish guides in Florida sometimes use leaders this long, and I use them regularly for stripers in shallow water. Needless to say, you should shorten your leader for easy casting as the wind picks up—the fish won't be as spooky in riffly water anyway.

If you need to lengthen a saltwater leader, you should lengthen the butt and not the tippet. For instance, let's say you are fishing for redfish on the flats with a seven and one-half-foot leader and you seem to be spooking the fish no matter how carefully you cast. Remove your leader from the line by unslipping the loops and cut the loop off your leader. Tie four or five feet of twenty-five- or thirty-pound monofilament (eyeball the butt of your leader and match it, or go slightly heavier) to your leader with a Surgeon's Knot. Tie a Perfection Loop onto the end of the new piece and re-attach it to the line.

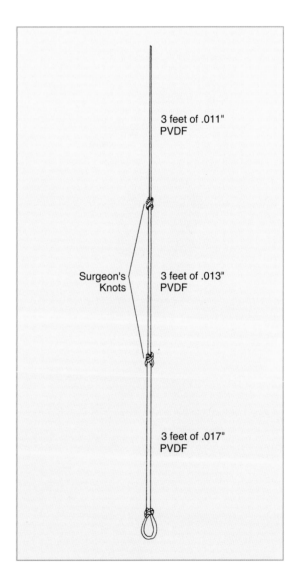

The three sections of this nine-foot knotted leader are joined with Surgeon's Knots.

KNOTLESS LEADERS

For most saltwater species that don't have sharp teeth (stripers, redfish, bonefish, permit, bonito, and false albacore), you can use a factory-made knotless tapered leader made from nylon or PVDF. For bonefish, permit, and redfish, especially where there are either weeds or coral in the water, a knotless tapered leader is recommended by most guides. Knots catch on weeds and ruin your presentation; they catch on coral and, well, ping! When the leader gets too short or too heavy, you can replace it or risk the annoyance of a knot and tie on a new tippet, just as you would for a trout leader.

THREE-KNOT LEADERS

For a simple knotted leader, perfect for striped bass or redfish (or bonefish over sand bottoms), tie a Perfection Loop in a three-foot piece of .0170 PVDF (about twenty-five pounds). Tie this to a three-foot piece of .0130 PVDF (about fifteen pounds) and then add a three-foot piece of .0110 (twelve pounds) for the tippet. The sections should be joined with Surgeon's Knots.

CLASS TIPPETS

By International Game Fishing Association (IGFA) rules, your tippet must be at least fifteen inches long between knots if you want your catch to be eligible for the record books. It's tough to determine if a knotless leader has a level piece of class tippet so most people going for records attach a separate class tippet that has a Bimini Twist in it. Why the Bimini? The weakest link in your leader will probably be the knot where the tippet attaches to the rest of the leader so you want to tie that knot with a doubled section of the weaker strand. This way the overall breaking strength of your entire rig is 100 percent of the breaking strength of the class tippet.

The easiest way to do this is to tie a Bimini Loop onto one end of the tippet and then knot this doubled piece to the butt section of your leader. In the three-knot leader above, for example, you'd tie the doubled twelve-pound-

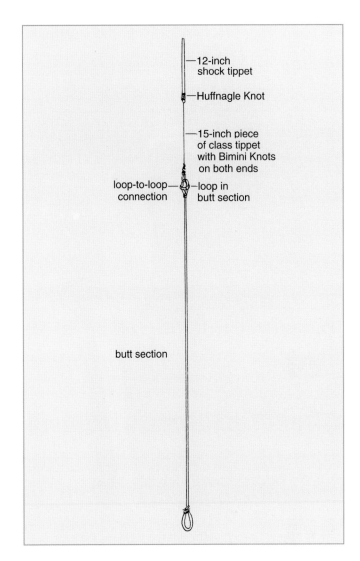

This class tippet with Bimini Twists at both ends is attached to the shock tippet with a Huffnagle Knot and to the butt section of the leader with a Surgeon's Loop.

class tippet to the .0130 section with a Surgeon's Knot. A better way to do it is to tie a Perfection Loop onto the end of the .0130 section. Tie up a bunch of tippets with Bimini Loops on them ahead of time. Put a Bimini in one end of each tippet and then tie a Surgeon's Loop in the doubled section—you will end up with a loop with four strands. These can be rolled around your hand like a leader for storage and kept in a leader wallet or small zip-lock bag until needed. In the heat of fishing, you can slip on a new tippet without tying any knots except for the knot that attaches your fly to the tippet.

Because of their abrasive mouths and sharp gill plates, even small tarpon require a shock tippet on the leader.

A wire shock tippet will keep sharks from biting through your leader.

SHOCK TIPPETS

For fish with moderately sharp teeth or abrasive mouths (such as mackerel, dorado, tarpon, big snook, tuna, and sailfish), you'll need to attach a monofilament shock tippet (PVDF is better than nylon) to the class tippet. These species don't chop through tippet the way sharks or bluefish do; instead their abrasive mouths wear through the tippet over the course of a long battle and you need a big-diameter material to cushion against breakoffs.

A single strand of tippet won't join securely to a piece of fifty- to one hundred-pound test material so you will need to prepare class tippets with Bimini Twist Loops on both ends. One end gets a Surgeon's Loop so it can be looped to the butt section of the leader while the other end is permanently tied to the shock tippet with a Huffnagle Knot. In practice, few people try to tie up shock tippet/class tippet combinations while tarpon are cruising past the boat. These pieces are tied up before a trip, in the calm comfort of your home. Many anglers tie these doubled Bimini sections to a shock tippet, attach a fly to the shock tippet, and store them in a stretcher box that keeps the leader straight. When a fish breaks off or a fly gets ruined, it's a quick step to loop a new class tippet/shock tippet/fly combination to the butt section with a loop-to-loop connection.

WIRE TIPPETS

Sharks, barracuda, wahoo, and bluefish need a wire tippet. I have seen sharks and bluefish bite through eighty-pound-test shock tippet before I have even felt the strike. Some newer forms of nylon-coated wire are very flexible and can be used like regular monofilament.

Braided wire is joined to the class tippet with an Albright Knot and to the fly with a Homer Rhode Loop.

Solid wire needs to have a loop put on each end: One loop goes through the eye of the fly and the other loop attaches to the class tippet with a Clinch Knot or Orvis Knot. This loop is made with a Haywire Twist. Wire tippets should be from four to eight inches long, depending on the size of the fish.

CHAPTER TWENTY-EIGHT

SALTWATER KNOTS

— TOM ROSENBAUER —

ALBRIGHT KNOT

This is a traditional saltwater knot that can be used to join materials that are quite different in diameter or to join two different kinds of materials. It is sometimes recommended for joining backing to fly line (I like a Nail Knot better) or to join a shock tippet to a class tippet (a Huffnagle is much better, though). The only place I use an Albright is to join a piece of braided wire to the tippet. This is one of those knots that must be tied and tightened precisely or it will slip.

1. Bend a loop in the tag end of the heavier leader material or wire, allowing at least four inches of overlap. Pass the lighter material through this loop and pinch it against the heavier material about two inches from the end. You should leave yourself at least three inches of material to work with beyond this point.

2. With smooth turns, wind the smaller material over the doubled section of bigger material, working toward the loop. Make at least twelve turns.

3. Pass the smaller material through the loop on the same side of the loop that it entered.

4. Slowly pull on the standing parts of the lighter material and heavier material (this is one knot that should never be tightened quickly!) and work the coils toward the end of the loop, being careful that they

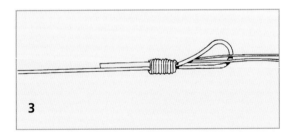

1

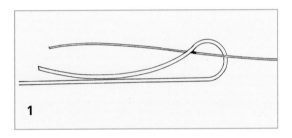

2

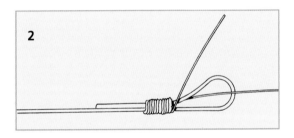

3

don't slip off the end. When the coils are near the end, pull gently on the tag end of the smaller material to snug the coils, then pull gently on the standing part of the lighter material. Keep alternating between pulling on these ends until the knot is tightened neatly against the loop. Now use a pair of pliers or forceps to hold the tag end as you take one last tight turn. Pull hard on the standing part of the light and heavy ends to make sure the knot will not slip. You can't be too careful with this one. Trim the tag ends of the heavy and light materials.

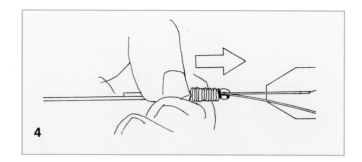

BIMINI TWIST

The Bimini Twist is a unique knot because it is not used to join anything. It is used to form a double strand in a piece of monofilament, and it is a 100-percent knot. Why do you want this?

When you join two pieces of material together, you never get a knot that is completely 100 percent—in other words, if you join a piece of twelve-pound monofilament to sixteen-pound monofilament, the resulting strand will break at the weakest link, the knot, and the strength of that link will be about 11.4 pounds, or 95 percent of the weaker piece. But if you double the twelve-pound section with a Bimini Twist, the weakest link is somewhere in the middle of the twelve-pound section; the breaking strength of the strand will be twelve pounds if there are no nicks or wind knots in the leader.

This becomes important when fishing for the record books, where you want your class tippet (the one you send in to the IGFA when you apply for the record) to break at no more than twelve pounds, but you want every bit of that twelve pounds.

1. IGFA class tippets must have a minimum single-strand section of fifteen inches. I find that I need about six feet of material to start if I am putting a Bimini on one end only; if I am putting a Bimini on both ends of the tippet, I might need ten or twelve feet. Double the strand and put one hand through the loop. The other hand pinches the tippet in the middle of the section. Put at least twenty-five twists

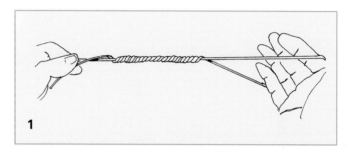

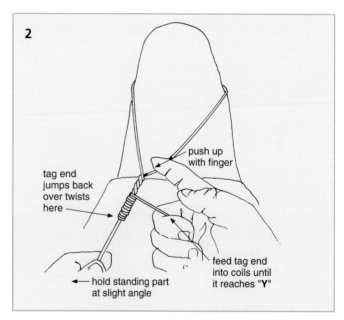

push up with finger

tag end jumps back over twists here

feed tag end into coils until it reaches "Y"

← hold standing part at slight angle

in the tippet by rotating your hand, letting the loop slip over the back of your fingers as you do.

2. Slip the loop over your knee. Hold the standing part of the tippet with one hand. Now grab the tag end with the last three fingers of your other hand and place the forefinger of this same hand at the **Y**

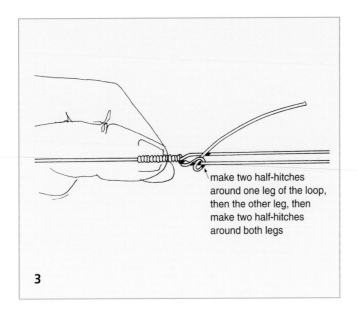

make two half-hitches
around one leg of the loop,
then the other leg, then
make two half-hitches
around both legs

3

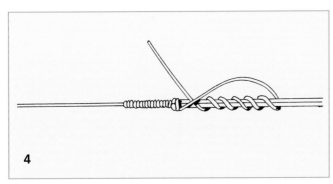

4

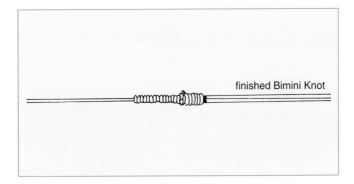

finished Bimini Knot

formed where the loop meets the twists. Now comes the trickiest part: By holding the standing end just a bit off the vertical, and the tag end at about ninety degrees away from the twists, push your finger gently against the fork of the **Y** while slowly releasing the tag end. You want the tag end to roll over the twists, toward your forefinger, in smooth even coils. Getting the twist started is the hardest part—once it starts rolling, it helps to move the hand holding the tag end upward to keep the coils neat. Most experts agree that a Bimini is tied correctly only when the coils are jammed tightly against each other so tightly that it looks like a solid piece. Don't let the coils jump over each other, either; there must be a single tight layer of them all the way to the forefinger. Keep rolling these coils until you reach the fork of the **Y**.

3. Pinch the twisted section to keep it from unraveling. Tie a single half-hitch or overhand knot around one leg of the loop and tighten the knot up against the twists. Repeat with the other leg of the loop. Now you can remove the loop from your knee. At this point, if your tag end is longer than four inches, it's easier to finish the knot if you cut the tag end back. Tie a half-hitch around both legs of the loop and tighten. Tie another one around both legs and tighten.

4. Tie one final half-hitch around both legs but in this case wind five times around both legs of the loop before tightening. You should be working back toward the coils. Tighten by moistening the knot and pulling the tag end up toward the coils. You will have to tighten a bit, work the turns back away from the coils with your fingernail, tighten a bit more, and keep going until the final turns are tight. If you don't back off the turns as you tighten, they won't tighten smoothly. Once the turns are neat and secure, give the tag end a good snugging with a pair of pliers, pulling it toward the closed end of the loop.

HUFFNAGLE KNOT

This is the neatest and most secure way of tying a heavy monofilament shock tippet to a section of class tippet that has been doubled with a Bimini Twist. It is far superior to an Albright Knot for this purpose.

1. Make a double overhand knot in the shock tippet, about two inches from the end of the tippet.

2. Tighten this knot until it forms a figure-eight, but leave both loops open because you will need to pass the class tippet through both of them.

3. Pass the loop at the end of a class tippet (to which you've already tied a Bimini Twist) through the loop of the figure-eight in the shock tippet. The class tippet should first be passed through the loop closest to the end of the tag end of the shock tippet and it should leave the loop through the same side where the tag end exited.

4. Pass the class tippet through the second loop in the figure-eight, again entering the loop on the same side that the standing part of the shock tippet exits.

5. Slide the figure-eight up against the Bimini Twist Knot and tighten it by pulling on both ends of the shock tippet. Trim the tag end of the shock tippet.

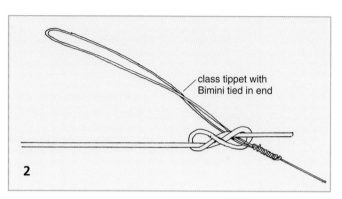

shock tippet

1

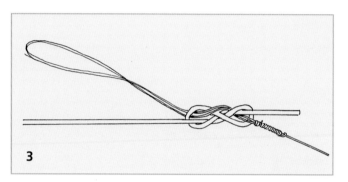

class tippet with
Bimini tied in end

2

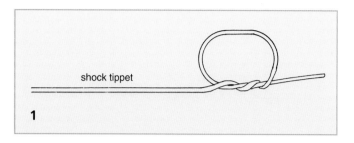

3

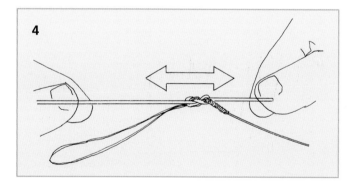

4

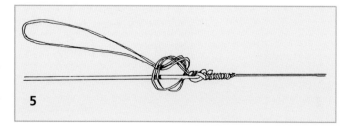

5

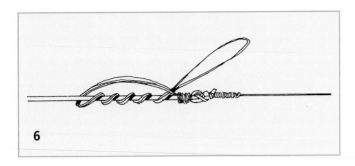

6

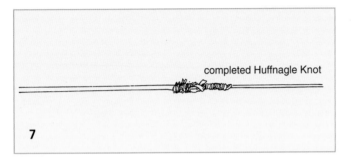

completed Huffnagle Knot

7

6. You will notice that the rest of this knot is the same as finishing a Bimini Twist so if you have mastered that knot, this one will be a snap. Make an overhand knot with the class tippet around the shock tippet. Tighten. Make another overhand knot and tighten.

7. Make a third overhand knot but this time take five turns around the shock tippet, working back toward the figure-eight. Tighten this, like the Bimini Twist, by pulling on the tag end, stroking the coils back toward the standing part of the shock tippet to keep the coils from wrapping over themselves, and repeating until the coils are snug against the rest of the knot. Tighten completely by pulling the tag end toward the class tippet, by pulling on the tag end of the class tippet and the standing part of the shock tippet.

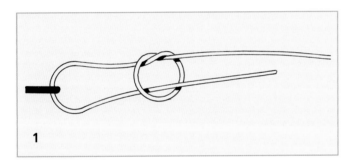

1

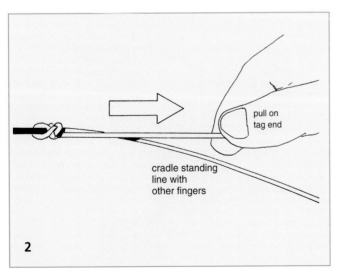

pull on
tag end

cradle standing
line with
other fingers

2

SALTWATER LOOP KNOTS

Because saltwater leaders are usually made from heavy material, tying the fly to the tippet with a loop lets the fly swing freely and gives it more action. Two knots are needed: One for heavy shock tippet (forty- to one hundred-pound monofilament, and plastic-coated wire) and one for standard class tippets (from four to twenty pounds). The Homer Rhode Loop is easy to tie but weak, so it is used on the heavier stuff. The knot tests at only 50 percent but with an eighty-pound shock tippet it will still be stronger than the class tippet by a comfortable margin. The Non-Slip Mono Loop is trickier to tie but it tests at nearly 100 percent, even with one-pound-test material.

HOMER RHODE LOOP

1. Make an overhand knot in the tippet, about six inches from its end. Insert the tag end of the leader through the hook eye.

2. Pass the tag end of the leader back through the overhand knot, making sure that it enters the loop on the same side it exited after you tied the overhand knot.

3. Tighten the overhand knot loosely against the eye of the hook by holding the fly in one hand and both pieces of the leader material in the other hand. Cradle the standing part of the leader with the last two fingers of this hand and pull on the tag end with your thumb and forefinger.

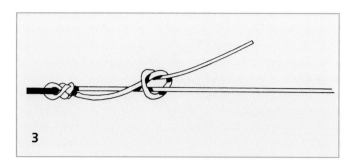

4. Now make another overhand knot with the tag end around the standing part of the leader. Position this knot at the point where you want your loop to end; about three-quarters inch to one inch is the standard size. This knot should be seated tightly against the standing part of the leader.

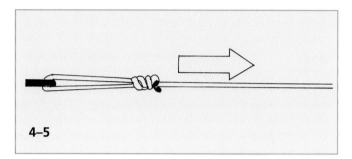

5. Pull on the fly and the standing part of the leader. The first knot will jam up against the second knot. Trim the tag end.

NON-SLIP MONO LOOP

1. Start this knot just as you would a Homer Rhode Loop, by making an overhand knot in the leader before doing anything with the fly. In this case, you should allow about ten inches of tag end. Don't tighten the loop. Pass the tag end of the leader through the hook eye.

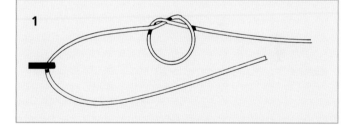

2. Bring the tag end back through the overhand knot, making sure that it enters the loop formed by the overhand knot on the same side as it exited when you tied the overhand. The distance between the fly and the overhand knot determines the size of your loop so work the knot up or down the standing part of the leader until you get the size loop you want.

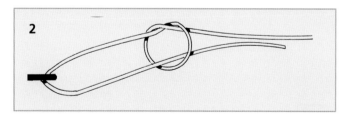

3. Wrap the tag end around the standing part of the leader, just as you would in tying a Clinch Knot. Make six turns for material less than eight-pound test, five turns for

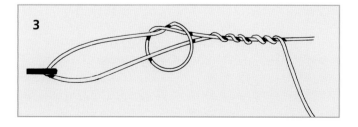

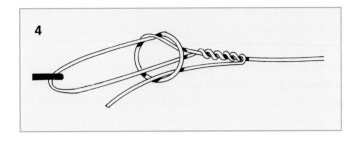

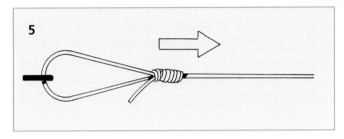

material from eight- to twelve-pound, and four turns for material up to forty-pound. (Use a Homer Rhode Loop for heavier material.)

4. Pass the tag end back through the original overhand knot one final time. Again, it must enter the loop on the same side you have been using.

5. Tighten the knot by first pulling on the tag end until the turns tighten against the overhand. Next pull tightly on the fly and the standing part of the leader to finish the knot. Trim the tag end.

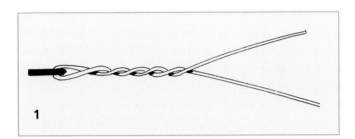

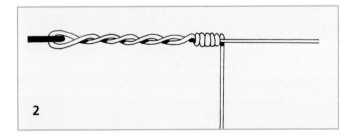

THE HAYWIRE TWIST

1. Pass the wire through the hook eye and bend it back towards the standing part of the wire. Twist the tag end around the standing part of the wire five times.

2. Now make five barrel coils around the standing part of the wire, close together and at ninety degrees to the standing part.

3. Make a handle by bending the tag end of the wire at two places. Crank this handle back and forth until the wire breaks. Never cut the end of a Haywire Twist; the sharp end of the wire can be extremely dangerous.

4. Now make another Haywire Twist in the other end of the wire and attach the tippet to this second loop.

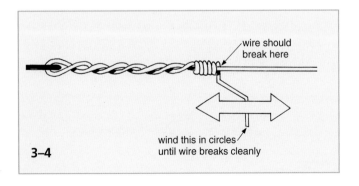

wire should break here

wind this in circles until wire breaks cleanly

CHAPTER TWENTY-NINE

BONEFISH AND PERMIT HABITAT

— JACK SAMSON —

Most bonefish habitat is basically the same: Long stretches of mud, sand, or coral marl flats interspersed with mangrove trees, the bottom sometimes covered with a variety of marine plants. In many places, however—such as Hawaii, Bermuda, and East Africa—bonefish live much of their lives in deep water.

For our purposes, most fly fishermen (and light-tackle anglers) are really only interested in one species of bonefish (*Albula vulpes*), which inhabits the flats of tropical seas worldwide. On some flats, there are deep channels, holes, and depressions within the mangroves where some bonefish may decide to stay even after the tide has gone out. They can be caught in these deep holes and channels with sinking or sink-tip lines and weighted flies, but I, personally, never considered that method very sporting—any more than I do dredging a deep-running fly through a bonefish mud in deep water. I feel that fly fishing for both bonefish and permit should be sight fishing—seeing the fish first, then casting to it. In the Yucatan—and in some places in the Bahamas —there are deep "blue holes," openings into underground caves in limestone. Sometimes—particularly in areas like Espiritu Santo Bay in the Yucatan—bonefish can be found near the surface of these big holes and occasionally they will take a fly.

But most bonefish and permit leave the flats at low tide and head for the deeper water near reefs or into deep channels, only to appear on

the flats again on the incoming tide. Nobody really seems to know exactly where bonefish spawn, although Dick Brown, in his excellent book *Bonefish,* writes:

> But we still do not know where and when the bonefish's spawning takes place and where the earliest stages of its life begins. Researchers offer two theories. One holds that bonefish spawn inshore during high tides, then currents and tides take the eggs offshore. Many weeks later as the larva develops, it returns to the shallows where it metamorphoses into a juvenile fish.

A second theory says that bonefish spawn offshore, in relatively deep water. The larva is then carried inshore to the shallows where it metamorphoses into a juvenile.

Ideal bonefish and permit habitat.

Poling for bonefish in the Yucatan.

I don't know where bonefish spawn any more than the next fisherman. The experts do know, however, where permit spawn.

Every bonefish fly fisherman and every guide I know has his own theories—and they're seldom based on scientific research. But we do observe bonefish behavior. A. J. McClane, longtime fishing editor of *Field & Stream* and the editor of *McClane's New Standard Fishing Encyclopedia,* did a lot of fly fishing and research on bonefish and permit in the Bahamas. He told me he had seen what he considered schools of spawning bonefish on the flats near Deepwater Cay in April and May and that they were performing what he considered a "daisy chain" circling motion—a ritual tarpon do while spawning in shallow water.

I have never seen that happen on the flats but while fishing at the island of Guanaja in the Bay Islands of Honduras one spring with

veteran guide and friend Robert Hyde, we did see something unusual. We came upon a school of about thirty to forty large bonefish (in the eight- to ten-pound category) quietly circling in the clear depths of a lagoon surrounded by mangroves. The lagoon was approximately fifteen to twenty feet deep. Still, the bonefish were not concerned with our boat, which constantly passed above them. They were not interested in our flies but continued in their slow circles. Robert, who was born on Guanaja and whose opinions on bonefish and permit behavior I greatly treasure, said the bonefish were "courtin'." That was proof enough for me that at least *those* bonefish were ready to spawn in inshore water.

I have noticed that bonefish on a grassy flat seem to select their prey more than those over sand. On a grassy flat, bonefish will pick out individual items—such as shrimp and clams—

whereas on a sandy bottom, bonefish do a lot more rooting and seem to be taking whatever they can find.

I have no logical explanation why bonefish and permit seem to prefer certain flats over others. They look exactly the same to me—miles of the same type of bottom. But local guides say certain flats contain lots more of the kind of food these fish prefer. That makes sense. Robert Hyde once told me permit like certain flats better because they have escape routes they know well and can use in emergencies. That also makes a lot of sense.

Bonefish leave signs that they have been feeding on a flat. Permit really don't leave that many signs. Bonefish leave small, cone-shaped holes in the sand or mud where they have been rooting. An expert can tell what sort of prey they have been after. Lots of pyramid-shaped piles of sand or mud indicate there are mantis shrimp or burrowing urchins on the flat. Small bulletlike holes mean there are clams and shrimp on the bottom, and debris mounds show that crabs have been burrowing.

Although it is very hard to see them over a dark, grassy bottom, bonefish feed on grassy bottoms more than anywhere else. There they can find an assortment of prey they want while they find concealment from predators. Their natural camouflage makes them almost impossible to see over grass. If grassy flats are abundant and if that is where the bonefish are, it is important to remember that almost all their prey species have adapted to the grass background and are the same color. Casting flies the same dark shade makes a lot of sense. Bright-colored flies against such a background tend to spook fish rather than attract them. The same can be said for flies over a white, sandy bottom. White or pink flies fished over glaring white sand take a lot more bonefish than dark-colored flies.

The feeding habitat of permit is basically the same as the bonefish—both grassy and sandy flats—but permit tend to feed more in rocky areas because their favorite food—crabs—cling to and live under such structure.

When not on the flats, permit may be found anywhere in deep water. They like to

The late A. J. McClane with a Bahama bonefish.

hover around sunken wrecks because of the preponderance of crabs, shrimp, and lobsters that gather there. Also, they cruise along the face of reefs, looking for crabs and other forms of marine life that live there. Divers have told me they see schools of permit close to reefs whenever they go there. Sometimes schools of permit will be seen in the depths simply floating quietly instead of swimming. That is true of a spot called the Elbow, close to a reef on the southern tip of Turneffe Island in Belize. Big-game fishermen have also told me they have seen schools of permit floating close to the surface of the ocean, quite far from shore.

CHAPTER THIRTY

FEEDING HABITS OF BONEFISH AND PERMIT

— JACK SAMSON —

WHAT BONEFISH EAT

Probably 98 percent of what bonefish eat is what they find on the flats. The other 2 percent, mostly small baitfish, is consumed in the depths.

I learned much from fishing with the late A. J. McClane, who was constantly searching the flats for more knowledge about both bonefish and permit. A. J. told me once that bonefish and permit will both eat lobsters—not only the regular spiny lobster of the region but also the smaller slipper lobster, which has no antennae. A. J. was constantly cutting open the stomachs of bonefish (for research on his encyclopedia) in the Bahamas to determine what they had been eating. He once told me that almost 20 percent of the diet of both bonefish and permit

A big bonefish taken on a Velcro crab fly.

that he had studied in the Bahamas was comprised of mantis shrimp. At the time (the early 1970s), I wasn't that interested in the diet of such fish and so I forgot it—until almost twenty-five years later, when I found mantis shrimp were a major prey food for permit and bonefish in the Yucatan and Belize.

A. J. also told me that bonefish ate other fish on the flats but I was such a novice know-it-all about saltwater fly fishing that I didn't believe him—at least not until his wife, Patti (in the presence of Bing McClelland, A. J., and me), caught a six-pound bonefish at Cat Cay on a spinning rod with a six-inch-long, yellow, floating Zaragosa plug, festooned with three sets of gang hooks.

"Bonefish will eat damn near anything when they're really hungry," he said, grinning at me.

Crabs

Crabs make up a large percentage of what the sleek game fish manage to dig out of the sand and mud. Crabs crawl out of their holes when the tide is out and forage for food on the wet surface of the sand or mud flats. When the tide inundates these flats, the crabs are quickly forced underground. Bonefish smell them under the surface and either root them up with their snouts or suck them from their burrows.

These small crabs vary over much of the world but those in the Bahamas, Florida Keys, and Caribbean are very similar. The common blue crab is found all over this region, as are spider crabs, green reef crabs, the various swimming crabs, fiddler crabs, and stone or mud crabs. Dozens of different hermit crabs are found mostly on the land, after taking over abandoned snail and small conch shells, but some do fall into the water from trees they climb, and some get washed out by tides and are crushed as food by bonefish.

There are all sorts of other crabs that make up the diet of the bonefish, among them the rough-clawed porcelain crab, spotted porcelain crab, purse crab, shamefaced or box crab, common coral crab, gall crab, small reef crab (when it is washed off rocks by waves), and urchin crab.

Mollusks

Of all the critters that bonefish eat, none are as uninteresting to we saltwater fly fishermen as the mollusks: Snails, clams, octopods, and squid. Although we do have a chance of tying flies to imitate the small squid (that is, the Squimp fly), I don't know of any fly imitation of snails, limpets, sea slugs, clams, oysters, or mussels, even though we know bonefish eat all these members of the phylum Mollusca.

Concerning the octopods, I have seen any number of small octopuses under rocks on the flats and am sure bonefish eat the small ones. I would be interested in seeing an imitation of that creature.

Shrimp

But when it comes to the shrimp (*Penaeidae*), we have enough individuals to keep a fly tier busy forever. The flats abound in all sorts of shrimp, from the big predaceous golden mantis and green mantis shrimp to the tiny bumblebee shrimp that is found hiding in weed beds.

Nobody but a marine biologist could name half the shrimp that bonefish feed on. They come in a wide range of sizes, but all can be found from the rocks and coral of the reef across the flats and up to the sandy shore of mangrove islands.

Sand crab, favorite food of the permit.

A small octopus on the flat.

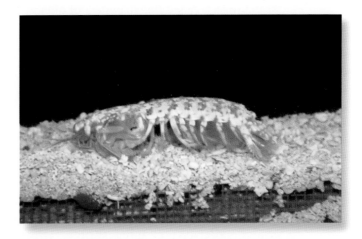
Mantis shrimp. (Carl Richards photograph)

Bonefish love mantis shrimp—and mantis shrimp flies.

The biggest individuals are the white, pink, and brown shrimp, which can grow to a length of six inches. The mantis shrimp—the golden mantis and the green mantis—can be three to four inches long or bigger and have the ability to slice their prey. The green mantis shrimp, for example, is called *thumb buster,* for obvious reasons. It took most of us saltwater fly fishermen a long time to realize that the mantis shrimp are a major portion of the bonefish diet because both are nocturnal feeders on the flats and hide in burrows all day. Most bonefish fly fishermen—of my acquaintance anyway— can be found in the flats resort bar at night rather than wading the tropical flats in the darkness looking for bonefish food.

Among the many medium-sized and small shrimp that bonefish eat are watchman shrimp, snapping shrimp, sponge shrimp, red cleaning shrimp, Pederson's cleaning shrimp, arrow shrimp, grass shrimp, and bumblebee shrimp.

Almost all of these creatures are distinctively shaped, looking much like water insects. They move forward slowly by using their small paddlelike legs but swim backward rapidly in a series of short jerks. Most shrimp feed at night and burrow into the sand or mud, or hide in dense weeds, during the day. Shrimp are not difficult to imitate, and there are dozens of excellent shrimp flies available to the fly fisherman.

Urchins

Of the echinoderms (sea stars, brittle or serpent stars, sea cucumbers, sea urchins, sea lilies, and feather stars), the only one I suspect bonefish eat is the sea urchin—that spiny black creature of the flats. Any number of guides— from the Bahamas to Belize—have told me they have seen both bonefish and permit tip up and "tail" over black sea urchins while eating them. Having had sea urchin spines penetrate wading shoes, I'll believe they eat urchins when I see it!

Rays

When it comes to the rays of the flats (of the order *Rajiormes*), I doubt that bonefish bother the smaller individuals, but I have no proof of that. I do know that the large bonefish sometimes stay quite close to both the common stingray and the eagle ray when churning up the bottom of a flat in search of food. Both bonefish and permit will follow close behind these rays when they are feeding and a veteran guide will caution a fly fisherman to look carefully behind these curious creatures.

The original "Nasty Charlie" bonefish fly invented by Bob Nauheim.

Baitfish

When it comes to the small fish that may become food for bonefish, there are any number of candidates. Perhaps the most famous bonefish fly ever devised was created by Bob Nauheim back in the early 1970s on Andros Island in the Bahamas when he and guide Charlie Smith tied up a fly to imitate the glass minnow. It was first called the Nasty Charlie but later became the Crazy Charlie when carried in the Orvis catalog by Leigh Perkins, Sr. It has scores of imitators and has caught bonefish all over the world.

When hungry, a bonefish will eat any small fish it can catch on the flats. That includes the fry of a whole lot of species. There are millions of tiny grunts, snappers, eels, toadfish, gobies, herrings, anchovies, needlefish, halfbeaks or ballyhoo, hardhead silversides, remoras, jacks, porgies, drums, mojarras, and Lord knows how many more juvenile forms of fish on the flats that a bonefish can catch and eat. The various colors and sizes of the popular Crazy Charlie fly probably imitate 90 percent of them!

Worms

A. J. McClane used to tell me that I wouldn't believe the number of marine worms bonefish

Modern Crazy Charlie bonefish fly.

dig out of the flats. He dug a bunch out of the mud to show me—big, ugly tube worms and a bunch of smaller, almost invisible, transparent worms he had scientific names for but which I have forgotten.

Bonefish root worms out of the mud and sand. These creatures make up a good portion of their diet. The only problem we have as fly fishermen is that it is very difficult to construct a fly to imitate a worm. Ingenious saltwater fly fishermen have done it, however. One of the great examples is the marvelous palolo worm fly tied in the Florida Keys to imitate a worm that hatches each spring and which tarpon take off the surface like trout taking mayflies.

The "Pop" Hill bonefish fly.

Some of the few successful bonefish worm flies I know of are the Mauna Worm Fly imitation tied for bonefish at Christmas Island in the Pacific; a very effective, spare, monobodied fly tied by the late Dr. "Pop" Hill of the Florida Keys, called the Pop Hill Special; and a sparse, thin plastic worm tube fly, called the Tube Fly, tied by Bonnie Beall.

All these flies make an effort to imitate such marine worms as fanworms, mudworms, threadworms, sandworms, tube worms, Christmas tree worms, and long-tentacled worms—a major portion of the bonefish diet.

WHAT PERMIT EAT

Permit—as much as bonefish—are what we call opportunistic feeders. In other words, they will eat just about anything edible they come across on the flats.

With a few exceptions, permit eat the same flats prey over almost all of their range. I am certain the Australian permit eat a different diet from our Atlantic permit, but there is not that much variance in diet between the fish in the Bahamas, the Florida Keys, Jamaica, Puerto Rico, the Yucatan, and Belize.

And although we think we know the diet of permit, we are constantly being surprised. I was fishing with David Westby, one of the great

guides of Belize, a few years ago, and we were leaning against a flats boat eating lunch.

"About all we use for these fish are crab flies," I said. "David, there must be *something* else these guys eat on a regular basis."

"Oh yeah, mon," David said casually. "I see them chasin' mantis shrimp all the time."

"Mantis shrimp?" I asked. "How come I never see them chasing them?"

"Two reasons," David said, simply. "You don't know what a mantis shrimp looks like and they only come out at night."

I stared at him. "Then how come you see them?"

"Mon," David said, "I *born* here."

He was absolutely right, and it was as simple as that.

It took about three months for me to obtain photos of a mantis shrimp and it was probably another three months before David, his brother Lincoln, Will Bauer, and I came up with two versions of the mantis shrimp fly. Both are very effective at taking permit. It is the only fly I know of that permit will *chase* in the shallow water of a flat.

But that experience taught me a lesson and illustrates a point: There are probably a lot of nocturnal creatures on the flats that serve as both bonefish and permit food but we hardly ever see them. The mantis shrimp digs into its burrow when the sun comes up, and both bonefish and permit smell them, root them out, and chase them. The vast majority of saltwater fly fishermen never see these encounters.

Like the bonefish diet, the food of the permit can be divided into groups: Shrimp, crabs, fish, worms, and clams. In the fish category, we can include such critters as the spiny-skinned brittle stars (*Ophiuroodae*) and the common sea urchin (*Echinoidae*). I have never seen permit eat either one but local guides tell me they do.

I have never seen permit crush and eat oysters either but my Australian guide friends tell me the Australian permit (*Trachinotus blochi*) is detested by the local oystermen for this practice and is actually called the oyster-catcher.

Shrimp

In our hemisphere, it is safe to say that the permit feeds on about every species of shrimp there is, from the common shrimp (*Penaeidae*)—which includes the pink, brown, and spotted shrimp—to the more exotic green, golden, and rock mantis shrimp (*Squillidae*). It also eats various members of the snapping shrimp family (*Alpheidae*): The short-clawed sponge shrimp, long-clawed sponge shrimp, banded snapping shrimp, red snapping shrimp, and common snapping shrimp.

And although the various smaller shrimp—such as the arrow shrimp, red-backed cleaning shrimp, bumblebee shrimp, and grass shrimp—average two inches long, they would certainly interest permit.

Crabs

Of the crabs, a permit will eat any it can find—even the big ones. For years I thought permit ate only the small ones (which is why we tie small crab flies) but I was fishing with that excellent guide, Robert Hyde, on the island of Guanaja in Honduras one day and asked him what size crabs were best for our flies. He hefted several of my crab flies—tied on 1/0 and 2/0 stainless steel hooks—then began to push the skiff toward the nearby shore. While I sat in the boat, he rummaged about in the thick mangrove bushes and sea-grape trees.

In a moment he came back with several large, dark red land crabs wrapped in a red bandanna. The biggest was at least six inches wide. Robert broke off its claws and reached for a spinning rod in the stern of the boat. He impaled a 4/0 hook through a hole in one edge of the big crab's shell.

"I'll show you," was all he said.

We had poled the boat along the shore for about twenty minutes before Robert shoved the push-pole into the sand and handed me the spinning rod, the big crab dangling from the tip on twenty-pound mono. He pointed toward the shore.

Will Bauer's Mantis Shrimp fly.

"See those permit?" he asked as I squinted. "Right next to that big log—three of them, right close to the bank."

I finally nodded.

"Throw that crab as close to them as you can," he said.

"You're crazy!" I said. "It'll spook the hell out of them."

"Go ahead," Robert said. "Cast it."

To my credit, I made a great cast—landing the big crab about six to eight feet to the right of the fish. The crab landed in the quiet, shallow water with a big splash. The permit closest to it immediately streaked for the crab and seized it. I set the hook by instinct and the fish was hooked. The other two thrashed away toward deeper water while my hooked permit streaked off to our right, for the depths.

"He took it!" I shouted, raising the rod high over my head.

"Sure, he took it," Robert said calmly. "These big land crabs fall in the water all the time."

It took about ten minutes to bring the approximately twelve-pound permit into the boat—where we released it. I handed the spinning rod back to Robert.

"I'll be damned," I said.

"Permit eat small crabs too," he said, grinning.

The hermit crabs of the species (*paguristes*) are the little critters that take over abandoned conch and snail shells and live on land. They

A big sand crab—but not too big for permit.

climb trees and bushes and frequently fall into the shallow water, where they are eaten by both permit and bonefish.

Permit also like the big, common blue crab (*Portunidae*)—as big as it is—and a whole bunch of the same species of swimming crabs, which we generally call sand crabs. They are also fond of the mud crabs (*Xanthidae*), which include the little black-tipped mud crab and the stone crab—much appreciated by gourmets.

Even the spider crabs (*Majidae*)—as ugly as they are—are eaten by permit. Permit also suck the green reef crab from the crevasses in the coral and enjoy the spotted and rough-clawed porcelain crabs when they find them. There is hardly a crab a permit will not eat.

Fish and Worms

I have been told that permit will eat baitfish in deep water and I am sure that is true. They will also catch small fish on the flats, and any small grunt, toadfish, gobie, snapper, or small eel that fails to spot a feeding permit in time will end up as a meal.

All sorts of marine worms also fall prey to searching permit. Anyone who has seen a big permit feeding on a flat—thrashing about in the shallow water, its huge, black, forked tail waving in the air as it throws mud and sand in all directions—knows it is a fierce feeder. It simply isn't selective. Permit that root in the mud or sand will produce fanworms, mudworms, threadworms, sandworms, big tube worms (*Onuphidae*), and long-tentacled worms.

Both the star and sea urchin—although not fish—interest permit. Permit will also closely follow rays as they churn across a shallow flat and leave a trail of mud and sand in their wake. Cast a fly into the muddy water behind the ray, and permit will think it is a crab disturbed by the digging.

Clams

Trying to categorize all the clams dug up by rooting permit would take a marine biologist all day to chronicle.

On the typical flat, some of them would include the tellins (*Tellinidae*); both the Caribbean and the candy-stick (*Lucinidae*); and the three-ridged, the Pennsylvania, the tiger, and the costate lucines.

Permit do not make the huge muds that bonefish schools do when they bottom feed. Instead, permit leave slight depressions and holes in the bottom. It is a sure sign they have been there.

CHAPTER THIRTY-ONE

FINDING BONEFISH AND PERMIT (AND HOW TO SEE THEM)

— JACK SAMSON —

The habitat of bonefish and permit is virtually the same: Flats inside reefs that are either bordering coastal shores or are inland, and vast shallows dotted with mangrove (*Rhizophora mangle*)-covered islands. Although bonefish and permit sometimes feed in the deep water outside the reefs and perhaps in the deeper channels inland, that does not concern us much as saltwater fly fishermen. We like to be able to see our prey in order to cast flies to it so we are mostly concerned with the shallow-water habitat of both game fish.

This shallow-water habitat can be either somewhat-barren-looking sand, coral-bottom flats, or flats mostly covered by turtle grass (*Thalassia testudinum*). Some minor grasses—such as shoal grass—grow closer to shore but turtle grass is where we find the small fish that make up the daily diet of both bonefish and permit.

And although those glaring white flats may look stark and barren to the casual observer, much of the food sought by bonefish and permit is buried in the soft bottom where it may be rooted out.

Bonefish and permit may feed together on the same flat. On a number of occasions, I have come across schools of feeding bonefish—usually on an incoming or high tide—with several small groups of permit and some singles busily tailing in the shallow water. That doesn't happen often but because they eat the same type of food, it is bound to occur now and then. It is a sight to gladden the heart and speed the pulse of any fly fisherman!

It takes some time to learn how to see bonefish. They are extremely difficult for the beginner to see. Bonefish live in a world of bright, ever-changing backgrounds, in which even a stationary, solid-colored object seems to be

A typical permit flat.

A bonefish suspended over a turtle grass bottom.

A permit over a muddy bottom. Note black dorsal fin and black, **V**-shaped tail.

moving at times. The bonefish is covered with several hundred tiny, mirrorlike, overlapping scales that reflect light in all directions, making the fish almost invisible under most conditions. At first, you have to learn to see the shadow of the fish rather than the fish. Later, as you become accustomed to looking at these fish, you become more adept at seeing them.

Bonefish are quite visible when they tail in shallow water: Their silvery tails reflect flashes of sunlight when they protrude above the surface. The other way they become visible—or at least their presence becomes visible—is when they are moving as a school in shallow water. The surface becomes rippled above them. Guides refer to this as "shaky" or "nervous"

water. Larger single bonefish, or pairs, do not cause such nervous water, but you can sometimes spot them by the **V** shapes they cause on the surface. Of course, the presence of distinctive "muds" indicates schools of deep-feeding bonefish.

Permit are relatively easy to see—compared with bonefish—although, at times, they too are tough to spot. In deeper water, a permit can become almost invisible because its silvery sides also reflect sunlight. The best way to spot this elusive fish is to look for the black, dorsal fin and black, forked tail moving horizontally. Tailing permit are easy to spot because the black, forked tail is highly visible above the surface, even hundreds of yards away. On the other hand, when wind is rippling the surface, schools of small permit can be almost as hard to see as a bonefish school. Permit schools make nervous water the same as bonefish schools but schools of large permit make a disturbance on the surface that can be seen from a long way off.

It constantly amazes me the way experienced guides see both bonefish and permit from a distance. It has taken me years to see and understand what these guides are seeing.

My favorite guides—Robert Hyde in Honduras, Lincoln Westby and "Dubs" Young in Belize, and Gil Drake, Jr. in the Florida Keys—can spot bonefish and permit when there doesn't seem to be anything on the horizon. Robert has taught me one secret: To look at a flat with the thought that any movement at all could be fish. It might be a small school of mullet, it might be a boxfish, it could be a barracuda or a school of small jacks, but at least it is something, and it could be bonefish or permit.

And after a while, you learn to recognize fish other than bonefish and permit by their distinct behavior. A boxfish "flutters" its tail when feeding nose down and scatters drops of water into the air. A lone barracuda may resemble a resting bonefish, but—on closer inspection—its tail waves slowly. A queen triggerfish, tailing on a distant flat, may speed the heart, but the black tail is blunt, not forked, and tends to stay in the air too long, much like a tailing redfish. Individual fish in a school of mullet in shallow

The author makes a perfect cast to several feeding permit—which totally ignore the crab fly, as usual. (Cam Sigler photograph)

water tend to weave about when swimming. A school of jacks disturbs the surface in its own way. It takes time—sometime years—to learn all this!

Seeing undisturbed bonefish in quiet water is unusual. They stand out quite clearly and you wonder why they are so difficult to see under most conditions. It is because they are motionless, nose down, and their dark markings show up against the bottom.

Occasionally there will be a school of bonefish at rest against the rocks on the inside of a reef. They might be all pointed in the same direction—facing into the slight movement of water coming through the rocks and onto the flat from the sea. Their white bellies and dark-barred backs do not blend with the rocky bottom. They seem to be asleep. But cast a fly close to the resting school and the odds are the entire school will churn up the flat and head for deeper water!

Seeing bonefish is one of the most difficult skills to learn. Dick Brown put it well:

The bonefish's camouflage is so effective that it prevents you from catching more than a glimpse of its body, a wisp of its shadow, or the quickest glimmer of its side as its body turns against the sun. If you are going to spot this fish, you have to carry a large inventory of visual patterns with you, and you must constantly scan the flat for every one of them.

Most of the time, seeing a bonefish requires making a positive match with a known bonefish pattern. You learn the different disguises or "looks" a bonefish adopts. Then you scan the water until you lock into one of these disguises long enough to identify it as a fish. But other times you will see a negative cue—a pattern breaker—that is not part of the background. You catch a glimpse of bonefish color, shape, pattern, and movement that says, "There is something here that does not fit."

I have never heard it put better.

CHAPTER THIRTY-TWO

SALTWATER WADING AND POLING, CASTING AND CATCHING

— JACK SAMSON —

It would be wonderful if all of us were able to find flats where we could wade to both bonefish and permit but that is seldom the case. Most bonefish and permit flats have soft, muddy bottoms or are in such remote areas that they must be reached by boat. And that boat—be it your own or one belonging to a friend—is costly. Fortunately for a lot of young, athletic flats fishermen, the kayak has come into its own. Lightweight and relatively inexpensive, one can be carried atop a vehicle and transported to areas that have both bonefish and permit—as well as snook, tarpon, and other flats game fish.

There are flats in the Bahamas and Florida Keys that have hard, sandy bottoms. They can be waded but you must know where they are.

A pair of flats wading boots can be invaluable.

Fly shops such as World Wide Sportsman, Inc., in Islamorada, Florida, can tell the novice where to go to find them. Most fly shops and outfitters, however, would rather recommend a guide who will take fly fishermen—mostly because they know the guides but also because they don't want to be held liable if some novice fly fisherman gets stuck in the mud or drowns on an unknown flat.

Some lodges on the outlying islands in the Bahamas are perfectly happy to point a fly fisherman toward wade-able flats. Needless to say, there are dangers in wading a flat—especially in remote tropical areas. If an angler is not properly equipped with the right footwear, for example, cuts from sharp coral can ruin a day. An ordinary pair of canvas tennis shoes is not enough protection from the spines of sea urchins—those prickly, black invertebrates that dot the bottoms of most flats. The sharp spines will easily penetrate such shoes—as will the toxic spines on tails of rays. There is a real danger of being jabbed by these highly poisonous spines if you are not careful while wading. The spines are not at the tip of the ray's long tail but *on top of the tail at the base—close to the body.*

If you plan to do much flats wading, buy a good pair of thick-soled wading boots with tough uppers. Wear heavy cotton socks to reduce sand blisters. To prevent sand and mud from entering the top of your boots, wear long trousers with heavy elastic bands about the bottoms of the pant legs. Long pants also prevent annoying bites from sea lice in certain areas. Sea lice are not poisonous but can be a real nuisance.

There is also a danger of sores to the feet from sand inside shoes and boots. Heavy socks can help prevent that. Soft bottoms and strong tides can be a dangerous combination, and care must be taken when wading in such conditions. Also, try not to play hooked bonefish or permit in fairly deep water. The splashes from their struggles may attract sharks and large barracuda, and although there is little danger of a barracuda attack, one might accidentally slice your hand or foot while chasing the hooked fish. Sharks are a different proposition. Bull sharks, in particular, have been known to attack wading anglers in thigh- to waist-deep water. Several other varieties of sharks must be watched for as well.

One time, I was digging conchs in a soft bottom in the Bahamas, near Deepwater Cay. I was handing a conch up to my guide in the flats boat when he suddenly shouted and yanked me violently into the boat. Just as he did, a six-foot-long lemon shark streaked into the cloud of mud I had stirred up and circled about violently, searching for the ray it thought had caused all the mud. I hate to think what it might have done to my legs had not the alert guide seen it in time!

I am not trying to frighten anyone away from wading a flat; just use a little common sense. Most flats creatures are far more afraid of you than you are of them and will try to get away when they sight you. I'd suggest, however, that you always wade a flat with a friend—not alone.

BONEFISH AND PERMIT ON THE FLY

Bonefish and permit live in similar habitats and feed on the same prey but they are worlds apart when it comes to the techniques needed to catch them on a fly. Bonefish are not easy to catch on a fly. They are spooky, difficult to see, and smart. Their instincts make them very wary in shallow water, as they are constantly in danger from barracuda and sharks and from ospreys and frigate birds above.

A big nurse shark cruising the flat.

Dark markings on the back of a bonefish taken over a grassy flat.

They have learned to fear anglers, be they in boats or wading. In places where they have been heavily fished, they are extremely difficult to approach, much less hook. Big bonefish—at such spots as Shell Key, near Islamorada, Florida; the flats at North Bimini; the Middle Bight at Andros Island in the Bahamas; and the flats on Turneffe Island—not only spook when they see bonefish flies, they probably know who tied them!

Even in areas where they don't see that many fly fishermen, the bonefish's natural instinct is to flee at the slightest suggestion of danger. I have seen them flee in a shower of

A nice Turneffe flats bonefish.

Yucatan guide holding a boxfish that took a fly.

sheep and will rip through them like silver arrows, cutting one of them in half as though sliced by a razor. Sharks, sometimes quite big ones, will also hunt close to bonefish schools, waiting for careless individuals to stray from the rest. Those sharks, which seem lazy as they weave slowly through the shallows, can move with the speed of light when attacking bonefish. I have lost hooked bonefish to both of these efficient predators.

All of which leaves the bonefish precariously balanced on the sharp edge of danger at all times so it seldom relaxes. It lives in a world where the slightest movement or vibration might mean threat of death.

Because of this, casting to bonefish must be done very carefully. The flash of sunlight on a leader or line can send the individual or school streaking away. The sound of a leader or line hitting the water can alert them. Any sound in a flats boat—a dropped push-pole, a chain striking the bottom of the boat, a dropped rod and reel, almost any sound—can make them wary.

When wading for bones, be very careful not to step on sticks, rocks, or brittle coral. Bonefish will pick up the vibrations and be gone by the time you begin to cast. Brightly colored clothing will spook them. I always wear neutral shirts and hats—preferably tan—when wading. Bright clothing in a boat also will alert them.

I certainly cannot prove it but I swear permit see more than bonefish and are far more wary. We can tell what frightens bonefish. There are times when I have no idea why permit spook. I personally believe they have some sort of extrasensory perception that sometimes makes them simply disappear—not quickly spook but just fade away quietly.

Permit are the most difficult of all flats game fish to cast a fly to. In the first place, they don't often *take* flies—as opposed to bonefish, which seem to like flies at times. When a permit finally takes a fly, it is usually an accident, sort of an afterthought. The only fly I have ever seen a permit deliberately *chase* is the mantis shrimp pattern. My guide friends tell me that's because any mantis shrimp that a permit sees on the flats has just been flushed from a bur-

spray from the shadow of a gull passing overhead. Low-flying cormorants will send them off for deep water in a panic. A pelican diving nearby will often cause them to churn up yards of bottom mud. They have good reason to be jittery: Barracuda in pods will sometimes circle their schools like wolves around a flock of row and is moving very rapidly—in quick spurts. They say the permit is acting by instinct when it chases this fly because it knows a mantis shrimp is only going to be there for a few more seconds before it burrows back into the bottom. Bonefish will chase mantis shrimp the same way.

Bonefish will readily take a fly under the best of conditions. There are also days when they will ignore every one cast at them—because of water temperature, barometric pressure, wind-whipped water, or just plain cantankerousness.

WADING FOR BONEFISH

Let's assume a beginner is wading his first bonefish flat somewhere in the Bahamas. What should he look for? Without a guide to point out fish, the novice will have to begin with the basics.

Bonefish are very difficult to see. Their skin is made up of dense, overlapping, shiny scales—much like tiny mirrors—that reflect light and make the fish almost invisible against any background. If there is bright sunlight, look for the fish's shadows on the bottom. Bonefish may be traveling in large schools, small schools, or even as single fish. Look for erratic movement. Bonefish (and permit) seldom remain still for more than a few seconds. They are constantly searching the bottom for food.

If you detect a shadow that remains still, it is probably a barracuda. It could be one of any number of snappers or grunts but these fish remain close to rocks, sunken logs, or other structure, such as dock pilings. Sometimes needlefish rest on the surface and cast a shadow on the bottom but bonefish do not stay on the surface. Small tarpon are silver and are often found floating immobile in the shallow water of flats but remember: Bonefish hardly ever stay still for more than a few seconds. Snook will lie close to mangrove roots in wait for prey but they too will remain very still for long periods of time.

If you are looking for tailing bonefish, remember that the tail is forked, silver, and—

Fisherman plays a big Yucatan bonefish.

when the fish is feeding nose down—will only wave in the air for a few seconds before the bonefish moves on to feed in another spot.

All this can be discouraging at first but take heart. After a few sightings, you will become used to the differences in these fish.

If the sky is overcast and there is wind blowing, there is almost nothing I can say that will help locate bonefish or permit—unless by a freak chance you spot tailing fish.

If the surface of the flat is calm, watch for surface movement. Fish moving in shallow water will cause a ripple effect on the surface. This condition (unfortunately) can also be caused by any number of other fish—mullet

A large school of bonefish.

A guide getting ready to tail a big bonefish.

If the school of whatever-it-is approaches, stand still if it appears to be approaching. If it seems as if it will pass to the left or right, move *slowly and quietly* in that direction while getting ready to cast.

When it is determined that the fish are bonefish and moving, cast ahead of the school and strip the fly in short jerks as it settles toward the bottom. Try to make only one backcast, then cast the fly. Line in the air can easily spook bonefish or permit, and the fewer the casts, the better.

If the bonefish or permit stop to feed and tail, cast directly at the closest fish (getting as close as possible) and allow the fly to settle to the bottom. In the case of bonefish, begin to strip. For permit, let the fly settle to the bottom and wait for the fish to discover the fly. If a permit ignores the fly, twitch it slightly to get its attention.

Years ago, when most of us began to learn saltwater fly fishing, we would raise the rod tip immediately and strike with the arm when a bonefish or permit picked up a fly. The fact that it worked is a testament to luck more than skill. As we became more experienced, we learned to strike with the free hand (in the case of right-handers, the left hand holding the loose fly line). The strip-strike is a quick jerk of the free hand backward, setting the hook. Then the fly rod may be raised to take up slack line and let the fish run "on the reel." This is very important in saltwater fly fishing because these game fish are fast and strong, and holding on to the line after the strike may well break the tippet.

Once the fish is on, hold the rod high overhead to keep the line as much out of the water as possible and away from obstacles such as mangrove roots, small mangrove trees, floating logs, coral heads, and other potential problems. Let the fish wear itself out against the drag of the reel. Don't put too much pressure on until the fish begins to tire and comes close to the boat (or your feet, if you're wading).

There are a few basic rules about casting to bonefish. Never cast into the center of a bonefish school, whether the fish are tailing or not. They will spook. Avoid false-casting over the

schools, baitfish, small jacks, needlefish, barracuda—all sorts of fish. But at least the surface movement gives the beginner a chance to get ready. When the commotion turns out to be caused by bonefish or permit, it will have been worth the wait.

school. Try to get the fly close to the school or in front of it on the first cast.

When casting to tailing bonefish, try to get the fly close to the side of the school nearest you. If casting to a single tailing bonefish, make sure there are no other fish feeding close to it. Wait until it is head down and tail up, and try to get the fly as close as possible.

When casting to a school of swimming bonefish—or even a single fish—get the fly some distance ahead of the fish and hope they (or it) will pass over your offering. As the fish approach, let the fly settle close to the bottom then begin to strip it in short jerks. If a fish begins to follow it steadily, speed it up a bit. If it continues to follow the fly but will not take it, sometimes letting the fly settle to the bottom will induce a strike.

I am not a big fan of fly fishing for bonefish in deep water, especially when they are on the bottom and creating big "muds" (because I don't consider it as sporting as casting to fish I see). But sometimes they are not feeding on the flats, and a guide will point to the muddy area.

In this case—and if you want to try for them—you should cast over the muddy area, let the fly sink slowly into the depths, then slowly strip the fly through the mud. This is blind casting and, for my money, a dull way to fish, but it does produce strikes. And once in a while a big bonefish will come out of a mud. What was that about even a blind hog finding the occasional acorn?

Finding, seeing, and casting to bonefish—even on a bright, sunny day—is not always easy. On a dull, overcast day—with wind and rain—it can be sheer agony. The bonefish are almost impossible to see, they don't feed and tail much under such conditions, and even if they *were* causing nervous water, no one could see it. On a day like this, even I might hope to find a big mud!

PERMIT ON THE FLATS

There is no mistaking a permit on a flat. If it is tailing, you cannot miss that huge, black tail. If it is swimming, the black dorsal and forked tail

Author with a nice Turneffe Island permit that took a small crab fly.

Small No. 4 hook Stone Crab fly, which works on Turneffe Island permit.

stand out clearly. Casting to swimming permit requires that the fly be cast far ahead of the fish so that it will be close to or on the bottom by the time the permit see it. *Don't start stripping the crab fly*—no matter how loudly the guide yells, "Strip, strip!" A guide who does this does not know much about permit fly fishing—either that or it is just perfectly understandable panic on his part.

A crab fly—the only acceptable fly for permit (besides the mantis shrimp fly)—should be left to rest on the bottom as the permit approaches it. Permit take live crabs on the bottom. If the permit begins to swim by the

Guide tails a big permit in Ascencion Bay, Yucatan.

Will Bauer releases a nice Belize permit.

immobile crab fly, the fly could be given a few slight twitches but not more than an inch each time. Permit will sometimes turn and take the crab fly. Eighty times out of one hundred, they will totally ignore the crab fly—because that is what permit *do*. Permit fly fishing is the most frustrating fly-fishing sport in the world! Catching Atlantic salmon on a fly is a lead-pipe cinch compared with permit and salmon are

difficult to take on a fly. But that is why we fly fish for permit.

As Al McClane used to say, "If they took flies every day, we'd never fish for them."

Those of us who have fly fished for permit over the years consider only those fish caught in shallow water, on the flats, as *legitimately* or fairly caught permit. There are all sorts of reports of permit caught on a fly that don't fall into that category. For instance, I do not consider catching permit over wrecks—by jigging a glistening, Mylar-type streamer fly deep in the midst of chum—catching a permit on a fly. Nor do I condone some other methods such as chumming with small live crabs or dead minnows thrown into deep holes or channels, and then stripping crab flies deep in the chum.

That is why I am not enamored with stripping flies through muds for bonefish. Fly fishing for both bonefish and permit should be sight fishing—casting flies at fish we can *see*.

LANDING FISH

It is preferable to use a long-handled landing net to scoop up bonefish while fishing from a boat. While wading, you simply have to use your hands and hope for the best. Bonefish are sleek and slippery but the best grip is just before the tail. Many experienced fly fishermen simply slide a hand beneath the belly and gently lift the fish.

Landing a permit is always a problem. It never really gives up; it makes sudden, strong runs, even when it reaches the boat or the legs of the wader. But if it comes within arm's reach, the narrow spot just ahead of the forked tail is the best place to grab it . . . and *hang on!* A big permit will put up a battle even after being grabbed.

While we are on the subject of grabbing bonefish and permit, why not release all your fish? Most serious fly fishermen do. Even if you think you have a world record, you can photograph it, weigh it, and measure it, and the International Game Fish Association (IGFA) will take your word for it on a world-record application if you have the weight (taken on an IGFA-certified scale) and a photo. Send your scales to the IGFA, 300 Gulf Stream Way, Dania Beach, FL 33004. There is a nominal charge.

As far as how to measure: The girth of the fish should be measured and that number squared. The girth is measured just ahead of the dorsal fin. That number is then multiplied by the length, measured from the tip of the nose to the base of the V in the fork of the tail. That number is then divided by eight hundred. The result should give you the weight. Taxidermists are so good today that they can make you an exact duplicate cast of that record fish.

CASTING FROM A BOAT

Casting from a boat gives you the advantage of height and better vision. (Given a choice, though, I'd rather wade to both bonefish and permit. I have all that solid ground to stand on when I'm wading and I can present a better silhouette against the sky background than in a boat.) Most guides would prefer you stay in the boat, probably because they feel they have better control over the situation, and they certainly can see the prey better from their elevated position. The trouble is that not all guides know how to position a boat to the fly fisherman's best advantage, and when they don't align the boat for a good cast, it is very difficult to present a fly properly. There is also a good chance of accidentally hooking the guide on the backcast.

Experienced professional guides immediately jam the tip of the push-pole into the bottom and swing the bow of the boat so the fly fisherman has nothing behind him to snag the fly. These veteran guides will also see bonefish or permit before the angler does and can give directions that will make it much easier for the angler to spot and cast to the quarry.

Distance and angle from the fly fisherman are vitally important in this sport when seconds count. "Forty feet at eleven o'clock" would be an ideal observation on the part of a good guide—when that is where the fish is. Unfortunately, most bonefish or permit are more likely to be eighty feet away—and moving fast!

Measuring a permit prior to release.

If a fly fisherman can cast easily to fifty to sixty feet, he should have no trouble reaching bonefish—and some permit. Those who can cast eighty to one hundred feet are in the minority. I know some fly fishermen who can cast an entire ninety-foot fly line outside the rod tip but they are few and far between, and even those experts cannot always do it while casting into the wind. Add a few other factors—a rocking boat, gusting winds, the fly line blowing about the deck around your feet—and the problem becomes compounded.

A stripping basket sometimes helps in keeping fly line unimpeded but I find them uncomfortable to wear. Keeping a plastic wastebasket at your feet and piling loose line in it is one solution but the wastebasket keeps getting in the way. If you're standing on the casting platform on the bow of a flats boat, letting the loose line pile up there works fine unless there is a strong wind—in which case the line can blow overboard and cause all sorts of problems. On windy days, I strip my loose line back into the bottom of the boat after making absolutely sure there are no protrusions there—such as cleats, nails, or loose tackle—to snag the line. On windy days, it is probably smarter to keep the line on the reel until needed but it always seems fish show up suddenly, and you don't have time to strip

Playing an Ascencion Bay bonefish.

Casting to bonefish at Guanaja, Honduras.

Being able to see bonefish and permit a distance away from the boat gives a saltwater fly fisherman a great advantage. I know veteran flats fishermen who regularly see fish before their guides do. A good, wide-brimmed hat helps greatly or a cap with a long bill. The underside of the cap bill should be a dark color to cut down on glare. Polarized glasses cut down on surface glare and are a must if you are to see fish against a varied background.

The direction of the wind is everything in casting a fly to these wary flats fish. Most of us are right-handed, and wind blowing from our right can be a real problem. The same is true in reverse for left-handed casters. And even the "experts" have problems with wind direction. The late, great Lee Wulff once told me he had a foolproof way to tell whether he had gone to heaven or hell.

"When I wake up and the wind is blowing toward my right shoulder, I'll know immediately," he said wryly.

I hope, where he is now, the wind is always blowing from his left.

There are those—like some of my tarpon guide friends who have spent a lifetime on the windy flats—who can hurl a big fly right into the teeth of a strong wind or backhand a big tarpon fly nearly one hundred feet with a 12-weight rod. I am not one of them nor are most fly fishermen I know.

It may be easier to control a hooked bonefish or permit from a boat than while wading because of the increased height and better visibility to see such obstacles as mangrove stalks, mangrove roots, coral outcroppings, and floating debris. But you sometimes sacrifice firm footing for height. I like to step down from the casting platform after hooking a fish and fight it while standing on the bottom deck of the boat.

While standing on the casting platform and waiting to spot bonefish or permit, hold the fly in your noncasting hand. Don't let it trail in the water close to the boat. It is likely to pick up small bits of debris that way (weed, grass, or leaves), or your fly may be neatly cut off by a small barracuda just about the time you spot a feeding permit.

that line off the reel in time. That is one reason I like to wade and let the line float behind me on the surface.

A lot of veteran saltwater fly fishermen go barefoot while standing on the forward casting platform. This is so they can feel the loose fly line beneath their feet and won't be standing on it when they cast. You always take a chance of getting sunburned feet that way and, personally, I find standing for hours in bare feet tends to make the arches ache and the legs cramp. I'd rather wear a good boat shoe with arch supports and gamble that I won't stand on the line.

CHAPTER THIRTY-THREE

FISHING DIFFERENT TYPES OF FLIES FOR STRIPERS AND BLUEFISH

— LOU TABORY —

Stripers and bluefish feed on many foods, with active baitfish such as sand eels, silversides, anchovies, and big-sided baits like herring and menhaden making up a good portion of the menu. I'll cover specific patterns and baits later but this is a good place to discuss basic fly types.

Although some flies copy certain baits, many are attractor flies that look like several food sources rather than one type of bait. Many attractor patterns simulate baitfish but might also look like a worm or an eel to the fish. Most attractors have flowing materials; this gives them movement even when they drift motionless in the water. I like flies with active materials because they look alive and they have great movement when a pulsating retrieve is employed.

ACTIVE MATERIALS

Flies made with active materials such as saddle hackle, marabou, and ostrich herl work with many different retrieves. In calm water, a fly with a spun deer hair head and active materials in the wing works well, particularly in low light. Fished with a clear-tipped line and long pulls, the fly leaves a wake, dips down, then bobs back to the surface like a crippled baitfish. This fly can also be effective at night when fished with a slow, crawling retrieve.

Flies with spun deer hair heads are also effective when used with a fast-sinking line because they keep nosing up toward the sur-

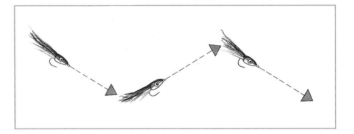

Fishing with fast sinking line will allow a buoyant fly to rise up toward the surface after each strip.

face. This up-and-down motion again makes the fly resemble a crippled baitfish. Make medium to long pulls, with a long pause between each, to let the fly wiggle, nose up, toward the surface. Work bigger flies that suggest herring or menhaden in the same manner. Most of the time I fish bigger flies on a sinking line, working them fast with long, hard pulls to make them bolt.

Letting flies with active materials move with the water's flow is another deadly tactic. Try letting the fly swing with the current, adding short pulls without bringing in any line. In strong currents, a fly that drifts with the flow like this can sometimes bring fish up from the bottom. In some moving water, there are times when letting a fly drift with no retrieve is the only effective way to present it. Dead drifting—getting the fly to swing and turn up current on a tight line—is also very effective.

Another deadly technique is to fish small to midsized active flies at different speeds with an

Several flies with active materials.

Small epoxy flies have little action, but can be extremely effective when they are fished correctly.

intermediate fly line. This also works with small to midsized epoxy flies. Some small flies have little action; they look very lifelike but their only movement is what you give to them. Sometimes small, bright flies are effective when fished with a fast, darting action. Epoxy flies look stiff in the water; they're most effec-

tive when moving because they look alive. They can, however, also produce strikes when drifted below a school of baitfish because they look like dead bait sinking to the bottom. Big bass often cruise below schools of feeding bluefish, picking up the pieces, so you're just as likely to hook a striper as you are a blue.

POPPERS

Topwater fishing for bluefish is fun and exciting. Getting the popper to generate a lot of noise and commotion is the key. A fast-moving bug is very effective on blues, particularly in rough or choppy water when a fly might become lost in the surface commotion. Topwater bugs are most effective in calm water or when a slight wind chop highlights the splash they make. On calm water, in low light, pop a big bug slowly, then let it sit for several seconds before moving it. Smaller bugs can also be effective in calm water when retrieved with a steady *pop-pop-pop* motion.

WEIGHTED FLIES

The Clouser Minnow is a very popular weighted fly pattern. The lighter ones are especially good flies for beginners, although some have eyes that weigh more than one-quarter ounce. These heavy flies are hard to cast, do not suspend in the water column, and can be difficult to use. Heavily weighted flies can also damage fly rods if they strike the rod during casting.

Still, weighted flies are effective because they hop like bucktail jigs. When retrieving a weighted fly, use hard, short pulls with a slight pause between each. Try different speeds and pull lengths; the longer the pause, the bigger the hop. Too long a pause will cause missed strikes because the fish will take the fly on the drop and you won't feel the hit.

Several different types of surface poppers.

BOTTOM FLIES

Two fishing methods work well when you're casting a crab, shrimp, or sand eel fly to a sighted striper in shallow water. One is to allow the fly to sink, then wait for the fish to attack it. After presenting the fly, let it settle; a fish may take it as it drops or settles on the bottom. If a fly moves too much, it can spook a fish. The other method is to let the fly sink, then hop it along the bottom when the fish approaches. At times one hop can be very effective; again, too many moves can scare off fish, particularly bigger stripers.

A weighted Clouser.

CHAPTER THIRTY-FOUR

SPECIAL TYPES OF WATER AND HOW TO FISH THEM FOR STRIPERS AND BLUEFISH

— LOU TABORY —

There are a variety of different water types to fish. Following are some of the most productive and most common fishing techniques for some of my favorite fishing waters.

FISHING SHALLOW FLOWING WATER FROM A BOAT

Drifting in a boat is an effective way to fish three to ten feet of fast-moving water. Big flats hold large numbers of fish that feed as the falling tide moves baitfish from their protected holding areas. As the water level drops, gamefish move slowly downcurrent with the

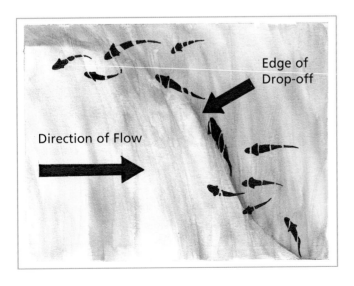

The edges of flats are good places to find feeding fish, especially on the last part of outgoing tide.

tide, feeding as they move off the flat into deeper holding areas. Run the boat away from the location you plan to fish, ease up into the shallow area, and begin drifting and casting. Pick spots with a good current and cast at different angles to the flow. I usually use a fast-sinking line but an intermediate will also work. Move the fly quickly, with long, quick pulls. My favorite patterns are a chunky white Deceiver and a heavily dressed olive Snake Fly. If the shallows are large, you must first find the fish, then keep drifting the same location until the fish move off with the tide. Look for the subtle rip lines that indicate a slight drop-off. Fish will hold behind the bars in the depressions, waiting for food to move off the flat. Cast above the rip lines, let the line settle, and begin retrieving so the fly flows over the bar, swimming through the hole at an angle. Cover as much water as possible because the fish might be moving quickly. They might hold for a short time but they're usually on the move, hitting the baitfish quickly as the water level drops. Fish will quicken their pace near the end of the tide as they don't want to be trapped in the shallows. You should also watch the end of the tide, particularly in big-tide areas, to avoid being trapped yourself. Some places in big-tide areas will drain out quickly, leaving you high and dry.

WADING THE EDGES

If you have a shallow-draft boat, carry waders and fish along the edges of flats at the bottom

High rocky cliffs like these often hold fish, particularly when there is white water rolling up against them.

of the tide or walk out to the edges from shore. These areas hold fish in low light, although they're also good locations for sighting fish when the sun is overhead. There might be hot sight fishing in places where the flats are exposed at low tide and along the edges when they begin to dry up. Walk along the flat, staying an easy cast from the edge. Look for fish feeding up on the flat while schools of sand eels are trying to vacate the shallows. I've seen large schools of small stripers feeding like trout as they sipped sand eels trapped on a flat. Stripers will also hold along the edges and pick up small baitfish as they spill into the deeper water over the edge.

FISHING ROCKY CLIFFS

Wave action around structure creates ideal feeding conditions, particularly for stripers.

Bluefish will venture along some cliff sections, usually in deep-water areas if there isn't too much white water. What makes fishing along cliffs unique is the way the fish feed in a location that seems uninhabitable. Coastal sections of Rhode Island, Massachusetts, and much of Maine have rocky shorelines that hold feeding fish right at your feet.

Some words of caution are necessary before you venture out on rocky cliffs. Never climb down if you'll need to climb back up to avoid breaking waves. Keep away from slippery rocks that angle into the water. Always watch the sea for rogue waves and move well back from the edge whenever you're changing flies. Watch the spot you plan to fish from for at least five minutes before venturing out. Dangerous times are during big seas and at night. My advice is to fish cliffs only in daylight. Common sense will keep you from getting into trouble. If you

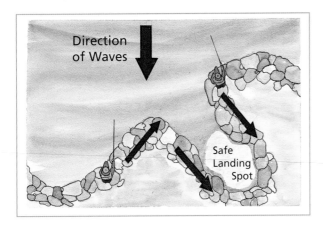

When the surf is large, look for safe places to land played-out fish. A channel, or large crack in the rocks, is an ideal spot.

This is a typical size striper from the cliffs.

Look for places with cracks and cuts for landing fish.

don't take chances, cliff fishing is safer than getting in a bathtub.

The best time to learn cliff fishing is in good light, at high tide, with light, two- to three-foot seas. Select a section of cliffs that has good footing, with places to land fish. Look for long cracks in the rocks that extend well back from the heavy surf; these alleys are ideal places for landing fish. The lee sides of points are also safe landing locations. When the waves are big, choose only the fishing locations with good, safe landing spots that you can lead fish into and land them safely.

Most cliffs have deep water right next to the rocks. You can expect to find fish in all the deep pockets but the best locations are those where billows of white water flow off the rocks into darker pockets of deeper water. These won't look very significant in small surf; in big seas of five to eight feet, though, you might not be able to fish them unless there's a high safe perch close by.

Working the Flow

Cast as the white water flows back into the sea, letting the flow sweep your line and fly into the deeper water. Keep casting, letting the white water carry the fly to the outer edges of the white water. You must keep working the water so the fly flows out and holds at the end of the flow. The white water will dissipate at

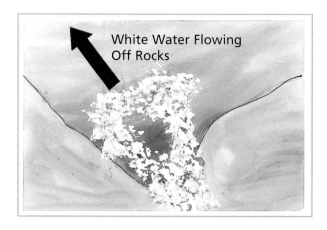

White Water Flowing Off Rocks

When fishing along rocky cliffs, look for places where the waves form billows of white water that flow into deeper water.

Fighting and landing fish from cliffs can be challenging.

the flow's end: This is the section of water to keep fishing.

If the waves are small, you can walk along and fish each little pocket, working the wave action around the structure. For smaller surf, an intermediate line is ideal when the fish are up in the water column feeding along the edges of the rocks. In big surf, a fast-sinking line will help get the fly down and will track better in the heavy flow. You can also use a fast-sinking line in small surf to work the deeper holes when the fish aren't feeding up in the water column.

Landing Fish

Landing fish along cliffs is challenging. You must be patient and try to finesse the fish, not outmuscle them. Usually fish don't run; instead, they sound, using structure to hide. If a fish gets around structure, raise your rod up high, putting a full bend in it. Such a full bend puts only slight pressure on the tippet. If the tippet touches the sharp structure with only light pressure, there is less chance of breaking off the fish.

Keep slight pressure on the fish and let the wave action work it away from the structure. Wait the fish out. Many times the fish will swim free after several minutes. With a big fish, you must hope that it swims into open

Keep the rod high, and with a full bend, if a fish gets behind structure.

water when it emerges from the structure. To improve your chances of landing fish, use bigger tackle—10-weights, twenty-pound tippets—but expect to lose most of the bigger fish anyway. When releasing fish, walk to a safe spot and slip them into a calm section of water. Because of the wave action, water along cliffs is rich with oxygen and fish generally revive quickly.

Mixed stripers and blues, feeding just outside the wash.

If you are casting into breaking fish with no success, try working the fly under the thick school of bait.

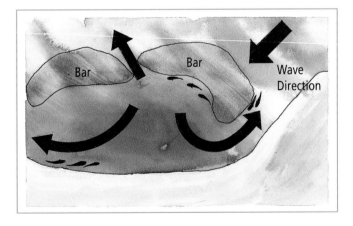

An ocean hole usually has a shallow outer bar or several bars that form a deep pocket next to the beach. Waves rolling over the bars form flows inside the hole that make feeding easier for the fish.

OPEN OCEAN BEACHES

Fishing rolling surf is not for the beginner unless the sea is small. The best time to learn how to fish a steep beach is when waves are smaller than two feet. The waves won't have knockdown power and all the water is fishable. In light surf an intermediate fly line is better for the beginner and it's the ideal line for fishing in low light or at night. I prefer a fast-sinking line, a two hundred and fifty- to three hundred-grain Depth Charge when fishing in the daytime. This line is effective when you need to get below thick schools of baitfish. In the fall, bass and blues will frequently drive large schools of juvenile herring and menhaden onto the beach. At times you must fish the fly below these schools of bait to have success. If you encounter thick bait when using an intermediate line, be sure to let the line sink for at least a ten-count to get the fly down.

How to Read a Beach

Deeper sections along a beach will have steep slopes right at the shoreline. Look for walls of sand, some four to five feet high, on the dry section of the beach. These walls mark the deeper holes and holding water near the shore. Many times the walls will be near a point or a bar that runs at an angle from the shoreline projecting into the sea. Fish and bait collect along these areas, holding in the deeper sections. Two hours on either side of high water is the most productive time to fish most ocean beaches. If you're fishing the bigger, deeper holes—some the size of many football fields—then all tides can be productive. When the surf is big, fly fishing is easier in the bigger holes during the lower phase of the tide.

Fish Close

When the surf is small, blind cast along the beach to cover as much water as possible. Concentrate on the edge where the waves are rolling along the beach. In small surf, I like to

Finding bait such as this along a beach means there is a good supply of food. The fishing should be hot.

A fish takes a fly right in the wash. When the surf is small and the fish are close, you'll have greater success with a short line.

The wash flowing down a beach creates a perfect feeding environment for both stripers and bluefish.

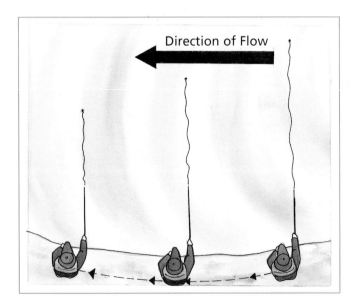

Direction of Flow

Moving with the flow, as you retrieve, will help you keep the fly in the strike zone for a much longer period of time.

cast quartering along the beach, working the edge of the white water. Fish feed right in, or just outside, the white water. The rolling water confuses the bait and permits easy feeding for both bass and blues. Even big fish will feed right next to the beach; this is an ideal opportunity to take a good-sized fish on fly tackle with only a short cast.

Last year I spotted several big fish cruising just outside the wash. I quickly walked down the beach and made a cast. Two fish turned and followed the fly, and one of them took. As the fish ran, my fly line knotted momentarily at the first guide, and the tippet parted with a "crack." It would have been the best surf fish I had taken in several years. Big fish have a knack for escaping by the simplest means.

Along ocean beaches you will, at times, encounter strong flows from wave action. Points, as well as different sections of the hole, will have water that is difficult to fish because the fly line is constantly being pushed away from the good holding water. In some cases the only way to present the fly in the best holding water and maintain a tight line is to move with the flow. Keeping the line perpendicular to the shoreline is the key to fishing the fly in the most productive water. After casting, walk at the same speed as the moving water along the beach, retrieving as you walk. This technique will help keep the line and fly from being swept onto the beach by both the flow and the waves.

Keep moving until you find fish. At times there will be concentrations of fish in a few spots along the beach. If you fish only one small section of the beach, you might believe there are no fish there. If the fish are moving, try to keep pace with them as they flow along the shoreline. Watch what other anglers are doing; this will help you determine how the fish are acting. Keep watching the surf line and just beyond.

Fish the Points

Work flowing water around points. The edges on either side of a point are always hot spots.

Points that protrude at an angle to the beach can be ideal fishing locations. Fish the flowing water along the bar's inside edge.

Cast up onto the point and let the fly flow into the deeper water along the edge. At times the shallow water right on the point is good; fish will feed right in the first wave. In small surf, keep retrieving if the fly doesn't have enough movement from the flow. If you feel the fly moving at a good pace, wait until it settles into the deeper water before retrieving. This water will be tough to fish if the waves are more than four feet high, and impossible in six- to eight-foot waves.

Any bar that runs from the beach into deeper water might have fish holding, usually along the inside edge. Watch the white water that rolls over the bar. If it spills across the bar and disappears, there's a hole behind the bar. Stand on the bar and cast into the white water, letting the fly flow with the white water so it swings into the hole. Fish should take as the fly flows into the drop-off. Once the fly settles into

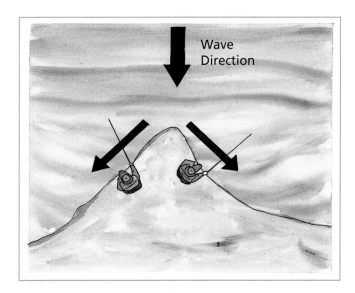

Along ocean beaches, both sides of a point can hold fish unless the waves create too much flow. Let the fly swing with the flow.

Lou Tabory displays a big bluefish that was blitzing the beach along the southern coast of Maine.

This is the backside of a bar on an ocean beach at low tide. Some bars might have a five- to six-foot drop-off behind the bar.

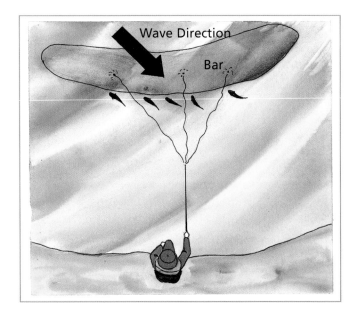

Cast onto the bar and work the fly so it flows with the white water into the pockets on the inside.

the hole, retrieve it slowly with short pulls. If that doesn't produce, try moving the fly quickly. Fish will take the fly aggressively in flowing white water and are seldom picky about patterns.

Bars that run parallel to the shoreline offer a similar fishing situation. With the bar straight out from shore, cast straight into the white water and bring the fly back toward you. The flow will be moving toward you, making a fast retrieve, at times, necessary to maintain contact with the fly. This can be tricky unless you can retrieve faster than the moving water, and are ready to retrieve as soon as the fly lands.

Use Waves to Land the Fish

Landing a fish of more than ten pounds in even moderate surf takes some skill. When it's in rolling water that surges up and down the beach, a fish will feel much heavier than it is. Fish use this surging water to their advantage. To land a fish in the wash, you must turn it so its nose is facing the beach. Then punch the fish, nose first, through the wave, and hold the fish from getting back into the wave as it flows down the slope. If the fish remains sideways to the waves, landing is difficult. It might take several tries to accomplish but be patient and remember that too much pressure will pop the leader. With a big fish, you might walk up and down the slope half a dozen times before you get it inside the first wave. Once the fish is inside that first wave, the next wave should put it high and dry. After hooking a fish, be sure to back up the beach so you're above the rolling waves.

Conditions are ideal for fly fishing when the surf along the steep ocean beaches is less than three feet. An increase of one foot in wave size increases the fishing difficulty by three times. Beaches with a longer, flatter slope are tough to fish in waves more than two feet high, unless you don't mind getting wet and getting knocked around by the surf. When the ocean beaches get big, move to more sheltered water; don't fight tough conditions.

SIGHT FISHING

One of the most difficult yet most exciting types of fly fishing is casting to a sighted fish in shallow water. You must spot a fish, calculate its speed and the water's depth and flow, then cast the fly quickly so it settles into the fish's view before the fish sees you.

Being able to spot fish quickly is the first concern. A group of fish usually shows up well over a light bottom but singles and pairs can be tough unless the water is very shallow. The keys are to look for movement and to look for the shadow below the fish. Once you learn to see moving shadows, spotting fish becomes easier. Being in a stationary position, either wading or fishing from an anchored boat, will help you see movement. If you're in a drifting boat, you're moving too and everything seems to have motion. Unless you're fishing with a guide who can spot fish for you, sight casting from a stationary position makes spotting fish easier.

Casting to the Fish

Wading is also an advantage because you can get closer to the fish. Spotting fish is easier from the height of a boat but the fish can also see you much better, and the boat makes noise. When you're sight fishing from a boat, you'll often need to make longer casts to avoid spooking the fish. A quiet wader can usually slip to within twenty-five or thirty feet of a fish.

Most sight casting is done at distances of thirty to sixty feet. The secrets of good sight casting are speed and accuracy. Spotting the fish at a good distance helps as it gives you time to set up. Most good sight-fishing anglers follow a routine to help the cast and presentation go smoothly: Start with about ten to fifteen feet of fly line outside the rod tip. Hold the fly in your noncasting hand. Now grip the fly line with the first and second fingers of your casting hand, holding it away from the rod. Pinching the fly line to the rod makes it difficult to pick up the line. When you're ready to cast, throw a forward loop, which should pull the fly from your hand. Rather than dropping the fly—it might end up in your leg—let the

Use the wave action along the beach to help land fish.

When landing a bluefish or striper on a steep beach, you must turn the fish and punch it headfirst through the inside wave.

Stripers will hold and feed in very shallow, clear water in the daytime.

Fish like this nice-sized striped bass might be feeding right in the wash, even in broad daylight.

When trying to spot fish in shallow water, look for the fish's shadow; then you'll be able to see the actual fish.

forward motion of the line take it from your hand. As the fly leaves your noncasting hand, reach over and grab the line between the two fingers of your casting hand and make a backcast. If you have enough line speed, shoot some line and decide if you can cast to the fish. Most anglers should make one false cast before casting to the fish. This gives you time to think and helps smooth out the cast. If the fish is more than forty feet away, you'll probably need the extra false cast.

Never rush the cast. Too many anglers try to hurry and miss opportunities because of it. Go at a comfortable pace and you'll get the fly to enough fish.

Either a floating, clear-tip, or full-clear intermediate fly line will work. Most anglers prefer a floating or clear-tip line because they can judge the distance between the fly and the fish. When you're using a full-length clear line, it's difficult to know how close the fish is to the fly if you lose sight of the fly's position. Use a nine-foot leader for a floating line and a three- to five-foot leader for the clear-tipped or fully clear line.

Don't Move the Fly

After casting to the fish, watch the fly as it settles to the bottom. If the fish is coming to the fly, let your offering keep falling. Stripers will usually hit the fly either as it drops or once it's on the bottom. Adding action to the fly can scare fish, particularly bigger stripers that have seen many flies, so be careful. Bluefish should attack the fly and will at times take a popper readily.

Keep watching both the fish and the fly to know when to set the hook. Sometimes you'll see the fish grab the fly. The fish's reaction will tell you that it has the fly. Look for the fish to turn, for a flash of its side, or for it to nose down on the fly. Then hesitate for one second and set the hook by making one long pull, called a strip strike. You can also take in line with a hand-over-hand retrieve if the rod is tucked under your arm.

Bluefish are great sport in shallow water. There are late-summer days in Long Island

Holding the line between the first two fingers allows you to grab it quickly when you're sight casting.

My wife, Barb, with a fat striper that took a fly in several feet of water.

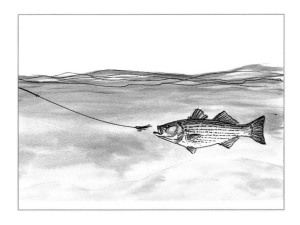

You usually want to present the fly at eye level or below. Stripers seldom look up when they are feeding in shallow water.

Stripers take a fly from the bottom by either nosing down or turning on their side. The angler will feel the fly stop abruptly in either case.

Look at the fish's body language to tell if it has taken the fly; the flash of a fish's side is a good indicator.

A bluefish takes the fly aggressively; stripers will usually feed cautiously in shallow water in the daytime.

Sound, at the mouth of the Housatonic River in Connecticut, when the blue fishing is absolutely out of this world. At low incoming tide, the outer bars have pods of fish milling on the surface. The water isn't clear but the fish are visible, leaving wakes on the surface. These fish will hit poppers with a vengeance. But they're spooky and you need to cast well away from them. When a group of fish swims across your path, cast well ahead of their direction of travel so the popper intercepts them. After a fish takes a popper, it either runs and jumps, or just starts jumping. Some fish go airborne half a dozen times. As one angler described it to me, "You could travel many miles and spend big money and not have fishing this good." The only area that might rival the Housatonic is in the Chesapeake Bay where some good flats in the lower bay offer good sight fishing for bluefish in spring if there isn't too much runoff to discolor the water.

BIG JETTIES, BAD WEATHER

I like fishing jetties when conditions are stormy and fishing is tough in other locations. The jetty must be high enough to offer protection from the wind, rain, and big seas. If the jetty's lee side offers protection from the wind and waves, it's fishable. The only way to check jetties in rough weather is to walk out and see how the water conditions are. From shore it can look worse than it really is. If the water is fairly free of floating weeds and not too riled up, start fishing. Look at the water movement along the jetty. There should be a flow coming from the shore out along the rocky side. Now look for a good safe access spot to fish in that flow.

Pick a place along the rocks and climb down, getting as close to the water as possible while still being safe. Most jetties have small pockets in the rocks that offer protection and a comfortable place to sit or stand. One of the best spots is where the moving water from inside, which flows along the jetty, ends. If there's a good place, begin fishing so you can cover this flow. Even if the wind is strong, all you need is a short roll cast to reach good holding water. The mistake most anglers

Bluefish are great performers in shallow water. Some fish will put on a real aerial display, and jump five to six times.

Where the jetty meets the beach is an excellent fishing location, particularly at low incoming tide.

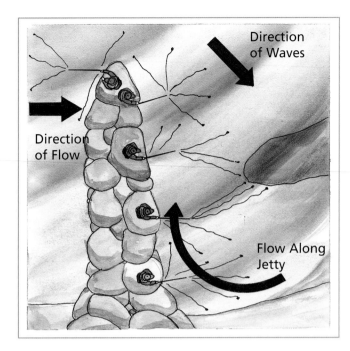

Work all the water around a jetty carefully, casting at different angles to the structure. Let the fly swing in the flow, then come to rest.

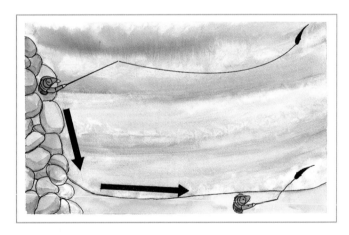

If you hook a big fish from a jetty, try to walk away from the jetty and fight the fish from the beach, where you can land him.

hold in the moving water next to the jetty. The fly will look like a baitfish trying to hide along the jetty's side. You'll find different types of baitfish, small bottom fish, and even eels hiding inside the structure. Wave action pushes this food out to gamefish that cruise the area, looking for a meal. One of the biggest bluefish I've seen taken from shore—an eighteen-pounder—took a swimming plug right next to a jetty. The angler thought he had a big striper.

The trick to fishing jetties in rough water is to hang tough and keep fishing the same few locations. If the water is working right, fish will keep searching the rocks for food. The best casting angle is often a quartering cast down the flow. Usually a slow retrieve with short pulls works best, although at times I let the line and fly drift with almost no retrieve. The fish will take softly, just a slight tightening of the line. It can be intense fishing, not a time to daydream. Jetties are perhaps the best opportunity for the fly rodder to hook a big fish on a short line.

If you do hook a big fish, the best landing technique is to walk toward shore and fight the fish from the beach. Let the fish run out from the structure while you walk toward shore; then get off the jetty and walk up the beach away from the rocks to land the fish. Trying to land a big fish from rocks is difficult and dangerous, as the only way is to climb down the rocks and try to grab it.

Even in big water, an intermediate line works well and is easy to pick up when making a roll cast. It's the best line to fish in low light. I might try a fast-sinking line in daylight if the water is very heavy but a slow-sinking intermediate line will make the fly come alive as it holds along the rocks.

BIG OFFSHORE RIPS AND ESTUARY RIVER SYSTEMS

I've already discussed some fishing techniques for deep, fast water but there are a few other methods that you need to know. You can find excellent fishing on some of the big offshore rips as well as in the rivers and shorelines of big estuaries. Some rips, like the ones around

make is trying to cast too far. Work the water close to the jetty, keeping your casts short to make line control easier. There are times when I'll cast only twenty-five feet. I've had several big fish take the fly within a few feet of the structure.

Let the fly swing in the flow and come to rest along the edges of the rocks. Allow it to

Martha's Vineyard and Nantucket, are all sand, while others, like the Sows and Pigs off Cuttyhunk in Massachusetts, are heavy structure. River systems of estuaries like the Chesapeake Bay, the Hudson River, or the Kennebec River in Maine are mixtures of rock, gravel, sand, and mud. Many of these places are five to forty feet deep with fast-moving water when the tide is at full flow. The heavy ocean rips have stand-up waves, formed because the water depth changes abruptly from several feet to thirty feet or more. The perilous rips are walls that can run almost straight up, pushing the flowing water to a boiling froth. No locations inside estuaries have dangerous waters like those of an offshore rip but when they flow into open water, sea conditions can be dangerous.

Leave the really big waters to the professional guides. Some of the heavy offshore rips will swallow a boat unless you're an experienced captain. There are many open rips that you can fish successfully, however. Most of the water inside estuaries doesn't have wave action but the flows can be strong, particularly around structure.

Use the Motor

On offshore rips, most guides will fish their clients with the motor running, stemming the tide and letting the angler cast to the side or behind the boat. Guides use both stemming the tide and drifting to position anglers just above the fish. Putting the boat in and out of gear lets the line and fly settle into the water column and swing to waiting fish. This works well in crowded locations as it allows many boats to fish one location. Another way to fish a location like this is to shut off the motor above the rip and drift down to the fish. This is a good technique unless the rip has stand-up waves or if there is structure just below the surface. Some rips are too dangerous to enter when the tide is flowing hard.

Drifting

In locations where drifting with the boat is possible, I like to work the water by flowing downcurrent while continually casting. This is

Captain Bob Luce holds a big fish for the camera. The offshore rips can have good numbers of large fish such as this.

John Posh, owner of Stratford Bait and Tackle in Stratford, Connecticut, with a bluefish that took a fly just after first light.

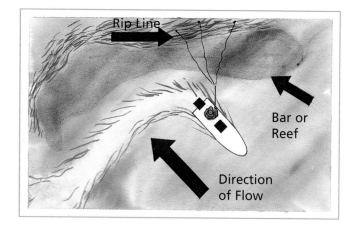

In tough-to-fish places, use the boat's motor to stem the tide. Then you can work the fish-holding water over a bar or reef.

If the rip is not too rough, drifting and casting can be productive.

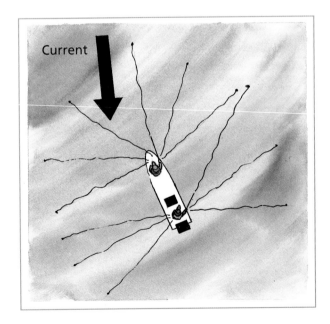

When drifting, try casting at different angles to the current until you find the most productive fishing angle.

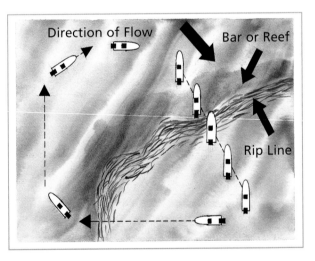

When continuously drifting over a fishing location, be sure to run around the area, not back over it.

very effective inside river systems, especially when the water is discolored. You can cover more water and go back over the same location several times. Drifting allows you to cover the water more efficiently, getting the fly deeper and fishing at different angles to the current. When you're drifting in a flow, keep casting at different angles to the current, and try letting the line and fly sink before starting the retrieve. As you retrieve, the line will swing, turning the fly toward the surface as it straightens out.

The boat should drift at the same speed as the current unless the wind is blowing. The fly, in turn, will act like a normal baitfish because it's moving with the flow. Use different retrieve speeds and pull lengths, depending on which bait type you're trying to match. If fish are feeding on squid or bigger batitfish (four to seven inches long), use long, sharp pulls and move the fly quickly. If they're on tiny, juvenile bait, try a slow retrieve with short pulls. If the fish are finning on the surface, use an intermediate line, a small white fly, and a slow retrieve with three- to four-inch pulls. If you're fishing a river system, expect to find hatches of small baits like worms, crabs, or shrimp. Match your fly to those baits.

With the boat drifting at the same speed as the flowing water, you can let the line sink and fish the fly deeper. Unless the water is shallow or a specific bait is bringing fish to the surface, getting the fly down will produce more strikes in fast-flowing water. If you're getting the fly down ten feet in fifteen feet of water, the fish might come up this short distance to take the fly. If the fly is on the surface, however, there's less chance of fish rising up that far to take the fly. Besides fish coming up to feed on bait, the only other times you're likely to find fish near the surface are in low light and at times of slack water.

Small Openings That Flow into Open Water

These are my favorite places to fish. If I could fish only one water type, it would be a creek or small river flowing into deeper water. I like places that you can cast across when the flow

Getting the fly down can be critical, especially on bright days.

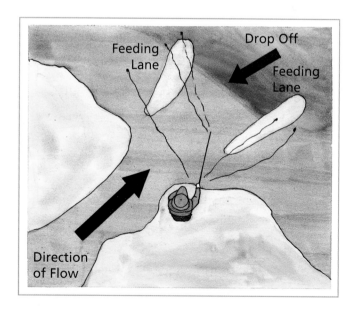

Work both the feeding lanes and the drop-off when fishing outlets.

Openings that run into the sea are great places to fish.

predict the most productive fishing periods so you don't waste your time.

Cast to different areas where the flow runs into the drop-off. Fish will often hold along the edges or just behind the drop-off. In a faster flow, the fish will take aggressively when they're feeding on baitfish. Outflows are grocery stores. As the estuary empties, it dumps food into the open water. The constant flow of food attracts gamefish, because the feeding is easy. A feeding frenzy can occur when there are large numbers of baitfish flowing out; the fish might hit anything that moves. This can be easy fishing. Just cast quartering downstream, then let the line and fly swing while making short pulls with a slow retrieve. Basic attractor flies work well, as do poppers.

When Fish Feed on Small Foods

If the food source is worms, shrimp, or crabs, stripers and blues will mostly be sipping them on or near the surface. You can often determine bait types by watching the feeding styles of the fish. If there are subtle swirls and small rings on the water's surface, the fish are usually feeding on small, immobile baits like spawning worms or shrimp. If the surface activity is loud with large splashes, and fish are crashing on top, they're feeding on fast-swimming baitfish such as herring or spearing.

When the fish are sipping, use small flies and try to cast the shortest line possible without spooking the fish. Cast above the feeding fish and let the fly swing to them on a dead drift. During worm and shrimp hatches, some fish will take up feeding stations like trout in a river, taking food only inside a small window. Even when the bait is thick, you can take fish if you keep putting your fly in that window.

Try to match the fly to the bait type, use a floating or intermediate line, and keep the cast short for better control. Keep in mind that the fish might feed more aggressively if the bait is spread out. Stripers will feed like this more often than bluefish will but don't be surprised to get cut off by the occasional big chopper bluefish that act like trout.

spills into six- to ten-foot drop-offs. Places like this have consistent action, are easy to fish, and usually remain the same for many years.

The Best Times to Fish

The first part of the outflowing tide and the first part of the inflowing tide are usually the most productive times to fish estuary mouths. The opening's size and the size of the backwater or estuary will determine how much lag time will occur. The flow won't begin moving out immediately after high water; most openings will have a delay, some up to several hours, before the water begins to run out. The inflow will have the same lag time. Here is where your fishing log becomes invaluable; it can help you

INDEX